The
North Carolina
Miscellany

The
North Carolina
Miscellany

CHAPEL HILL
THE UNIVERSITY OF NORTH CAROLINA PRESS

edited by
RICHARD WALSER

drawings by PAUL GRAY

Grateful acknowledgment is extended to numerous authors and publications for permission to reprint copyright material: an excerpt from *Old Bethesda*, by Bion H. Butler, published by Grosset & Dunlap; passages from articles by Jonathan Daniels and Ovid Williams Pierce, reprinted by special permission from *Holiday*, copyright 1956 and 1957, by The Curtis Publishing Company; an excerpt from *Our Incredible Civil War* by Burke Davis, published by Holt, Rinehart and Winston; LeGette Blythe's Foreword to *Miracle in the Hills*, published by McGraw-Hill Book Company; Frank Holeman's column "North Carolina and the Civil War," reprinted by courtesy of *The News*, New York's Picture Newspaper; Karl Kohr's article on Ava Gardner, reprinted from *Parade*; selections from books by Zoe Kincaid Brockman and Thad Stem, Jr., published by William E. Loftin, Charlotte; an essay from a book by Weimar Jones, published by John F. Blair, Winston-Salem; "The Whang Doodle" and "Tom Dula" from publications of the Duke University Press; excerpts from the writings of Adelaide L. Fries, John Harden, Guion Griffin Johnson, Hugh T. Lefler, Wm. T. Polk, Phillips Russell, Cornelia Phillips Spencer, and David Stick, all published by the University of North Carolina Press; an extract from *The Big Money*, in *U.S.A.*, by John Dos Passos, by special permission of the author; and other selections from books and publications cited hereafter.

EDITOR'S FOREWORD

This book of miscellaneous selections about North Carolina or by North Carolinians was projected on the assumption that there are thousands of readers, like me, who have an unashamed curiosity about what has transpired on the byways as well as the throughways of life in our state. To have covered only a portion of this spacious and varied panorama would have demanded dozens of books the size of the one you have before you. Even so, it seemed to me, a trip here and there into the expanse of North Carolina deeds and documents was better than no trip at all, especially when one recognizes the impossibility of satisfying a total wanderlust.

Consequently, I have fashioned a book in which my reader can once again experience with me some of the more familiar proceedings in North Carolina affairs, but with generous excursions into the less familiar and even forgotten side roads. Though Virginia Dare and Thomas Wolfe are of course met with, I have neglected neither the Siamese Twins nor Tom Dula. Though Duke University is on our journey, we travel also to Knott's Island.

The five sections into which the book is divided are not exclusive; they are merely convenient. Needless to say, Places are usually dull unless People are there, People are static unless they are involved in some Incident or other, and Incidents generally provoke Observations. The section on Folklore would seem to be a thing apart. But not so. For all I know, every page in the book may be compacted of Folklore. I have tried to reproduce my contributors and my sources faithfully, whether primary or occasionally secondary; yet I do not vouch for their validity. For instance, I am prone to question the yarn about Calico King, to say nothing of the story of the Great Fall of Flesh and Blood, but

I have cited my sources and the reader, according to his bent, may place credence in them or not. Furthermore, I have a feeling that Folklore, not hard facts, characterizes a regional people.

At this point, I must affirm that I make no apology for the omission of certain favored selections, or material about certain popular subjects, which someone may think ought to have been included. There must have been a quarter of a million possibilities—all of them, certainly, not read by me. The final choices are those which I personally liked and felt would provide variety for a miscellany, and which I hope readers will like. If a majority of the recent pieces come from rather restricted sources, this is due to my greater acquaintance with certain books, periodicals, and newspapers.

And now a final word: Gathering together the materials for this NORTH CAROLINA MISCELLANY has been a pleasure which I wish could have been every reader's. Never was there a boring moment. If an iota of this pleasure can be communicated, I and my helpful associates at The University of North Carolina Press shall be abundantly compensated.

R. W.

North Carolina State College
Raleigh, 23 February 1962

CONTENTS

PLACES

"North Carolina begins with the brightness of sea sands and ends with the loneliness of the Smokies reaching in chill and cloud to the sky."

—OVID WILLIAMS PIERCE

WHEN I THINK OF NORTH CAROLINA
1873

Cornelia Phillips Spencer

When I think of North Carolina abstractly there are a hundred things that go to make up her image in my mind,—not only does there rise up her geographical figure,—her profile from the sand-bars to the mountains,—not only a thought of her commercial and political status, not only a reminder of her history, or her pro-verbial character, of the gallantry of her men and the fair fame of her women; but somehow mixed up with all these comes a vision of her humblest, homeliest aspects,—of her red gullies, and her broom straw, her persimmon trees. I recall her may-weeds as well as her yellow jasmine,—her sassafras as well as her white oaks.

—*Selected Papers* (1953)

CLIMB TO BEAUCATCHER MOUNTAIN

Christian Reid

"And this is Beaucatcher in front of us!" says Sylvia. "Such a fine height deserves a better name."

"The name is vulgarly foolish," says Eric, "but, as far as absolute ugliness goes, there are worse within the borders of Buncombe. What do you think of creeks named Hominy, Cane, Turkey, Sandy Mush—?"

"O Eric!"

"Literally true, I assure you. Then there are Beaver Dam, Bull, and Flat—all clear, rushing mountain-streams."

"It is infamous!" says Sylvia, with the most feeling indignation. "Something ought to be done—the Legislature ought to interfere! If the Anglo-Saxon settlers had no sense of poetry in their own rude organizations, they might at least have spared the Indian nomenclature, which is beautiful and appropriate wherever it is found."

"Yes, it is beautiful," says Eric, who has a passion for all Indian names, and repeats them with the lingering intonation which makes them thrice musical. "Compare with such a nomenclature as I have just mentioned, Swannanoa, Nantahala, Tuckaseegee, Hiawassee, Cheowah, Feloneke, and Tahkeeostee—all Cherokee names, and all possessing excellent significations."

"What are the significations?" I ask.

"Swannanoa means 'Beautiful'; Nantahala, 'Woman's Bosom,' from the rise and fall of its breast of waters; Tuckaseegee, 'Terrapin Water'; Cheowah, 'River of Otters'; Feloneke, 'Yellow River'; and Tahkeeostee—the Cherokee name of the French Broad—is the most expressive of all, for it means 'Racing River.'"

"And no doubt there were any number, just as admirable, which have been lost," says Sylvia. "It is unbearable! We do not find that the French or Spanish settlers left such barbarities behind them."

"No," says Victor Dupont, who is walking by her side, "I have been thinking, while Mr. Markham spoke, of the names in Louisiana and Texas. None of them are ugly unless—forgive me!—they are English. Many melodious Indian names are left, and those which the first settlers gave are full of a religious poetry—such as Laguna del Madre, Isla del Padre, Bay of St. Louis, Bayou St.-Denis, Ile au Breton."

"Those are certainly very different from Smithville and Jonesville, and Big Pigeon River," says Sylvia, "but I wish the Indian names could have been preserved everywhere."

This conversation takes place as we walk out of Asheville along the winding road which leads to Beaucatcher. The sun is sinking low toward the western mountains, spreading a mantle

of gold over the uplands, and leaving the glades and dells full
of softly toned shadows. Eric and I form the advance-guard of
the party. We have been tried friends and comrades for many
a day, and, when we were younger, he often paid me the com-
pliment of wishing I were a boy. Sylvia and Victor come next,
Charley and Adele loiter in the rear. Scattered around in every
direction are villa-like houses "bosomed high in turfted trees";
before us are the green hills—that in a different country would be
esteemed mountains—behind, the marvelous peaks at which we
are forbidden to glance.

"Nobody must look round," cries Adele, playfully, waving a
flowering branch. "You shall all be turned to stones, like the
princes in the story of the singing water, if you do!"

"The view is not to be devoured piece-meal," says Charley,
"but to be taken whole—like an oyster—from the top of the knob
to which we are bound."

So we go on, with our backs to the glory which is behind. The
ascent of Beaucatcher is not difficult. A very excellent road leads
over it to a highly cultivated cove in the mountains behind, where
day begins an hour or two later, and ends an hour or two earlier,
than in Asheville. We leave this road at the gap where it crosses
the mountain, and follow a steep path to the top of the knob
which rises on the right.

"One could not easily drive up here," says Sylvia, as we
clamber over the rocks, "but it would be quite possible to ride
without difficulty."

"Shall we try it tomorrow, if saddle-horses are to be found in
Asheville?" asks her attendant.

"I thought we were to return to the Sulphur Spring tomorrow,"
she says, laughing.

Eric and I reach the summit first. It is smooth, level, and
green. There is a grass-grown fortification where a Confederate
battery was once planted, and close behind it a dead tree that
from Asheville, and miles beyond, presents the perfect appearance of a large cross.

We mount the fortifications just as the sun sinks behind the
distant mountains. At our feet Asheville is spread, but we scarcely

glance at the picture which the town presents, crowning the verdant beauty of its summer hills, with the fertile valleys of the French Broad and Swannanoa on each side. Our gaze turns beyond—to the azure world that stretches, far as the eye can reach, to the golden gate-way of the sun—an infinity of loveliness, with the sunset radiance trembling on the crests of more than a hundred peaks. The atmosphere is so transparent that it is impossible to say how far the range of one's vision extends. Mountains rise behind mountains, until they recede away into dimmest distance, their trending lines lying faint and far against the horizon. Blue as heaven, and soft as clouds, the nearer ranges stand—serried rank behind rank, and peak upon peak.

The view is so boundless and so beautiful that the imagination is for a time overwhelmed. Are those sapphire heights the Delectable Mountains—and do those dazzling clouds veil the jasper walls of the city of God? It almost seems so. The sunset sky is a miracle of loveliness—of tints which it would be presumption to attempt to describe—and the majestic sides of Pisgah grow softly purple as the incarnadine glow falls over its towering pinnacle.

"Oh, what a scene!" says Sylvia, with a long sigh. She stands like one entranced, gazing at the farthest peaks where their blue outlines melt into the sunset gold.

"I scarcely thought there were so many mountains in the world," says Adele Dupont.

"It is one great charm of the Asheville views," says Eric, without looking round—he is standing in front, with his arms folded—"that they possess such magnificent expanse, and all the effect of farthest distance. It is difficult to exaggerate the advantages of the incomparable situation of the town—especially in the fact that, although surrounded by mountains, it is not overshadowed, but regards them from a sufficient distance, and a sufficient elevation, to behold them like this."

"I see several depressions, like gaps, in the chain," I observe. "What are they?"

"They *are* gaps," Eric answers. "That farthest west is the gorge of the French Broad. Yonder is the Homminy Gap—there the Hickory Nut. Swannanoa is in the east."

" 'Don't let us go home," says Sylvia. "Let us live in this land of the sky forever. It is enchanted."

... With the enthusiasm of ignorance, we cannot believe that any thing—not even the view from the Black Mountain itself— can surpass the scene spread before us in softest beauty, to the farthest verge of the dying day. We sit on the fortification and watch the fires of sunset slowly face, and the lovely dusk of summer steal over the land. Winds laden with the freshness of the great hills come to us from remote distances. Venus gleams into sight like a tremulous diamond in the delicate sky. The immense expanse, the great elevation, seem to embody at once infinity and repose.

"This is delightful!" says Charley. "We may fancy ourselves lotus-eaters, 'propped on beds of amaranth' far above the world.". . .

"The enchanted hours of life are short," says Victor Dupont. "Let us enjoy them to the last minute."

"Let me know when the last minute comes," says Eric, walking away.

It does not come for some time. We cannot resolve to break the spell which rests over us. We talk very little, and that little in low tones. It is enough to see the splendor of the west grow faint and more faint, while the far, heavenly mountains change from blue to tender gray. Suddenly Charley lifts himself on his elbow and points toward the east. We turn and see the silver face of the full moon rising slowly over the tree-tops into the hyacinth sky.

The appearance of her pale, pure majesty above the chain of hills that stretch eastward to the Black, fills our cup of pleasure to the brim. It is a scene to hold in remembrance while life shall last. We linger until we see lights like stars, gleaming here and there in Asheville. Then we know that our enchanted hour has ended.

"At least *one* enchanted hour," says Sylvia, as Mr. Dupont folds her shawl around her, "but I hope that there are many more in reserve for us. Like Moses, I have had a glimpse of the Promised Land, and now I shall not be content till I have seen every thing that is to be seen."

Silver lights and dark shadows are lying on the streets of Asheville when, foot-sore and weary, we cross the large open square in the business part of the town, and turn into the street which leads to our hotel. To tired and hungry humanity, the lights blazing out from the last are more cheerful than the beauty of the great constellations shining overhead; and, although Eric has made one or two astronomical remarks, we have not paid them the attention which no doubt they deserve.

"Tomorrow night we will go to Battery Porter and study astronomy at our leisure," says Sylvia. "Tonight I shall first do full justice to the *cuisine* of the 'Eagle,' then I shall beg Mr. Dupont to play for me the 'Cradle Song,' and perhaps a strain or two of Mendelssohn. After that I shall say good-night to everybody, I shall go to bed, and I shall sleep—like a top!"

"I thought you would have said like an angel," says Victor. "But angels never sleep," says Charley. . . .

—*The Land of the Sky* (1876)

TO TARHEELIA WITH LOVE

Julian Scheer

Nobody asked me . . . But . . . the things I like best about North Carolina include:

Names like Chunky Gal, Whynot, Saxapahaw.

Ham gravy at Henry Franklin's near Linville Falls and barbecue from anywhere.

The glow of fires in tobacco barns.

A hundred fishing holes in a hundred counties.

Lighthouses on the coast.

The brilliance of mountain color in the fall.

Sunrise over the Atlantic near Wilmington.

Christmas lights in Charlotte.

An air drop at Ft. Bragg.

Wide highways like US 29.

Carnivals and fairs—anywhere.

Blue windows on textile mills.

Black bears in the Smokies.

High Point furniture.

Chimes at Chapel Hill after a football game.

Country schools and yellow buses.

Damp caverns like Linville.

Stately architecture of Duke.

Scottish plaids of Laurinburg.

Impressive Fontana Dam.

Charlotte's Coliseum, Raleigh's Cow Palace.

Monuments to Confederate soldiers.

Tom Wolfe, Proff Koch, Hugh Lefler, Frank Graham, Olla Ray Boyd.

Red clay, green fields, orange sunsets.

Tobacco fields, cotton harvest, strawberry patches.

Shrimp and menhaden boats.

Hot sausage, persimmon pudding, homemade liquor.

Arthur Smith, N. C. Symphony, Wake Forest drum majorettes.

Winston-Salem, Asheville, Tryon, Elizabeth City.

Smell of cigarette plants, Cannon towels, Drexel tables, Jugtown.

Duke-Carolina football, semipro baseball, Dixie Classics basketball.

Blowing Rock, Grandfather Mountain, Cape Hatteras, Lake James.

Pinehurst, Edenton, Mattamuskeet.

Ava Gardner.

The houses of Biltmore, Marsh, Bellamy.

Sir Walter Hotel when General Assembly in session.

Square dancing, folk music.

Crooked country roads.
Picnic tables.
White frame churches.

—Charlotte News (January 1, 1957)

THE ATLANTIC SANDBANKS
1524

Giovanni da Verrazzano

We saw in this Countrey many Vines growing naturally, which
growing up, tooke holde of the trees as they doe in Lombardie,
which if by husbandmen they were dressed in good order, without all doubt they would yeeld excellent wines: for hauing oftentimes seene the fruit thereof dryed, which was sweete and pleasant, and not differing from ours, wee thinke that they doe
esteeme the same, because that in euery place where they growe,

they take away the under branches growing round about, that the fruit thereof may ripen the better.

We found also roses, violets, lilies, and many sorts of herbes, and sweete and odoriferous flowers different from ours. . . .

—Hakluyt's Voyages (1600)

FIRST PUBLIC LIBRARY

Mary L. Thornton

On October 21, 1703, Governor Henderson Walker of North Carolina, writing to the Bishop of London, said:

. . . God, of his infinite goodness, was pleased to inspire the Rev. Dr. Bray, some time about four years ago, to send in some books of his own particular pious gift, of the explanation of the Church catechism, with some other small books, to be disposed of and lent as we thought fit . . . and about a year after did send to us a library of books for the benefit of this place, given by the honorable the Corporation for the Establishing the Christian Religion, by one Mr. Daniel Brett, a minister appointed for this place.

The library referred to is the one established at Bath, about 1700 or 1701, the first public library in the province. Bath, the first town incorporated in North Carolina, is described in a letter of William Gordon to the Secretary of the Society for the Propagation of the Gospel in Foreign Parts, written in 1709:

Here is no church, though they have begun to build a town called Bath. It consists of about twelve houses, being the only town in the whole province. They have a small collection of books for a library, which were carried over by the Reverend Doctor Bray, and some land is laid out for a globe; but no minister would ever stay long in the place, though several have come hither from the West Indies and other plantations in America; and yet I must own, it is not the unpleasantest part of the country—nay, in all probability it will be the centre of trade, as having the advantage of a better inlet for shipping, and surrounded with most pleasant savannas, very useful for stocks of cattle.

... The three precincts of Bath County did not contain as many inhabitants as any one of the precincts of Albemarle. The Albemarle section was naturally favored by the clergy as a place of residence. They constantly complained about the great distances to be covered and the many rivers to cross in carrying on the duties of ministry.

Efforts were made to have the library moved to the Albemarle region. On July 7, 1711, the Rev. John Urmstone, who had recently established residence in Chowan Precinct, asked the Society for the Propagation of the Gospel in Foreign Parts to direct the Governor and Council regarding the library "which Dr. Bray sent to Bath in Pamlicough thro' mistake and being informed that there was the Seat of Government."

On March 2, 1713, the Vestry of St. Paul's Church, Edenton, petitioned the Society:

The First Library of Great Value Sent us by the Direction of the Rev. Dr. Bray, thro' an unhappy inscription on the Back of the Books or Title page, Vizt. Belonging to the Parish of St. Thomas of Pamlico, in the then rising but now miserable County of Bath, falsely supposed to be the Seat of government, was lodged there, and by that means rendered useless to the Clergy, for whose service it was chiefly intended and in what Condition We Know not. We fear the worst by Reason of the late War.

Bath had declined in importance by this time following the Indian Wars, 1711-12. In 1712, the Rev. Giles Rainsford, who had arrived in Edenton, complained that Dr. Bray's library "is all dispersed and lost by those wretches that don't consider the benefit of so valuable a gift." In no less than four letters written in the period from 1714 to 1718, Urmstone denounced the location and treatment of the library, one written in 1718 ending in this angry note:

... the library at Pamptichoe, sent in for the use of Clergymen by Dr. Bray in all appearance will be to all destroyed, that place being abandoned and so will all the county be in a short time, for fear of 7 or 8 Indians.

But Urmstone's influence must have declined by this time. In the many letters that he wrote to the Society he shows a uniformly venomous pen. The opinion of his parishioners is expressed in an anonymous letter of May 26, 1721, that he was "very unfit for that or any other place ... so much disliked of the people he was among that scarce any of them came to hear him."

In spite of his efforts, the library remained at Bath. The House of Assembly valued it highly enough to place it among the laws of the province in 1715 when an extensive act for its preservation is recorded.

This act is remarkable for two reasons: first, because it was the only law for the encouragement of learning passed by the North Carolina Assembly under the Proprietary government; second, because it presents ideas of that day in regard to the proper administration of public libraries.

It is much like the act for a similar purpose passed by the South Carolina Assembly in 1700, and may have been drawn up by the Society as legislation recommended to the various colonies. It provided for a librarian, called Library-Keeper, to preserve the books from "damage, imbezzlement, and all other destruction," the librarian being personally responsible for twice the value of the books, if destroyed. He was to be appointed by a Board of Commissioners, selected from the Council and the Precinct Courts of the colony.

The books were to be catalogued and annually inspected by the Board. Rules for borrowers were rather lenient. The inhabitants of Beaufort Precinct had the right to borrow any book, giving a receipt for it, a folio to be returned in four months' time, a quarto in two months' time, an octavo in one month's time, but for refusal to return, a borrower had to pay three times the rated value of the book.

A manuscript catalogue of the Bath library has been preserved in London in the records of the Society for the Propagation of the Gospel in Foreign Parts. It lists 176 volumes, only one of which is known to exist as an identical copy. It is Gabriel Towerson's *Explication to the Catechism*, a folio printed in London in 1685. This copy was discovered by the Rev. R. B. Windley of Bunyan, N. C., in the 1880's, and presented to the Episcopal

Diocese of East Carolina. Other copies of the titles listed in the catalogue might possibly be located by circulating a want list among British book dealers.

—*News and Observer*, Raleigh (October 25, 1959)

LAND FOR SALE

TO BE SOLD, half part of the Island of Roanoke . . . containing about six Thousand Acres of Land and Marsh, as it was surveyed in the Year 1718, by William Maule, Surveyor General. . . . Any Person . . . may apply themselves to Samuel Swann, Esq; of the Precinct of Perquimmans . . . ; or to Doct. Belcher Noyes, of Boston in the Province of the Massachusetts Bay in New England, who is the rightful Owner thereof. Boston, May 26th, 1740.

—Broadside (Duke University Library)

TRAVELING PREACHER DOWN EAST
March, 1785

Bishop Thomas Coke

Wednesday 23.—I went to *Edington* [Edenton], a most wicked place. Here Mr. *Pettigrew* preaches; but the church is like a pig-stie. The people in general seemed to prefer the court-house, which is an elegant place; so I went there and preached to a very large congregation. The preachers ought really to take this place into their plan, and there is a person who will receive them. There seemed nothing but dissipation and wickedness in the tavern at which I set up, and yet the landlord would take nothing for my entertainment. In the afternoon I went with brother *Dameron*, one of our preachers who came to meet me, to Mrs. *Boyd's*, a widow lady, who rode to *Edington* to hear me. She lives about seven miles off on my way, and has good desires.

Thursday 24.—I arrived at Colonel *Campbel's, in North-Carolina*, the gentleman and the Christian united. He sat in the Senate of this State as long as he chose, and I have been persuading him to resume his seat. He is the first of our friends in the Upper House, that I have met with. I am vastly pleased with him. On the 25th, I preached in the parish church, in which we do regular duty; but, alas! Religion is at a very low ebb in this neighbourhood.

Saturday 26.—I preached in the house of one Mr. L——, rich man, but of no religion. We usually preach in the church. But he has the gout, and therefore requested me to preach in his house, which is large. It was really a profitable time.

St. John's Chapel, Sunday 27.—This belongs to the church of *England*, and we do regular duty in it. I preached here to an attentive people, and administered the Lord's-Supper.

Bridge's Creek Church, Monday 28.—This also belongs to the Church of *England*, and we do duty in it whenever we please. I had a large congregation, but our friends thoughtlessly neglected to provide the elements for the Lord's-Supper. I have been travelling in a very low, wet country for these three weeks, and it is astonishing what a number of frogs there are here.

Roanoak Chapel, Wednesday 30.—I found in this chapel a serious, attentive people. Here I met with Mr. *Jarrat*. After duty he went with me to one brother *Seaward's* (in the State of *Virginia*) about eight miles off. We now talked largely on the minutes concerning slavery: but he would not be persuaded. The secret is, he has twenty-four slaves of his own: but I am afraid, he will do infinite hurt by his opposition to our Rules.

—*Extracts of the Journals of the Late Rev. Thomas Coke* (1816)

TARBOROUGH AND GREENVILLE
April, 1791

George Washington

Monday, 18th. Set out by six o'clock—dined at a small house kept by one Slaughter, 22 Miles from Hallifax and lodged at Tarborough 14 Miles further.

This place is less than Hallifax, but more lively and thriving; it is situated on Tar River which goes into Pamplico Sound and is crossed at the Town by means of a bridge a great height from the water, and notwithstanding, the freshes rise sometimes nearly to the arch. Corn, Porke, and some Tar are the exports from it. We were recd. at this place by as good a salute as could be given by one piece of artillery.

Tuesday, 19th. At 6 o'clock I left Tarborough, accompanied by some of the most respectable people of the place for a few miles; dined at a trifling place called Greenville 25 miles distant, and lodged at one Allan's 14 miles further a very indifferent house without stabling which for the first time since I commenced my Journey were obliged to stand without a cover.

Greenville is on Tar River and the exports the same as from Tarborough with a greater proportion of Tar, for the lower down the greater number of Tar makers are there. This article is contrary to all ideas one would entertain on the subject, rolled as Tobacco by an axis which goes through both hands—one horse draws two barrels in this manner.

Wednesday, 20th. Left Allans before breakfast, and under a misapprehension went to a Colo. Allans, supposing it to be a public house; where we were very kindly and well entertained without knowing it was at his expense, until it was too late to rectify the mistake. After breakfasting, and feeding our horses here, we proceeded on and crossing the River Neuse 11 miles further, arrived in New Bern to dinner.

—*The Diaries* (1860)

ON GRANDFATHER MOUNTAIN
August, 1794
André Michaux

Le 30 monté au sommet de la plus haute montagne de toute l'Am. Sept. et avec mon compagnon Guide, chanté l'hymne des Marseillois et crié Vivre l'Amerique et la Républiq. Française, Vivre la Liberté &c &c.

[On the 30th climbed to the summit of the highest mountain in all North America and, with my companion guide, sang *La Marseillaise* hymn and shouted "Long live America and the French Republic! Long live liberty!" and so on.]

—*Proceedings of the American Philosophical Society* (1889)

NAG'S HEAD

We learn from a gentleman who has just returned from Nag's Head that the visitors at this delightful watering place number 500 and that the ocean sea bathing is very fine. Much of the intelligence, beauty and wealth of North Carolina are now assembled there.

—*Spirit of the Age*, Raleigh (August 30, 1854)

TRAIN RIDE FROM GREENSBORO TO SALISBURY

A few days since, myself and one or two friends concluded to take a ride on the North Carolina Rail Road to Salisbury. I was forcibly struck with the improvements on the road when I contrasted it with our own quiet town, and could but see the advances.

A small improvement has been made at the first station, Jamestown. Proceed on to the next, where the plank road and rail road cross at High Point, and there you find a village springing up as if by magic. The new buildings show that enterprise marks the place, and that ere long it will be numbered and ranked as one of the most important places on the Rail Road. Although in its infancy, the traveler will be obliged to say here is a place of considerable business.

From High Point you are carried on to the next station, Thomasville, some ten or twelve miles distant—another town which owes its existence to this noble rail road; a town which certainly has been laid out with much taste by its founder. It has a female Academy, and you would judge from the large brick building which has been erected expressly for the purpose, that it is a School of some size. It takes its name from its former owner, who first established it one mile from Thomasville, and called it in honor of his inestimable lady, ANNA—(Glen-Anna). This school, if attended to, the writer thinks, is bound to succeed, from its easy access and commanding location on the rail road. Thomasville has other attractions to the traveler. It has a Hotel, one or two stores, several handsome residences, all being new and just in the forrest, which gives the traveler a favorable opinion and certainly reflects much credit on its founder, John W. Thomas, Esq., a sterling Whig and a very enterprising man.

After five minutes stop, you then proceed on, and over creeks, and rivulets, passing through a portion of fertile country you next arrive at Lexington. The rail road does not pass immediately through this town, and the writer had very little opportunity of forming an opinion. This town is behind many others of its sister towns on the road. It has not recently used as much white lead and oil as it might have done to improve its appearance. Lexington is quite an important Depot on this road, much freight and considerable travel starts from this point.

Immediately after leaving this place, you are carried over one of the most fertile regions of North Carolina. We cannot pass

over it without noticing one farm which the road passes immediately through; it is the farm of Dr. Wm. R. Holt. Those who
have a taste for farming could not spend the same amount of
money more pleasantly and probably more advantageously than
a visit over this road, and view the farm. Dr. Holt has great taste
for fine stock, fine farm, and is a specimen of a good farmer,
North or South. Visit his farm; it will richly repay you for the
ride. You will find the Doctor a very gentlemanly man, and like
to tell you about farming, phosphates, blooded stock, &c.—The
road passes about one mile through his farm, and through some
of the finest farming land, called the Jersey settlement, up the
banks of the Yadkin, one of the noble streams of the Old North
State,—crossing on a fine bridge, which gives the traveler a fine
view of the stream, and the surrounding country.

A few miles more, and you are landed at the ancient town of
Salisbury; I say ancient, because it dates back nearly as far as
any town in the State. This town is located in a level country,
soil red. It has a population of some 2500 inhabitants. When we
landed at the Depot, we found two omnibusses, both bearing the
marks of age; we listened carefully to what the representative
of each omnibus had to say, for we soon found they were representing two hotels; we, like a majority of other passengers, got

into the largest omnibus, drawn by four splendid bays: with the crack of the whip, and a few turns of the corners, and we were landed at Col. Roberts' Hotel, where we found a good dinner prepared to satisfy our hungry appetites. We found our old friend Adam from Salem, one of waiters. Col. Roberts is an accommodating landlord, and with the aid of a little white lead and oil, would have a good house.

We had a fine walk around the town, and found it quite a business place, some ten or twelve dry goods stores, some of them large for retail stores in an inland town. Salisbury has three churches, Presbyterian, Methodist, and Episcopalian. It, being the county town, has one of the finest court houses, just built, in the State: nearly all the residences wear the appearance of age, built in the old fashioned style of architecture; a little white lead and oil would improve wonderfully. In passing around, I had nearly forgotten to mention some of the new buildings under way. 1st, Shaver's Hotel, a fine commanding looking building from the out side, it is situated near the Depot. Boyden has also a fine house, which I learned was for a Hotel; it reflects credit on the founder and the town. I was surprised to find so many factories in this ancient town of Salisbury. There is near the Depot, a large Machine Shop and Foundry, where agricultural implements and other articles are made to a considerable extent, promising a rich return to its owners and proprietors; everything was neat, and things were done up with despatch. In the west part of town is a large Factory, which I did not visit, but heard was doing quite a profitable business. Also our neighbors, Messrs. Dowlers, have opened a large factory for the manufacturing of wheat fans, doing quiet a large and profitable business. There is also the large Cotton Factory which has been in operation for a number of years.

A large machine shop built for the manufacture of Rail Road cars on the Western Road, and last, but not least, is the large steam distillery of Mr. Myer Myers, a gentlemanly man, and a man of great energy. This factory is situated about half a mile from the Depot, in a beautiful grove, called Rock Spring, and driven by a thirty-horse-power steam engine runs two pairs of Burt Stones, which I was told would grind 1,000 bushels of corn in twenty four hours. This establishment is well worth a visit to, by any person visiting Salisbury. Corn is put into elevation, carried into the hoppers of the mill, ground, carried up, marked, put through the different operations until it comes out whiskey, then rectified and put up in barrels and casks, for market,—everything done by machinery, and after extracting all the spirits out of the grain, the slop made is forced off in pipes some hundred yards distant, and fed out to hogs. This gentleman has now five hundred hogs fattening for fall trade, says he will be able to have one hundred, which will average two hundred by Nov. next. This establishment will be able to use up five hundred bushels grain per day, and make from twelve to fifteen hundred gallons whiskey. Everything about the establishment is done in the cleanliest and neatest manner, and reflects much credit on the proprietor. I learned from him, that there is invested some $30,000, and he hopes when grain gets plenty, and price down, to make it a very profitable investment. . . .

After bidding our hospitable landlord adieu, we got into the same large omnibus, drawn by four fine bays, and driven by an old stager who we shall take the liberty of calling Moses. He drove us down to the Rail Road, crossing the track at full speed, turning his four steeds and the omnibus around in a circle of ten feet, to the satisfaction of all parties; we bid our friend Moses adieu, promising ourselves to take a ride with him the next time we went to Salisbury. After 2¼ hours of as pleasant a Rail Road ride as we ever had, with the gentlemanly conductor, Mr. Bradshaw, we were landed safely in our own quiet town to enjoy the past as a pleasant dream.

—*Patriot and Flag*, Greensboro (June 26, 1857)

BAKERSVILLE

Porte Crayon

The town of Bakersville, being a place of some mark, should not be passed over without befitting notice; for we are persuaded there are many persons, considering themselves very well informed, who are totally ignorant of its locality and resources. It is situated on the main road from Grey Briggs's to Young's, about eight miles from the former place. Its principal street is built up one side with a rail-fence, and on the other with two cabins, set back from the street. The back streets and alleys, which are laid off *ad libitum*, contain the stables, cowsheds, and hen-houses. The only public buildings worthy of note are an apple-jack distillery, where the best may be obtained for twelve and a half cents a quart, and a spring-house, covering a fountain of cool, pure water, which has no commercial value, although some persons affect to prefer it to the former as a beverage. During the dark of the moon the town is lighted with pine-knots; and its police force, consisting of six big dogs, is at all times uncommonly vigilant and active.

—*Harper's New Monthly Magazine* (November, 1857)

IN WARMER AIR

Walt Whitman

. . . In lower latitudes in warmer air in the Carolinas the large black buzzard floating slowly high beyond the tree tops,
Below, the red cedar festoon'd with tylandria, the pines and cypresses growing out of the white sand that spreads far and flat,

Rude boats descending the big Pedee, climbing plants, parasites
with color'd flowers and berries enveloping huge trees,
The waving drapery on the live-oak trailing long and low,
noiselessly waved by the wind...
Southern fishermen fishing, the sounds and inlets of North Carolina's coast, the shad-fishery and the herring-fishery, the large
sweep-seines, the windlasses on shore work'd by horses, the
clearing, curing, and packing-houses;
Deep in the forest in piney woods turpentine dropping from the
incisions in the trees, there are the turpentine works,
There are the negroes at work in good health, the ground in all
directions is cover'd with pine straw....

—"Our Old Feuillage," *Leaves of Grass* (1860 ed.)

A TOMATO-CATSUP FARM

The soil and farms upon Knott's Island are rather stiff and very
prolific in the culture of corn and marketable vegetables. For the
first time, we saw upon this Island a Tomato-Catsup plantation—
where the tenant cultivates tomatoes entirely, and stills them into
Catsup, which he sells and ships by the barrel, as the people of
Edgecombe and Nash do their "apple jack."

—*Times*, Greensboro (October 20, 1860)

HERRING FISHERIES

Doubleyou Vee

At Avoca on the more western extremity of Albemarle Sound
are situated the Capehart fisheries. We saw here at one haul of
the seine 50,000 herrings landed. This we were told was only a

small haul. It appeared not to be a good day for fishing! So they said. But to a mountaineer it looked like a pretty lucky haul. Piled up on the beach they look more like a busting big corn pile just after "shucking." The seine here used was a mile long, and had attached to each end a half mile of inch-and-a-half rope. It took four 8-horse-power steam engines to manage it. They were located in this way: two of them were stationary on the beach, about a hundred yards apart, and each of the other two ran a steamboat. These boats were used in casting the seine. They went out side by side for nearly three quarters of a mile and separating they would go in opposite directions for a few hundred yards and then strike towards the shore until they let out all the rope. The engine on the beach then would pull it in. About every five hours a landing was made. The process of taking care of the fish, of shipping, and the other details we will give the *Herald* in a subsequent letter.

—*Independent Herald,* Hendersonville (May 18, 1882)

LAKE WACCAMAW

This is one of the most beautiful of all the Southern lakes. It is situated in Columbus county, North Carolina, near the line of the Wilmington, Columbia & Augusta Railroad, fifty miles from Marion and about forty miles from Wilmington, and although it was described one hundred and fifty years ago by a young Englishman who was making a tour of America as "the pleasantest place I ever saw in my life," it is comparatively unknown to the pleasure seeker of to-day. The lake is oval in shape, and covers about twenty-seven thousand acres of ground, and is five and a half miles broad and eight miles long. It is almost entirely surrounded by a magnificent growth of forest trees which bathe their hoary feet in the beautiful flood, and with their charming colors of leaf and branch, festooned by fragrant honey suckle vines and gay colored flowers draped with bright trailing moss, present a panorama of exquisite beauty and loveliness. The lake is supplied by a number of creeks which empty into it and springs which send up their never failing currents from the bottom of the basin.

The water near the shore is shallow, but elsewhere reaches an average depth of thirty feet, the greatest depth being about thirty-five feet. By the course of the Waccamaw river, which is said to form the eastern boundary of the republic of Horry, the lake is one hundred and eight miles from the Atlantic ocean. In an air-line the distance to the sea is not more than twenty miles. The water is perfectly fresh and strongly impregnated with the juniper berry. This whole section of country is on an almost dead level of slight elevation above the sea, and no reasonable account of the origin of this inland sea has ever been given. One theory is that in the remote past there was an immense deposit of vegetable mould which was burned out and formed a basin for the lake. This is not a reasonable theory, and the origin of the lake can only be attributed to those tremendous convulsions of Nature which elevated the mountain ridges and hollowed out the seas. There can be but little doubt, however, that this entire section of country was at one time covered by the waters of the great deep. Oyster shells and sea shells of almost every variety have been found in excavations which have been made for wells, and only a few days ago in digging a well near the lake an immense block of marl filled with sea shells was brought up thirty feet from the surface of the earth. Immense beds of marl have been found all through this section, and those who have given the matter a great deal of attention are satisfied that there are rich phosphate deposits underlying the lake, which could be worked to very great advantage. Several analyses of marl have been made showing that it contains a percentage of the most valuable fertilizing properties, and experiments have fully established its value as a cheap manure for all the crops that are cultivated. The marl is found in regular strata, and is ready for use as soon as it has been mined. Surrounding the lake are immense swamps, filled with forest growths of cypress, oak and hickory. On the north east side lies the Great Green Swamp, which covers an area of two hundred square miles. This swamp is an evergreen jungle, containing, however, many patches of highland, which are called islands, and are covered with hickory, oak, juniper, long leaf pines, birch and other forest trees. These swamps have been penetrated in many directions by train railways, and a very large lumbering business has been developed in cypress shingles and staves and sawed lumber of oak and hickory. Col. H. B. Short owns about 60,000 acres of land at the lake and does an immense business. He employs 200 hands and ships his lumber to New York, Philadelphia, Baltimore and largely to the West Indies and South America. About one half of his products are sold in foreign markets by direct shipment from Wilmington.

The "Islands" which are located in the swamps are very fertile and yield large crops whenever they are under cultivation. The earliest vegetables in this section are raised on these islands, only a few of which, however, have any population. It would pay well to develop the business of truck farming for the Wilmington and Northern markets. The lake is well stocked with fish, and some almost fabulous stories are told of the wonderful catches that have been made in its waters. All varieties of perch are to be found, and the white perch is peculiar to this lake. In addition there are trout in abundance, blackfish, pickerel and catfish, and Col. Short is now experimenting with German carp and the landlocked salmon. To give some idea of the great number of fish in the lake it is stated upon good authority that a party consisting of three went out last week and in about one hour's time caught 263 white perch with the hook, "and it wasn't a good day for fishing either."

The swamps around the lake are filled with game of all kinds—squirrels, raccoons, deer, black bear, beaver, otter, &c. Two hundred deer have been killed here within sixty days and an old man named Hudson who lives on "Cusoe's Island," has for years done a very profitable business in trapping. There are also a great many wild cattle in the swamps and many of the people around

here winter their cattle in these swamps, which furnish an in-
exhaustible supply of green food the year round.

There are many romances connected with the lake. It is said
Osceola, the great Indian chief whose modest tomb may now be
found beneath the frowning walls of fort Moultrie, on Sullivan's
Island, was born on the banks of Waccamaw Lake, and his father
was a white man named Powell. Other stories are told of many
terrific encounters between the old Indian tribes upon the shores
of this lake and several mounds may be seen where the dead were
buried. During the war a great many deserters found a safe hid-
ing place in the swamps around here, but the wilderness is as
dense almost as it was a hundred years ago, and the solitude as
grand.

—*Carolina Watchman,* Salisbury (July 27, 1882), as reprinted
from the Charleston (S. C.) *News and Courier*

ESEEOLA INN, LINVILLE

Shepherd M. Dugger

Three thousand years ago Solomon said: "There is nothing new
under the sun"; but if he could come back to this world and engage board at Eseeola Inn, he would find that something new has
been invented; for he could hollow "halloo" in a telephone and
receive an answer from a social-minded fellow in the telephone
office over at Cranberry, and he could chalk his cue and try his
luck on a billiard-ball, like which no rotary object ever revolu-
tionized across a rectangular game-table in the city of Jerusalem.

This splendid building has hot and cold baths, smoking and
reception rooms, broad stairways of easy ascent, carpeted rooms
and hall-ways, marble-topped office counters, extensive piazzas
for promenades, and a beautiful dining-room, whose sumptuary

ingatherings are guaranteed by the proprietors to be equal, if not superior, to those of any other house in the mountains of North Carolina.

Such is the variety and flavor of the food that, when you place your foot on the threshold of the masticating department, your nasal proboscis is greeted with the aroma of roasted mutton or beef, and the alimentary pupils of your orbicular instruments are fixed upon large slabs of comb honey, consisting of the gathered sweets from mountain flowers, and rivalling in delicacy the nectar of the gods.

Among the delicious dishes of Eseeola's tables is pure maple syrup, manufactured from maple orchards on the Company's lands, and those popular mountain batter-cakes, made from that peculiarly-shaped grain, about which a lady recently interrogated a gentleman, as follows:

"Kind sir," said she, "do you know how buckwheat came into this country?"

"No, madam," replied the man; "but I will thank you for any information you may give me on that point."

"Well, sir," said the lady, "I will tell you. It came into this country three-cornered."

—*The Balsam Groves of the Grandfather Mountain* (1892)

TERRAPIN WATCHING

Holley Mack Bell

Sunday is not a good day for the terrapins of the Cashie River.

The terrapins I'm speaking of are the half a dozen or so which try to sun themselves on a log at the bend of the river just up-stream of the Cashie River Bridge here.

Sunday is a bad day for the terrapins, big, little, and middle-sized, which try to sun themselves on these bright, sunshiny days.

There are too many motorboats. Just about the time three or four—or sometimes five or six—terrapins have climbed up on the log and have begun soaking up sunshine, zoom, comes a motorboat and upsets their siesta.

Sometimes the terrapins hop off log at the first sound of the motor. Sometimes a brave one will hold on for dear life. The motorboat will go putting by, the swells from the boat will rock the log like a storm-tossed vessel. The brave one will hold on, but finally the swells become so big he's shaken off.

The boat passes; the swells subside; the peaceful, placid Cashie becomes its own again and, one by one, the terrapins begin to climb back on the log.

Apparently the log is the exposed portion of a submerged tree, because it doesn't move with the wind currents. It's a grand spot for the terrapins every day except Sunday when there are lots of motorboats out.

Terrapin watching is an absorbing subject and is practically my full-time operation on Sundays since we moved to a house on the banks of the Cashie at the bend of the river just above the bridge.

Terrapin watching is a delightful pastime because at the same time you can engage in reading the Sunday papers, sipping pineapple juice or eating a sandwich while lounging away a lazy Sunday afternoon in a hammock on a screened-in porch on the Cashie.

I start the morning when upon arising I announce to my wife, "Four little ones and two big ones on the log." Throughout the day I give the regular Terrapin Report. "One big one and two little ones," or "Motorboat came by—no terrapins," until the final Terrapin Report for the day: "Sun down; terrapins left log." Terrapin watching is a fascinating pastime.

—*Bertie Ledger-Advance*, Windsor (June 9, 1955)

THE BROWN MOUNTAIN LIGHTS

John Parris

Jutting out of the Catawba Valley like a grim prophecy is the mountain that provided the locale for a best-selling mystery novel, *Kill One, Kill Two*.

It is the famous Brown Mountain where mysterious balls of fire gambol across its summit in the night when the moon is down and the stars are too sleepy to wink.

Since time out of memory folks have looked upon the mountain with awe and with wonder, and there are some who say anything can happen there. The old-timers shake their heads when you talk of Brown Mountain and say there is a spell on it. Hunters have told strange tales about it. Like how their dogs come whimpering back whenever they get to a certain spot on the long, flat-topped mountain.

For fifty years the Brown Mountain lights have puzzled scientists. They first attracted nationwide interest in 1913 when the U. S. Geological Survey became interested in the mysterious fire-ball capers and sent one of its scientists into the hills to study their origin. He was here only a short while before reporting that they came from the headlights of locomotives flashing up over the mountain.

The old-timers listened and then laughed. They had seen the lights over the mountain before a train ever ran through the valley. Besides, these were balls of fire that popped up over the Brown Mountain, and any fool knew that a locomotive threw out a beam.

Then the automobile came along, and the scientists laid the phenomenon at the door of Henry Ford. In time, there were almost as many theories to their origin as there were lights over Brown Mountain.

In 1922 another government geologist arrived for a more thorough investigation, determined to lay the spooks of the old mountain once and for all. This was his report after two weeks:

47 per cent of the lights originated from car headlights.

33 per cent from locomotive headlights.

10 per cent from fixed lights.

10 per cent from brush fires.

The old-timers laughed some more and reckoned there was a sight of addle-brained folks drawing down good hard money up in Washington.

Some folks who remembered the 1916 flood in the mountains wrecked the geologist's report. They recollected that the flood put the local trains and the automobiles out of business and that the electric power lines were down, too. It was a wet time, they recalled, and even the devil couldn't have started a brush fire. While all this was taking place, they pointed out, the Brown Mountain lights still put in their regular appearance.

But the geologist did clear up one point. Over the years the lights popped up in different colors. One would be orange, another blue, and another white. The geologist said dust and mist caused the lights to have various tints. The old-timers reckoned maybe that could be so.

Through the years there have been many explanations given as to the origin of the lights but none has proved correct. Some have suggested the will-o'-the-wisp, albeit there's no marshy ground on the mountain. Some have suggested foxfire, the glowing light often seen on pieces of decaying wood. But no one has ever known of a piece that could be seen seen eight miles away. A piece of pitchblende was discovered near the mountain and this was offered as the cause until somebody pointed out that the emanations from radium are invisible.

Some wag suggested they were the reflections from the fires of corn likker stills. Others have suggested they came from nearby towns which can be seen from here. But at night the lights from these towns are steady. They don't stray off, zoom and zig-zag through the sky.

Of course, there are legends to account for the mysterious lights. One is that it is the soul of an Indian maiden who seeks her warrior brave killed in a bloody battle.

Fall is considered the best time of year to see the lights. And Wiseman's View is one of the favorite spots to come and watch the mysterious phenomenon.

You'll know when you see them. Suddenly, as you look toward Brown Mountain, a light pops up on the horizon. It shines steadily for a few seconds. Then it rises in the air. It wavers as if hesitating which way to go. Then it winks out.

Back in 1940, a friend of mine with the Associated Press in New York decided to write a mystery. A South Carolinian by birth, he was familiar with the Brown Mountain lights. So he took Brown Mountain and its mysterious lights and wove them into his novel, writing it, strangely enough, in the AP morgue.

In his book, Andy Anderson put a lodge on Brown Mountain and peopled it with a lot of folks. Every time the lights started popping up over his Brown Mountain somebody got murdered. He called it *Kill One, Kill Two*.

But like the old-timers here in the hills, Andy didn't try to explain the mysterious lights.

—*Roaming the Mountains* (1955)

DEBUTANTES AND CULTURE

Jonathan Daniels

The Debutante Ball in Raleigh, which adds 165 young ladies to North Carolina's social "400" each year, apparently is unique. Elsewhere society is centered in cities. In North Carolina, so long without cities, the state is the unit of society and the state capital its center. So in September (a hot time chosen because it is a vacation time too) girls from everywhere in the state are presented to society in Raleigh in a process which combines the best features of the industrial assembly line and the old South of crinoline and roses.

The town is full of mothers as well as daughters at Deb Ball time. Fathers come with their checkbooks, though, except for the clothes, being presented to Society in North Carolina is an eighty-five-dollar bargain.

There is a similar sharing of the arts two months after the Debutante Ball, in what was once called facetiously and now is known almost officially as Culture Week. So far as I can learn, this also is a unique Raleigh affair.

Mild-mannered Dr. Christopher Crittenden, head of the State Department of Archives and History, serves as shepherd for the cultural flock. Other males—college professors, editors, writers and artists—do much of the formal speaking. The ladies crowd to overflowing the Sir Walter Hotel, and if no great halls are required to receive those saluting the various native arts, it must be realized that these ladies combine the arts with cookies, punch and conversation to make Raleigh the good gathering place they insistently want it to be in terms of "culture."

—from "Tarheel Capital," *Holiday* (February, 1956)

SEVEN WONDERS OF NORTH CAROLINA

What are the seven wonders of North Carolina? Editor Don Shoemaker of the Asheville Citizen entertains himself and others by speculating on this. The Seven Wonders of the Ancient World, as our readers will recall, were:

> Great Pyramids
> Pharos Lighthouse
> Phidias' Statue of Zeus
> Mausoleum of Halicarnassus
> Colossus of Rhodes
> Temple of Diana at Ephesus
> Hanging Gardens of Babylon

Editor Shoemaker nominates for North Carolina wonders the following among others:

> The Cow Palace at Raleigh
> The Old Fort-Ridgecrest Southern Railway
> The Blue Ridge Parkway
> A mammoth textile mill such as Cone
> The carillon tower at Duke
> The Playmakers building at Chapel Hill
> The State Capitol building
> Wright Memorial at Kill Devil Hills

But wait a minute. That's already eight, and Don hasn't even mentioned Dr. Archibald Henderson or Harry Golden.

—*Greensboro Daily News* (April 22, 1956)

DUKE UNIVERSITY

Ovid Williams Pierce

Beginning at a circular drive, there is a long beautiful approach to the tower. The road rides high above the slopes and gardens below, which, in spring, drop down and down in terraces of color. The tower ahead reaches up, overlooks the forest around. Then, suddenly, to the right and left, the quadrangle, perhaps the largest university court in the world, has received you—a vast greensward enclosed by buildings of greenish-gray stone.

It is strange to pass a tobacco barn, a crossroads store, a little white church in a grove as fresh as a primer drawing, and to come suddenly to the center of this Gothic world. Here in the middle of the North Carolina woods is a re-creation of the Middle Ages, as complete as a town.

The story is that in 1925 James B. Duke looked over the forests around Durham and, coming upon this spot, exclaimed, "Here's where it ought to be." Here, accordingly, a complete university sprang from the woods.

The chapel tower reaches above the lesser towers. Arches and cloisters are worked into a unifying design. Flagstone walks cross the green. Chimneys and spires rising from the deep slope of moss-gray slate reach into the sky with the tops of the pines. And there inside the chapel are the bodies of the founders of the Duke dynasty, each marble sarcophagus as cold, as permanent as that of any European saint.

Comparison with the University of North Carolina is of course inevitable. By its very nearness to Chapel Hill, Duke has had a difficult role to play. To many, it has seemed to be a foreign thing on native soil. But Duke, too, is North Carolina—an old school, in fact, founded in 1838 as Union Institute, with a history of more than a hundred years of service to the South.

Now as you follow the serpentine road around the campus, you see the cars of all the states. Here is a school for the Eastern seaboard: New York, New Jersey, Pennsylvania, as well as the South. A little farther around the circle is the hospital area, one of the great medical centers of the South, a complete world within itself.

You can't help remembering again what a short time ago it was that Mr. Duke walked into this forest and said, "Here's where it ought to be." The making of a myth out of marble tombs inside the Duke Chapel seems not so strange as the story of this school translated from tobacco farms, from North Carolina land.

—from "North Carolina," *Holiday* (February, 1957)

BREVARD FOR SUMMER MUSIC

Thelma Harrington Bell

Brevard, the seat of Transylvania County, lies in a high region of mountains, forests, and waterfalls. One of the busiest, friendliest towns imaginable, it has a special music story of its own.

Along about May, within a thirty-mile radius of the town, large musical eighth notes suddenly appear on telephone poles and trees. Brightly-colored red or yellow, they point the way to the Transylvania Music Camp. Any time after June 27 you can follow the notes a mile out of town along a pleasant country road to the open entrance gates of a rustic camp beautifully situated in rolling Blue Ridge mountain country. Below you lie the camp buildings. A sky-reflecting lake, fed by a mountain stream, invites you to linger on a warm day.

From various small practice cabins, scattered up and down the slopes, come the full-bodied sounds of violin and cello and the call of flute and oboe. In the community building beside the lake a youthful band is testing the intricacies of one of the modern compositions. In the auditorium at the foot of a long grassy slope, a symphony orchestra is rehearsing a Berlioz score under the baton of the camp musical director, James Christian Pfohl.

In this camp, the oldest and most progressive in the South, young people between the ages of twelve and twenty gather each summer to study and to make serious music. If you should catch sight of a Tiny Tim, a potential concert master, no doubt, carrying a *violino piccolo* (a half-pint violin), he would be one of the faculty children. Even a quarter-size, or pocket violin, was in evidence one year!

The heads of the various teaching departments, almost without exception, are first chair men from the nation's symphony orchestras. During the camp session, advanced students play in the concert orchestra side by side with their faculty instructors.

All summer long the town is alive with music. Everywhere one is aware of a unique feeling that is inspired by a bond of music appreciation. There are thrice-weekly camp concerts featuring guest artists, faculty members, or talented students as soloists. There is a weekly student concert, and a weekly lecture on the compositions to be played at the weekend symphony concert. The public is admitted free to both.

To those people who derive special enjoyment from the musical efforts of young fry, the concerts of the Hilltopper Orchestra and Band are available every Sunday afternoon.

In mid-August at the close of the camp season, the town's population expands with the advent of the Brevard Music Festival, a full week of nightly concerts. An augmented Festival orchestra of about eighty players, supplemented by a full chorus for such works as Mendelssohn's *Elijah,* presents programs in which a classical repertoire rubs notes with modern compositions and occasional world premieres. In a delightfully congenial setting, patrons may enjoy such solo virtuosi as Isaac Stern, Ruth Slenczynska and Eileen Farrell.

James Christian Pfohl, through whose efforts the Transylvania Music Camp was founded in 1936, is also the conductor of Florida's Jacksonville Symphony Orchestra.

The activities of both camp and Festival receive the enthusiastic support of civic-minded citizens and local industry. Many of the practice cabins carry the names of states above their doors; they were donated by the Federation of Music Clubs of those states. "I'll be practicing in Alabama," or "They're working on Mozart in Maryland," have special meaning in camp. . . .

—*Ford Times* (May, 1959)

CREEKS ARE PEOPLE

Thad Stem, Jr.

A man can do far worse than be a lover of creeks, especially in the divinely inspired blue-green days when the earth all but explodes at the seams with green fulfilment.

Have you watched a creek lately, watched it with your heart, taken time out to draw its picture in your mind? The principal trouble is that a creek's personality is so devious he is likely to leave you flabbergasted in your efforts to keep up with him. Watch him intensely. One minute he's playing a game of leap-frog with fallen logs and stolid, squat rocks. He's Huck Finn playing hooky in the woods, chewing sassafras and giving cities a wide berth and taking no stock in dead folks.

Or, he becomes confused and runs in a semi-circle, an irate dog chasing his own tail. Then he straightens out like a Saturday night drunk on Monday morning and goes humping across the sweet meadowland twirling a stick in his supple fingers, playing at drum-major for a caravan of naive saplings, garrulous blue-jays, and neurotic bumble bees. But his mood of gallantry he can't long sustain. He blows up his wet sleeve and changes himself into a roll-a-coaster and hurtles down the hill at prodigious speed, grits his teeth and climbs the next knoll to spend himself in undulating paroxysms to reach the place where someone who thinks he is a silver stallion put a bridge across his back for a saddle.

Yep. You can do much worse than be a lover of creeks. Just watch him crawling on his belly under the willows, emulating an Indian scout, and then pausing briefly to tease the lady-birds about their fellows. His history is short to the eye but long to the heart. He swaggers down from the spring, a boy dwarfing the mother who bore him. He pauses at the corner oak to wave farewell, as a boy off to high adventure whose mind leaps between the magic he's read and the safe comforts he's known at home.

Then, proudly and wistfully, he races headlong to the bridge to mingle with the fellows who're off to see the whole, wide world.

—*The Perennial Almanac* (1959)

A COPPER MINE AND A DESERT

To be Sold, by Charles Evans, *Ferry-keeper on* Tar *River,* 15 *Miles from* Speere's *Ferry on* Roanoke *River, in* North-Carolina, *at Ten Pounds* Virginia *Currency per Hundred, Two Thousand Acres of very good land, being Purchase Land, granted in the Proprietor's Time, at Six Pence per Hundred Quit-Rents, for ever: And in the Banks thereof is a Copper Mine, twice tried in* England. *It runs 5 Miles on the River, is very commodious for Trade, with two Cyprus Swamps thereon, full of vast large Cyprus, and near adjoining to a Desart, called the* Canetar; *which is suppos'd to be 10 Miles wide, and 30 Miles long; and when fenced to the Desart at each End, you may keep 1000 Head of Cattle, without any Feeding, for 1000 Years, being full of vast high Reeds, and there is brave hunting the Bear.*

—*Virginia Gazette,* Williamsburg (February 23, 1739)

ALPHABET POEM

Among the foremost of all lands,
Behold old North Carolina stands.
Colossal mountains pierce her sky;
Delightful valleys among them lie;

Entombed beneath her surface deep,
Full mines of precious metals sleep.
Grand, grand, magnificently grand,
Her noble hills majestic stand;
In rich luxuriance covered o'er
Just like the fabled fields of yore,
Ken the delightful scenery round;
Landscapes more grand nowhere are found.
Majestic groves of forest trees
Nod gently to the passing breeze;
Orchards and fields in rich array,
Plenteous fruit and grain display,
Quelling every want and need,
Rendering man happy indeed.
So let all with heart and hand
Try to improve our goodly land,
Until each hill and vale shall be
Vocal with life and industry;
We then can boast a State, I vow,
X (10) times as great as she is now.
Youth, noble youth, with hearts elate,
Zealous be for the good old North State.

—*Murphy Bulletin* (October 11, 1888),
copied from the *Patriot* (Greensboro)

PEOPLE

"The Inhabitants of Carolina, through the Richness of the Soil, live an easy and pleasant Life."

—JOHN LAWSON

WHAT MANNER OF MAN?

William T. Polk

What manner of man is a North Carolinian? How can you tell a Tar Heel? What ingredients went into his making? Is he different, and if so, how and why?

There is no slide-rule answer to these questions, but it may be interesting to explore them. The Tar Heel is not a distinct species, but he may have some distinguishing marks.

North Carolinians are what they are largely because of racial heritage. This is mainly Anglo-Saxon with a strong infusion of Scotch and a weaker one of German blood; about a third of the population is Negro. The Anglo-Saxons account for the law-making, law-abiding, commercial-minded, self-reliant, practical and determined strain; the Scotch are the proud, stoical, imaginative, high-tempered, democratic folk, their heroes being the parson, the teacher and the statesman; the Germans are the shrewd, the economical, the hard-working and the good-humored, placing much stress on church, school and business, but not much on politics; the Negro is the one who works most and loafs most, suffers most and rejoices most, is the most violent and the most patient, the one who enjoys and endures most and absorbs the shocks of life as a rubber tire absorbs the shocks of the road.

The environment plays its part too. The State was not settled from the sea as Virginia and South Carolina were; its Outer Banks fended off immigration from Britain and Europe; North Carolina was settled at second hand from its neighbor states to the north and south, with some Scots and Germans from Pennsylvania sliding down the Appalachians and rolling off into Tarheelia. So it came about that North Carolina did not develop either urban life or the big plantation system—for better for worse—to anything like the extent that Virginia and South Carolina did. There was more of isolation and homogeneity, less of caste and culture in North Carolina. So Tar Heels adopted the somewhat invidious motto "*Esse Quam Videri*," and took perhaps excessive pride in referring to their state as "a vale of humility between two mountains of conceit." We were mighty proud of not being proud.

We did, however, in such a historical setting, become independent, courageous, resourceful, democratic, gregarious and individualistic, although we would use plainer words than these Latin terms to describe ourselves. . . .

—*The North Carolina Guide* (1955), ed. Blackwell P. Robinson

ON ROANOKE ISLAND
1587

John White

The 13 of August our Sauage *Manteo,* by the commandement of Sir *Walter Ralegh,* was christened in *Roanoak,* and called Lord thereof, and of *Dasamonguepeuk,* in reward of his faithfull service.

The 18 *Elenor,* daughter to the Gouernour, and wife to *Ananias Dare* one of the Assistants, was deliuered of a daughter in *Roanoak,* and the same was christened there the Sunday following, and because this child was the first Christian borne in *Virginia,* shee was named *Virginia.* By this time our ships had unladen the goods and victuals of the planters, and began to take in wood, and fresh water, and to new calke and trimme them for *England:* the planters also prepared their letters and tokens to send backe into England.

—*Hakluyt's Voyages* (1600)

HEREDITARY NOBILITY
IN NORTH CAROLINA

Wingate Reed

Two hundred and ninety years ago, the "true and absolute" Lords Proprietors of Carolina conceived and attempted to spawn a government of landed aristocracy in the sparsely populated wilderness of Carolina.

To judge fairly the grandiose plans of those eight Earls, Lords, Dukes, and Baronets, one must consider the political climate and human relations of England at that time. After their success in restoring Charles II to the throne of England, the creation of a *Palatinate* of Carolina must have seemed a relatively easy project. They saw nothing wrong in a privileged class of nobility, nor an underprivileged class of leetmen and serfs, subject to the will of their masters. Both were accepted by all Englishmen.

In addition to the vast area of land, the King's charter included the "jurisdiction and privileges of a County Palatine of Durham." This included the right to create an order of nobility in Carolina, provided the titles used were not those common to England. "Only God could create a King with divine rights, and only a King could create a Lord."

Inspired by visions of a principality in Carolina as great as the German *Palatinate* on the Rhine, the Lords Proprietors borrowed the title or *dignity* of *Palatine* for the ruler of their domain. *Landgrave*, also a German title, borrowed from the ruler of Hesse-Kassel, was next in *dignity* to the *Palatine*. *Cacique*, the Spanish equivalent of a Count, and a title used by Spaniards to designate a native chief or ruler of their American possessions, was selected as the third *dignity*. For each *Landgrave*, there were to be two *Caciques*.

The eldest member of the Lords Proprietors was to be the *Palatine* of Carolina, the pinnacle of this pyramid of nobility. He, with the seven other Lords Proprietors, each having a resounding but empty title such as Admiral, Chancellor, or Chamberlain of

Carolina, formed the *Palatine* Court, which was to rule the Province or *Palatinate* of Carolina. Upon his death, the *Palatine* was to be succeeded by the next older Proprietor.

Initially, Carolina was to be divided into twelve counties of 480,000 acres each. Each county was divided into seignories, baronies, and colonies. A barony consisted of 12,000 acres, "in one single piece." A seignory was one or more baronies. A provision was made for "manors" of from 3,000 to 12,000 acres, so designated by grant, for commoners.

For each county, there would be one, and only one *Landgrave*, and two *Caciques*. These *dignities* were to be bestowed upon "such of the inhabitants of the said Province," as the Lords Proprietors thought deserving of the honor.

Within each county, each Proprietor was to have a seignory of 12,000 acres. The *Landgrave* was to have four baronies, totaling 48,000 acres. Each *Cacique* was to have two baronies, totaling 24,000 acres. This accounted for two-fifths of the land area of the county. The remaining three-fifths, or 288,000 acres, was to be divided into four colonies (precincts), for the use of freeholders. The possession of land was a legal requirement for the holder of any *dignity* or office within the Province....

Colonel Robert Daniel was the first *Landgrave* to reside in North Carolina. Appointed while serving on the Governor's council in Charles Town, Daniel came to North Carolina as deputy Governor. He received no barony in North Carolina, but purchased a plantation on the Pamlico, now known as Archbell's Point, across Bath Creek from Bath Town. Later, Daniel returned to Charles Town, as deputy to Governor Craven. After Craven returned to England, Daniel assumed the governorship.

The Swiss Baron Christopher von Graffenreid, who founded New Bern, was the second *Landgrave* to reside in North Carolina. He wrote that during the Cary Rebellion, while Governor Hyde was in Virginia, "a small crowd of North Carolina inhabitants offered the government to me, ... as in the absence of a Governor, the *Landgrave* occupied the first rank and held the presidial. ..." Graffenreid declined, explaining, "I had been an ocular witness to his [Hyde's] election by the Lords Proprietors, and had congratulated him ... far more, he was a near relative of the Queen."

Governor Charles Eden was the third and last *Landgrave* to live in North Carolina. ...

After more than a quarter of a century of trying to get the "assent and approbation of the Freemen," or their Assemblies, to the Fundamental Constitutions, the Proprietors abandoned the hope and directed the Governor to "come as nigh as possible" in the laws passed by the Assembly.

This failure was not because the Constitutions created class distinction in Carolina. Such distinctions were there. The bell tolled for hereditary nobility in Carolina because the Constitutions threatened the two things the Freemen of Carolina prized most: their freedom and "good bottom land."

They had no intention of surrendering the "liberties, franchises, and privileges of the King's subjects resident within the realm of England," guaranteed them by the charter. Their greatest objection was the grant of vast tracts of 12,000 to 48,000 acres of choice land to a single individual. These land-hungry Freemen saw this as the greatest threat to their future and that of Carolina.

Over half a century elapsed before the Lords Proprietors finally abandoned their hope of creating a Palatinate in Carolina, and surrendered their charter to the Crown, leaving their hereditary nobility in Carolina to wither on the vine.

This desire for "nobility" did not expire easily. Forty years after the Revolution, a lady in South Carolina, whose husband was a descendant of Sir John Colleton, signed herself "Baroness of Fairlawn and *Landgravine* of Colleton."

—*The State* (May 27, 1961)

INDIANS ON THE ENO RIVER
1670

John Lederer

The fourteenth of *June*, pursuing a South-south-west course, sometimes by a beaten path, and sometimes over hills and rocks, I was forc'd to take up my quarters in the Woods: for though the *Oenock*-Indians, whom I then sought, were not in a direct line above thirty odde miles distant from *Akenatzy*, yet the Ways were such, and obliged me to go far about, that I reached not *Oenock* until the sixteenth. The Country here, by the industry of these Indians, is very open, and clear of wood. Their Town is built round a field, where in their Sports they exercise with so much labour and violence, and in so great numbers, that I have seen the ground wet with the sweat that dropped from their bodies: their chief Recreation is Slinging of stones. They are of mean stature and courage, covetous and thievish, industrious to earn a peny; and therefore hire themselves to their neighbours, who employ them as Carryers or Porters. They plant abundance of Grain, reap three Crops in a Summer, and out of their Granary supply all the adjacent parts. These and the Mountain-Indians build not their houses of Bark, but of Watling and Plaister. In Summer, the heat of the weather makes them chuse to lie abroad in the night under thin arbours of wilde Palm. Some houses they have of Reed and Bark; they build them generally round: to each house belongs a little hovel made like an oven, where they lay up their Corn and Mast, and keep it dry. They parch their Nuts and Acorns over the fire, to take away their rank Oyliness; which afterwards pressed, yeeld a milky liquor, and the Acorns an Amber-colour'd Oyl. In these, mingled together they dip their Cakes at great Entertainments, and so serve them up to their guests as an extraordinary dainty. Their Government is Democratick; and the Sentences of their old men are received as Laws, or rather Oracles, by them.

—The Discoveries (1672)

CHRISTIAN NATIVES OF CAROLINA

John Lawson

The *Christian* Natives of *Carolina* are a straight, clean-limb'd People; the Children being seldom or never troubled with Rickets, or those other Distempers, that the *Europeans* are visited withal. 'Tis next to a Miracle, to see one of them deform'd in Body. The Vicinity of the Sun makes Impression on the Men, who labour out of doors, or use the Water. As for those Women, that do not expose themselves to the Weather, they are often very fair, and generally as well featur'd, as you shall see any where, and have very brisk, charming Eyes, which sets them off to Advantage. They marry very young; some at Thirteen or Fourteen; and She that stays till Twenty, is reckon'd a stale Maid; which is a very indifferent Character in that warm Country. The Women are very fruitful; most Houses being full of Little Ones. It has been observ'd, that Women long marry'd, and without Children, in other Places, have remov'd to *Carolina* and become joyful Mothers. They have very easy Travail in their Child-bearing, in which they are so happy, as seldom to miscarry. Both Sexes are generally spare of Body, and not Cholerick, nor easily cast down at Disappointments and Losses, seldom immoderately grieving at Misfortunes, unless for the Loss of their nearest Relations and Friends, which seems to make a more than ordinary Impression upon them. Many of the Women are very handy in Canoes, and will manage them with great Dexterity and Skill, which they become accustomed to in this watry Country. They are ready to help their Husbands in any servile Work, as Planting, when the Season of the Weather requires Expedition; Pride seldom banishing good Houswifry. The Girls are not bred up to the Wheel, and Sewing only; but the Dairy and Affairs of the House they are very well acquainted withal; so that you shall see them, whilst very young, manage their Business with a great deal of Conduct and Alacrity. The Children of both Sexes are very docile, and learn any thing with a great deal of Ease and Method; and those that have the Advantages of Education, write good Hands, and prove good Accountants, which is most coveted, and indeed most necessary in these Parts. The young Men are commonly of a bashful, sober Behaviour; few proving Prodigals, to consume what the Industry of their Parents has left them, but commonly improve it. The marrying so young, carries a double Advantage with it, and that is, that the Parents see their Children provided for in Marriage, and the young married People are taught by their Parents, how to get their Living; for their Admonitions make great Impressions on their Children. I had heard (before I knew this new World) that the Natives of *America* were a short-liv'd People, which, by all the Observations I could ever make, proves quite contrary; for those who are born here, and in other Colonies, live to as great Ages as any of the *Europeans,* the Climate being free from Consumptions, which Distemper, fatal to *England,* they are Strangers to. And as the Country becomes more clear'd of Wood, it still becomes more healthful to the Inhabitants, and less addicted to the Ague; which is incident to most new Comers into *America* from *Europe,* yet not mortal. A gentle Emetick seldom misses of driving it away, but if it is not too troublesome, 'tis better to let the Seasoning have its own Course, in which case, the Party is commonly free from it ever after, and very healthful.

—A New Voyage to Carolina (1709)

LUBBERLAND
1728

William Byrd

The only Business here is raising of Hogs, which is manag'd with the least Trouble, and affords the Diet they are most fond of. The Truth of it is, the Inhabitants of N Carolina devour so much Swine's flesh, that it fills them full of gross Humours. For want too of a constant Supply of Salt, they are commonly obliged to eat it Fresh, and that begets the highest taint of Scurvy....

We had encampt so early, that we found time in the Evening to walk near half a Mile into the Woods. There we came upon a Family of Mulattoes, that call'd themselves free, tho' by the Shyness of the Master of the House, who took care to keep least in Sight, their Freedom seem'd a little Doubtful. It is certain many Slaves Shelter themselves in this Obscure Part of the World, nor will any of their righteous Neighbours discover them. On the Contrary, they find their Account in Settling such Fugitives on some out-of-the-way-corner of their Land, to raise Stocks for a mean and inconsiderable Share, well knowing their Condition makes it necessary for them to Submit to any Terms.

Nor were these worthy Borderers content to Shelter Runaway Slaves, but Debtors and Criminals have often met with the like Indulgence. But if the Government of North Carolina has encourag'd this unneighbourly Policy in order to increase their People, it is no more than what' Ancient Rome did before them, which was made a City of Refuge for all Debtors and Fugitives, and from that wretched Beginning grew up in time to be Mistress of a great Part of the World. And, considering how Fortune delights in bringing great things out of Small, who knows but Carolina may, one time or other, come to be the Seat of some other great Empire? . . .

One thing may be said for the Inhabitants of that Province, that they are not troubled with any Religious Fumes, and have the least Superstition of any People living. They do not know Sunday from any other day, any more than Robinson Crusoe did, which would give them a great Advantage were they given to be industrious. But they keep so many Sabbaths every week, that their disregard of the Seventh Day has no manner of cruelty in it, either to Servants or Cattle....

Surely there is no place in the World where the Inhabitants live with less Labour than in N Carolina. It approaches nearer to the Description of Lubberland than any other, by the great felicity of the Climate, the easiness of raising Provisions, and the Slothfulness of the People.

Indian Corn is of so great increase, that a little Pains will Subsist a very large Family with Bread, and then they may have meat without any pains at all, by the Help of the Low Grounds, and the great Variety of Mast that grows on the High-land. The Men, for their Parts, just like the Indians, impose all the Work upon the poor Women. They make their Wives rise out of their Beds early in the Morning, at the same time that they lye and Snore, till the Sun has run one third of his course, and disperst all the unwholesome Damps. Then, after Stretching and Yawning for half an Hour, they light their Pipes, and, under the Protection of a cloud of Smoak, venture out into the open Air; tho', if it happens to be never so little cold, they quickly return Shivering into the Chimney corner. When the weather is mild, they stand leaning with both their arms upon the corn-field fence, and gravely consider whether they had best go and take a Small Heat at the Hough: but generally find reasons to put it off till another time.

Thus they loiter away their Lives, like Solomon's Sluggard, with their Arms across, and at the Winding up of the Year Scarcely have Bread to Eat.

To speak the Truth, tis a thorough Aversion to Labor that makes People file off to N Carolina, where Plenty and a Warm Sun confirm them in their Disposition to Laziness for their whole Lives. . . .

Most of the Rum they get in this Country comes from New England, and is so bad and unwholesome, that it is not improperly call'd "Kill-Devil." It is distill'd there from forreign molosses, which, if Skilfully manag'd, yields near Gallon for Gallon. Their molosses comes from the same country, and has the name of "Long Sugar" in Carolina, I suppose from the Ropiness of it, and Serves all the purposes of Sugar, both in their Eating and Drinking.

When they entertain their Friends bountifully, they fail not to set before them a Capacious Bowl of Bombo, so call'd from the Admiral of that name. This is a Compound of Rum and Water in Equal Parts, made palatable with the said long Sugar. As good Humour begins to flow, and the Bowl to Ebb, they take care to replenish it with Shear Rum, of which there always is a Reserve under the Table. But such Generous doings happen only when that Balsam of life is plenty; for they have often such Melancholy times, that neither Land-graves nor Cassicks can procure one drop for their Wives, when they ly in, or are troubled with the Colick or Vapours. Very few in this Country have the Industry to plant Orchards, which, in a Dearth of Rum, might supply them with much better Liquor.

The Truth is, there is one Inconvenience that easily discourages lazy People from making This improvement: very often, in Autumn, when the Apples begin to ripen, they are visited with Numerous Flights of paraqueets, that bite all the Fruit to Pieces in a moment, for the sake of the Kernels. The Havock they make is Sometimes so great, that whole Orchards are laid waste in Spite of all the Noises that can be made, or Mawkins that can be dresst up, to fright 'em away. These Ravenous Birds visit North Carolina only during the warm Season, and so soon as the Cold begins to come on, retire back towards the Sun. They rarely Venture so far North as Virginia, except in a very hot Summer, when they visit the most Southern Parts of it. They are very Beautiful; but like some other pretty Creatures, are apt to be loud and mischievous. . . .

Within 3 or 4 Miles of Edenton, the Soil appears to be a little more fertile, tho' it is much cut with Slashes, which seem all to have a tendency towards the Dismal.

This Town is Situate on the North side of Albemarle Sound, which is there about 5 miles over. A Dirty Slash runs all along the Back of it, which in the Summer is a foul annoyance, and furnishes abundance of that Carolina plague, musquetas. There may be 40 or 50 Houses, most of them Small, and built without Expense. A Citizen here is counted Extravagant, if he has Ambition enough to aspire to a Brick-chimney. Justice herself is but indifferently Lodged, the Court-House having much the Air of a Common Tobacco-House. I believe this is the only Metropolis in the Christian or Mahometan World, where there is neither Church, Chappel, Mosque, Synagogue, or any other Place of Publick Worship of any Sect or Religion whatsoever.

What little Devotion there may happen to be is much more

private than their vices. The People seem easy without a Minister, as long as they are exempted from paying Him. Sometimes the Society for propagating the Gospel has had the Charity to send over Missionaries to this Country; but unfortunately the Priest has been too Lewd for the people, or, which oftener happens, they too lewd for the Priest. For these Reasons these Reverend Gentlemen have always left their Flocks as arrant Heathen as they found them. Thus much however may be said for the Inhabitants of Edenton, that not a Soul has the least taint of Hypocrisy, or Superstition, acting very Frankly and aboveboard in all their Excesses.

Provisions here are extremely cheap, and extremely good, so that People may live plentifully at a triffleing expense. Nothing is dear but Law, Physick, and Strong Drink, which are all bad in their Kind, and the last they get with so much Difficulty, that they are never guilty of the Sin of Suffering it to Sour upon their Hands. Their Vanity generally lies not so much in having a handsome Dining-Room, as a Handsome House of Office: in this Kind of Structure they are really extravagant.

They are rarely guilty of Flattering or making any Court to their governors, but treat them with all the Excesses of Freedom and Familiarity. They are of Opinion their rulers wou'd be apt to grow insolent, if they grew Rich, and for that reason take care to keep them poorer, and more dependent, if possible, than the Saints in New England used to do their Governors. They have very little coin, so they are forced to carry on their Home-Traffick with Paper-Money. This is the only Cash that will tarry in the Country, and for that reason the Discount goes on increasing between that and real Money, and will do so to the End of the Chapter.

Our Time passt heavily in our Quarters, where we were quite cloy'd with the Carolina Felicity of having nothing to do. . . .

—*History of the Dividing Line* (1841)

COLONIAL GOVERNORS WERE DISLIKED

Bion H. Butler

The antagonisms that arose between the governors of the province and the people ... came to such a stage that in many cases the people were defiant of law. Governor Burrington, in 1731, before the Cape Fear had become much of a settlement north of Wilmington, writing to the Duke of Newcastle, said, "The inhabitants of North Carolina are not industrious, but subtle and crafty; always behaved insolently to their governors; some they have imprisoned, others they have drove out of the country, and at other times they set up a governor of their own choice, supported by men under arms." However, Burrington was not rated high as a governor, and a few years later he was murdered. William Byrd, one of the commissioners who ran the dividing line between Virginia and North Carolina, was scarcely more complimentary of the Carolina people, for he said in his narrative about the survey that the folks along the border "much rather belong to Carolina, where they pay no tribute to God or Caesar." They complained if the survey set them over in Virginia.

—Old Bethesda (1933)

DANIEL BOONE

Lord Byron

Of all men, saving Sylla the Man-slayer,
  Who passes for in life and death most lucky,
Of the great names which in our faces stare,
  The General Boon, back-woodsman of Kentucky,

Was happiest amongst mortals any where;
    For killing nothing but a bear or buck, he
Enjoyed the lonely vigorous, harmless days
Of his old age in wilds of deepest maze.

Crime came not near him—she is not the child
    Of Solitude; Health shrank not from him—for
Her home is in the rarely-trodden wild,
    Where if men seek her not, and death be more

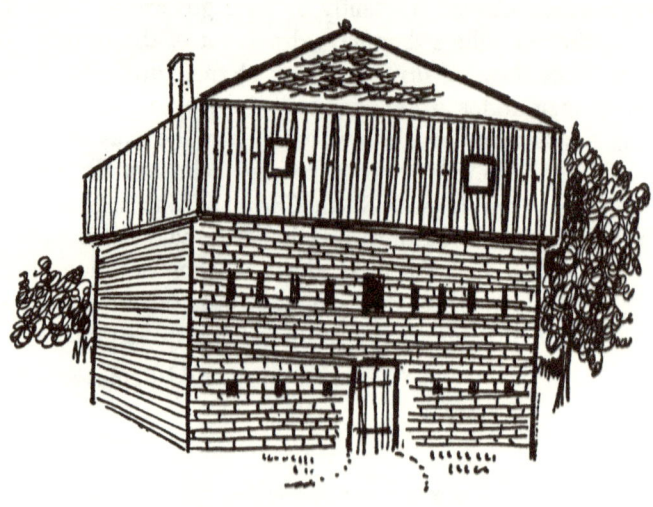

Their choice than life, forgive them, as beguiled
    By habit to what their own hearts abhor—
In cities cage. The present case in point I
Cite is, that Boon lived hunting up to ninety;

And what's still stranger, left behind a name
    For which men vainly decimate the throng,
Not only famous, but of that *good* fame,
    Without which Glory's but a tavern song—

Simple, serene, the antipodes of shame
  Which hate nor envy e'er could tinge with wrong;
An active hermit, even in age the child
Of Nature, or the Man of Ross run wild.

'Tis true he shrank from men even of his nation,
  When they built up unto his darling trees,—
He moved some hundred miles off, for a station
  Where there were fewer houses and more ease;
The inconvenience of civilization
  Is, that you neither can be pleased nor please;
But where he met the individual man,
He shewed himself as kind as mortal can.

He was not all alone: around him grew
  A sylvan tribe of children of the chase,
Whose young, unwakened world was ever new,
  Nor sword nor sorrow yet had left a trace
On her unwrinkled brow, nor could you view
  A frown on Nature's or on human face;—
The free-born forest found and kept them free,
And fresh as is a torrent or a tree.

And tall and strong and swift of foot were they,
  Beyond the dwarfing city's pale abortions,
Because their thoughts had never been the prey
  Of care or gain: the green woods were their portions;
No sinking Spirits told them they grew grey,
  No Fashion made them apes of her distortions;
Simple they were, not savage; and their rifles,
Though very true, were not yet used for trifles.

Motion was in their days, Rest in their slumbers,
  And Cheerfulness the handmaid of their toil;
Nor yet too many nor too few their numbers;
  Corruption could not make their hearts her soil;

The Lust which stings, the Splendour which encumbers,
    With the free foresters divide no spoil;
Serene, not sullen, were the solitudes
Of this unsighing people of the woods.

                                —*Don Juan*, Canto VIII (1823)

THE SIAMESE TWINS

Our village has been gratified with a sight of the far famed phenomenon which has so much puzzled Physiologists and astonished the rest of the world. The curiosity consists in two completely formed human bodies being indissolubly bound together with a strong cartilagenous substance about eight inches in circumference, and about 4 inches long, also in the perfect coincidence of the motions and in the facility of which they each perform the ordinary functions of life. We have not time nor disposition to add our speculations to the mass of wisdom and nonsense which has been written about this singular freak of nature; they who wish more minute information can be gratified by procuring a historical and scientific treatise which the twins have had published and have for sale and for the perfect accuracy of the historical part of which they vouch. We advise every curious visitor to procure one of these pamphlets, as without it one's curiosity is only irritated and left unsatisfied.

The Siamese brothers were brought to this country in August, 1829, by Capt. Coffin of Newburyport, Mass., under a contract with the mother, which we are sorry to learn has not been fulfilled by him. In November following, they were taken to England, where they remained 18 months, after which time they came back to this country, and have visited most of the States of the Union (this being the 21st). They are now 23 years old, and of course are their own men, acting as the law expresses it "for their own behoof and emolument." They speak the English language with ease and distinctness and from what we can infer are more than ordinarily sprightly in intellect.

We learn from them that they intend making a tour through the whole State. They intend to be in Raleigh on the 4th of July next: In the mean time, they will visit the following places, Salem, Germanton, Wentworth, Leaksville, Yanceyville, Roxborough, Oxford, Louisburg, and possibly Chapel Hill at the commencement.

—*Carolina Watchman*, Salisbury (June 14, 1834)

**

We learn through the medium of a friend that our old acquaintances, the Messrs. CHANG and ENG, have purchased a tract of land near Trap Hill in Wilkes County, where they intend establishing for themselves a home.

We learn that they do not intend travelling much more, perhaps not at all, for exhibition. But will probably make a visit to their native Country and return. We have it from good authority that they have been able to lay up a sum of money which will put them quite at ease for the remainder of their lives. They came into Court on Saturday of Wilkes Court and took the preliminary steps for becoming citizens of the U. States. They seem much delighted with their mountain settlement, particularly from the opportunities afforded them of hunting. Our informant says that he had often seen these two young men before, but that they appeared in their unconstrained condition much more amiable and interesting than when encountering the gaze of the wondering crowd. They seem to take considerable interest in the affairs of the County and neighborhood, and what speaks for their taste as well as intelligence, they are GENUINE WHIGS.

—*Carolina Watchman*, Salisbury (November 1, 1839)

A LONG LIFE

Baley, John, remarkable for longevity; he was baptized and died in North Carolina in 1789, aged 136.

—*Highland Messenger*, Asheville (August 11, 1843)

OBITUARY

by Uncle Jake Carpenter

Charley Kiney age 72 dide may 10 1852
 wars farmer live in mt on bluey rige at kiney gap
 he had 4 wim[min] cors ["of course"] marid to one
   res[t] live on farme
all went to felde work to mak gra[i]n
 all wen to crib for ther br[ea]d
 all went smok ho[u]s for there mete
 he cilde bote 75 to 80 hoges eve[ry] yere
and wimen never had worde[s] bout him
  haven so many wimin
 [if] he wod be [living] this times
  wod be hare pulde
 thar wars 42 children blong to him
 th[ey] all wento preching togethern
noth[ing] sed des aver bod[y] go long smoth
  help one nother
  never had any foes
 got along smoth with avery bodi
  I nod him

—*American Folk Tales and Songs* (1956)
Compiled by Richard Chase

A. LINCOLN'S FATHER A CAROLINIAN?

Burke Davis

A lingering legend is that Abraham Lincoln was the son of a mountaineer (Kentuckian or North Carolinian, in various versions), at whose home Nancy Hanks lived briefly.

This tale has more than once reached the dignity of treatment in books, and many people in the hill country profess to believe it today. According to this story, Nancy Hanks, who spent some years in the North Carolina hills, remained for months in the home of Abraham Enloe, in western North Carolina, on a main wagon route to the west.

She became pregnant by the master of the house, and was banished by Mrs. Enloe. The master of the wagon train taking her West was Thomas Lincoln, to whom she was soon married. Lincoln is said to have agreed to accept the paternity of the child who was to become the most renowned American of his era.

A book of James A. Cathey claimed, on the basis of interviews with elderly mountain people held just before 1900, that the Enloe story was true. Photographs stress the resemblance of face and figure between Lincoln and his "half brother," Wesley Enloe, those of the latter made at the age of eighty-one. The "evidence" ends there.

The dates given do not bear out this tale, for Kentucky documents make it certain that Abraham Lincoln was born three years after Nancy Hanks married Thomas Lincoln. Citation of these facts by biographers has not checked the popularity of the story in the Southern mountains.

Other versions of the Enloe story are laid in various parts of Kentucky. Among even more unlikely tales are those crediting the siring of Lincoln to John C. Calhoun, to a stepson of Chief Justice John Marshall, to Henry Clay, and even to Patrick Henry, who died a decade before Lincoln's birth. This is in the familiar vein of ancient folklore, in which the parentage of great men is attributed to distinguished men on the ground that the common people, as represented in this case by the Hanks-Lincoln strain, cannot produce an Abraham Lincoln.

—*Our Incredible Civil War* (1960)

ON TO LIBERIA

A number of Free Negroes,—nearly forty—left Raleigh on Wednesday, for Norfolk, with the purpose of embarking for Liberia. The vessel which is to convey them is at present in Hampton Roads, and has on board already a number of passengers, who embarked from Baltimore.

—*Spirit of the Age,* Raleigh (May 4, 1853)

SLAVE-OWNERS

Two former slaves, Gooden Bowen of Bladen and John Walker of New Hanover, after being freed became slave-owners themselves. Both were listed as owning 44 slaves each.

—*The State* (June 25, 1960)

RECALLED TO LIFE!

John A. Oates

Luzene Chipman was supposed to have died on the 13th day of April 1874. She was bathed and dressed for burial and put on the bed awaiting the making of the casket. On the 14th of

April when parties started to put her in the casket one man felt a warm spot under her left shoulder and all proceedings were stopped and the doctors began working to restore her to life. On the night of the 14th she opened her eyes and began getting better. She got well and lived two years longer.

—*The Story of Fayetteville and the Upper Cape Fear* (1950)

THE HEAVIEST MAN ON HISTORIC RECORD

The biggest man this country ever knew was Miles Darden. A writer of the Richmond Dispatch thought he was a Virginian, but was corrected by Mr. B. W. L. Holt, who furnishes the following from an old copy of the Wilmington Journal:

"Miles Darden, probably the largest man on record, born in North Carolina, 1798, died in Henderson county, Tennessee, January 23, 1857. He was seven feet and nine inches high, and in 1845 weighed 851 pounds. At his death his weight was a little over 1,000 pounds. Until 1843 he was active and lively and was able to labor, but from that time was obliged to stay at home or be hauled about in a two-horse wagon. In 1839 his coat was buttoned around three men, each of them weighing more than 200 pounds, who walked together in it across the square at Lexington. In 1850 it required thirteen and one-half yards of cloth one yard wide to make him a coat. His coffin was eight feet long, thirty-five inches deep, thirty-two inches across the breast, eighteen inches across the head, and fourteen across the feet, and twenty-five yards of black velvet were requisite to cover the sides and lid. He was twice married and his children are very large, though probably none of them will ever reach half the weight of their father."

—*State Chronicle*, Raleigh (June 9, 1891)

CALICO KING OF NEAR LOUISBURG

U. U.

Several accounts of large families are going the rounds of the papers, and not to be behind in such matters, the following is the Franklin County record: Calico King, a colored man living near here, aged 55, is the father of thirty-six children. He has been married three times, and his last wife is thirty-one years old, and is the mother of fifteen children. There is one other family in the county, also colored, which but for the above would be moderately large, but as they have only twenty-six children (only four being boys), the name will not be given.

—*News and Observer*, Raleigh (August 25, 1891)

WOLF HUNTER

Mr. Jonathan Moody, the veteran bear hunter, caught six young wolves last week in the mountains near here. He is 82 years old but still delights in hunting. He killed seven bears and one large wolf last year. His catch last week will amount to $60, as the county pays ten dollars each for wolf scalps.

—*Waynesville Courier* (June 2, 1893)

ON THE NAMING OF A BOULEVARD
FOR O. HENRY

Edwin Gill

It is, I think, a particularly happy idea to dedicate this Boulevard to the memory of O. Henry. His was a restless spirit, always seeking the story that bordered the road and which awaited him at the end of the journey. His genius was stimulated by meeting new people and by visiting new places. It was this roaming spirit, this continual questing for something novel and unique, that marked and colored his life.

It was no accident that he called one of his books *Rolling Stones*, for O. Henry was a rolling stone himself! Nor is it strange that one of the most famous of all his volumes is called *Roads of Destiny*. In fact, the image of the road was often in his mind. Other stories were called by him "The Lonesome Road" and "The Roads We Take."

The journeys of O. Henry were not, as a rule, carefully planned as to time and place, but were delightfully aimless and pleasantly casual. He was seldom in a hurry because there must always be time for him to make new friends and to glean from them in fragmentary talk the seeds that would flower later into his famous stories.

O. Henry reached the high tide of achievement in the city of New York. There he wrote some of his greatest stories of the little people who were lonesome and forgotten in the great metropolis. One reason the great city appealed to him was that it had many streets that crossed and recrossed each other, making an endless pattern of new and interesting communities in which he could usually find adventure. New York was to him an endless road, turning now this way and now that, always bringing him in contact with interesting people and novel situations. And yet, O. Henry never lost his love for the South, for the seeming security of the small town, for the remembered charm of the countryside. He recalled the days of his youth, and would have liked nothing better than to sit on the edge of the porch, singing the Swanee River to the accompaniment of a guitar, amid the scent of the honeysuckle. But O. Henry knew better than anyone that the fugitive moments of youth could never be regained, and that true to his destiny he must press forward on the ever-winding road of life.

Today we pay tribute not only to O. Henry, but to Will Porter whose sensitive spirit was cradled here in this community. We can well believe that as this likable young man worked in Clark Porter's Drug Store on Elm Street, his eyes frequently came to rest on the beautiful apothecary globes—red, blue, or perhaps green—symbols of an ancient art suggesting to his imaginative mind the alchemy by which the ordinary events of life are transmuted into the gold of adventure. These colored symbols doubtless told him of the medieval world in which love philtres were seriously regarded, and medicine was endowed with a magic which promised revivals of youth to the aged, to say nothing of pills calculated to tranquilize and thus remove the troubles that beset us.

Although Will Porter left us at an early age and lived in Texas, in New Orleans, in Honduras, and finally in the city of New York, it was here in Guilford County that he was born and reared. It was here in the decisive years of childhood and adolescence that O. Henry's mind received its curve and slant, and the development of his personality received impetus and direction. Here he was called Will Porter, and as such is remembered for his gentleness, his warmness of heart, his buoyancy of spirit, the almost indolent delight that he took in the passing scene and the sense of wonder that he felt in the presence of nature....

This is neither the time nor the place to attempt a critical evaluation of O. Henry. Suffice it to say that he ranks as one of the four or five greatest masters of the short story. But, as a great critic once said: "It is idle to compare O. Henry with anybody. No talent could be more original or more delightful . . . [he] is actually that rare bird of which we so often hear false reports—a born story teller."

So here in the land of O. Henry we acknowledge our debt to him. With his humor and pathos, he illuminated the lives of ordinary people. With a lightness of touch, he uncovered for all of us to see the indomitable courage and the nobility of spirit with which the little people of the world often face the daily crises of their lives. Unerringly he diagnosed the malady of the human race, and expertly he prescribed the cure. Notwithstanding the role of fate and the element of chance, in the eyes of O. Henry, the disease that afflicts mankind is selfishness and the cure is love.

Yes, it is a happy thought to give the name of O. Henry to this Boulevard. I like to think that as thousands of people travel this way, they will feel that O. Henry, the gay and diverting companion, travels with them; and I am sure that they will learn from him (if they are willing to listen) that no matter what road we take, it is the heart of the traveler that counts.

—From manuscript (January 14, 1957)

THE CAMPERS AT KITTY HAWK

John Dos Passos

On December seventeenth, nineteen hundred and three, Bishop Wright of the United Brethren onetime editor of the *Religious Telescope* received in his frame house on Hawthorn Street in Dayton, Ohio, a telegram from his boys Wilbur and Orville who'd

gotten it into their heads to spend their vacations in a little camp
out on the dunes of the North Carolina coast tinkering with a
homemade glider they'd knocked together themselves. The telegram read:

SUCCESS FOUR FLIGHTS THURSDAY MORNING ALL AGAINST TWENTYONE
MILE WIND STARTED FROM LEVEL WITH ENGINEPOWER ALONE AVER-
AGE SPEED THROUGH AIR THIRTYONE MILES LONGEST FIFTYSEVEN
SECONDS INFORM PRESS HOME CHRISTMAS

The figures were a little wrong because the telegraph operator
misread Orville's hasty penciled scrawl
    but the fact remains
    that a couple of young bicycle mechanics from Dayton, Ohio
    had designed constructed and flown
    for the first time ever a practical airplane.

*After running the motor a few minutes to heat it up I released
the wire that held the machine to the track and the machine
started forward into the wind. Wilbur ran at the side of the machine holding the wing to balance it on the track. Unlike the start
on the 14th made in a calm the machine facing a 27 mile wind
started very slowly. . . . Wilbur was able to stay with it until it
lifted from the track after a forty-foot run. One of the lifesaving
men snapped the camera for us taking a picture just as it reached
the end of the track and the machine had risen to a height of
about two feet. . . . The course of the flight up and down was
extremely erratic, partly due to the irregularities of the air, partly
to lack of experience in handling this machine. A sudden dart
when a little over a hundred and twenty feet from the point at
which it rose in the air ended the flight. . . . This flight lasted only
12 seconds but it was nevertheless the first in the history of the
world in which a machine carrying a man had raised itself by its
own power into the air in full flight, had sailed forward without
reduction of speed and had finally landed at a point as high as
that from which it started.*

A little later in the day the machine was caught in a gust of wind and turned over and smashed, almost killing the coastguardsman who tried to hold it down;
it was too bad
but the Wright brothers were too happy to care
they'd proved that the damn thing flew.

When these points had been definitely established we at once packed our goods and returned home knowing that the age of the flying machine had come at last.

They were home for Christmas in Dayton, Ohio, where they'd been born in the seventies of a family who had been settled west of the Alleghenies since eighteen fourteen, in Dayton, Ohio, where they'd been to grammarschool and highschool and joined their father's church and played baseball and hockey and worked out on the parallel bars and the flying swing and sold newspapers and built themselves a printingpress out of odds and ends from the junkheap and flown kites and tinkered with mechanical contraptions and gone around town as boys doing odd jobs to turn an honest penny.

The folks claimed it was the bishop's bringing home a helicopter, a fiftycent mechanical toy made of two fans worked by elastic bands that was supposed to hover in the air, that had got his two youngest boys hipped on the subject of flight
so that they stayed home instead of marrying the way the other boys did, and puttered all day about the house picking up a living with jobprinting,

bicyclerepair work,
sitting up late nights reading books on aerodynamics.

Still they were sincere churchmembers, their bicycle business was prosperous, a man could rely on their word. They were popular in Dayton.

In those days flying machines were the big laugh of all the crackerbarrel philosophers. Langley's and Chanute's unsuccessful experiments had been jeered down with an I-told-you-so that rang from coast to coast. The Wrights' big problem was to find a place

secluded enough to carry on their experiments without being the
horselaugh of the countryside. Then they had no money to spend;
    they were practical mechanics; when they needed anything they
built it themselves.

    They hit on Kitty Hawk,
on the great dunes and sandy banks that stretch south towards
Hatteras seaward of Albemarle Sound,
    a vast stretch of seabeach
    empty except for a coastguard station, a few fishermen's shacks
and the swarms of mosquitoes and the ticks and chiggers in the
crabgrass behind the dunes
    and overhead the gulls and swooping terns, in the evening fish-
hawks and cranes flapping across the saltmarshes, occasionally
eagles
    that the Wright brothers followed soaring with their eyes
    as Leonardo watched them centuries before
    straining his sharp eyes to apprehend
    the laws of flight.
    Four miles across the loose sand from the scattering of shacks,
the Wright brothers built themselves a camp and a shed for their
gliders. It was a long way to pack their groceries, their tools,
anything they happened to need; in summer it was hot as blazes,
the mosquitoes were hell;
    but they were alone there
    and they'd figured out that the loose sand was as soft as any-
thing they could find to fall in.
    There with a glider made of two planes and a tail in which
they lay flat on their bellies and controlled the warp of the planes
by shimmying their hips, taking off again and again all day
from a big dune named Kill Devil Hill,
    they learned to fly.

    Once they'd managed to hover for a few seconds
    and soar ever so slightly on a rising aircurrent
    they decided the time had come
    to put a motor in their biplane.

Back in the shop in Dayton, Ohio, they built an airtunnel, which is their first great contribution to the science of flying, and tried out model planes in it.

They couldn't interest any builders of gasoline engines so they had to build their own motor.

It worked; after that Christmas of nineteen three the Wright brothers weren't doing it for fun any more; they gave up their bicycle business, got the use of a big old cowpasture belonging to the local banker for practice flights, spent all the time when they weren't working on their machine in promotion, worrying about patents, infringements, spies, trying to interest government officials, to make sense out of the smooth involved heartbreaking remarks of lawyers.

In two years they had a plane that would cover twentyfour miles at a stretch round and round the cowpasture.

People on the interurban car used to crane their necks out of the windows when they passed along the edge of the field, startled by the clattering pop pop of the old Wright motor and the sight of the white biplane like a pair of ironingboards one on top of the other chugging along a good fifty feet in the air. The cows soon got used to it.

As the flights got longer
the Wright brothers got backers,
engaged in lawsuits,
lay in their beds at night sleepless with the whine of phantom millions, worse than the mosquitoes at Kitty Hawk.

In nineteen seven they went to Paris,
allowed themselves to be togged out in dress suits and silk hats,
learned to tip waiters
talked with government experts, got used to gold braid and postponements and vandyke beards and the outspread palms of politicos. For amusement
they played diabolo in the Tuileries gardens.

They gave publicized flights at Fort Myers, where they had
their first fatal crackup, St. Petersburg, Paris, Berlin; at Pau they
were all the rage,
    such an attraction that the hotelkeeper
    wouldn't charge them for their room.
Alfonso of Spain shook hands with them and was photographed
sitting in the machine,
    King Edward watched a flight,
    the Crown Prince insisted on being taken up,
    the rain of medals began.

They were congratulated by the Czar
and the King of Italy and the amateurs of sport, and the society
climbers and the papal titles,
    and decorated by a society for universal peace.

Aeronautics became the sport of the day.
The Wrights don't seem to have been very much impressed by
the upholstery and the braid and the gold medals and the
parades of plush horses,
    they remained practical mechanics
    and insisted on doing all their own work themselves,
    even to filling the gasolinetank.

In nineteen eleven they were back on the dunes
    at Kitty Hawk with a new glider.
Orville stayed up in the air for nine and a half minutes, which
remained a long time the record for motorless flight.
    The same year Wilbur died of typhoidfever in Dayton.
    In the rush of new names: Farman, Blériot, Curtiss, Ferber,
Esnault-Peltrie, Delagrange;
    in the snorting impact of bombs and the whine and rattle of
shrapnel and the sudden stutter of machineguns after the motor's
been shut off overhead,
    and we flatten into the mud
    and make ourselves small cowering in the corners of ruined
walls,

the Wright brothers passed out of the headlines

but not even headlines or the bitter smear of newsprint or the choke of smokescreen and gas or chatter of brokers on the stock-market or barking of phantom millions or oratory of brasshats laying wreaths on new monuments

can blur the memory

of the chilly December day

two shivering bicycle mechanics from Dayton, Ohio,

first felt their homemade contraption

whittled out of hickory sticks,

gummed together with Arnstein's bicycle cement,

stretched with muslin they'd sewn on their sister's sewing-machine in their own backyard on Hawthorn Street in Dayton, Ohio,

soar into the air

above the dunes and the wide beach

at Kitty Hawk.

—The Big Money (1936), in *U. S. A.*

❦❦❦❦❦❦❦❦❦

HE WROTE "THE BIRTH OF A NATION"

F. B. Dedmond

North Carolina's Thomas Dixon knew his life story would make good reading.

Before his death on April 2, 1946, he prepared his autobiography, which he dedicated to "the large flock of black sheep known as ministers' sons—by one of them."

The man who wrote *The Clansman,* from which the movie *The Birth of a Nation* was made, had some lively tales to tell.

When he was 10, for example, he was stopping on his way from school at Aaron Mooney's barroom not far from his Cleveland County home, and buying his Grandma Dixon a bottle of

Bourbon. Thomas's father found out about the purchase and soundly thrashed the boy. When Grandma Dixon heard of the whipping, she got her things together and in a huff left the Dixon house.

Thomas found a good deal of Grandma in him. When things didn't go to suit him, he turned in another direction.

Because he was 6-feet-3½ and weighed only 150, he failed to get a part in a New York play. On his way home to Shelby from New York, he decided to be a lawyer.

Later, at the suggestion of his father, he ran for the North Carolina Legislature and was elected before he was 21 years old.

Then Dixon gave up both law and politics and entered the ministry. Shortly afterwards he received a call to the First Baptist Church of Goldsboro. After six months there, he was called to the Tabernacle Church in Raleigh. Dixon stayed in Raleigh about a year and a half, and then in November, 1887, became pastor of the Dudley Street Church in the Roxbury section of Boston, Massachusetts.

While in Boston, something happened which determined what he called his life's work. At a mass meeting in Tremont Temple, Dixon listened to a man make a speech on the "Southern Problem," which, as he put it, "sent a shock down my spine that lifted me from my seat." The speaker had just returned from a journey where he had spent six weeks in "an exhaustive study of Southern life from car windows." The speaker declared that "the rebel flag still floats over every Southern town and village. The only way to save this nation from hell today is for Northern mothers to rear more children than Southern mothers!"

Dixon, on the front row, sprang to his feet and shouted with laughter.

"Who are you, sir?" thundered the speaker.

"A Southern white man who has lived in the South 23 years since the war and never saw a Confederate Flag," Dixon shouted back.

After the meeting, Dixon said, "I made up my mind...to write a trilogy on the South after the model of Henry Sienkiewicz's novels of Poland, *With Fire and Sword*, *The Deluge*, and

Pan Michael." He was determined to destroy sectionalism and reunite the nation with a single pen.

Dixon, already famous as a lecturer, took 20 weeks of speaking on a guarantee of $10,000. As he traveled from place to place, he worked on his first novel. Into the book (*The Leopard's Spots*) went "more than 10 years of reading and preparation and this period of work had been preceded by a quarter of a century of living its scenes." From Dixonville, Va., the manuscript was mailed to Walter Hines Page of Doubleday, Page and Company. Within 48 hours, Page sent a telegram of congratulation.

The novel was a best seller from the beginning, and sales reached 100,000 copies before the first semi-annual report of royalties reached Dixon. The reviews of the book were generous.

For the second part of the trilogy (*The Clansman*), Dixon "dug through more than 5,000 pamphlets and books in preparing the notes." He wrote the novel in 30 days, working 16 hours a day. It contained, according to Dixon, the first full-length portrait of Thad Stevens that had ever been written and proved a greater sensation as a book than *The Leopard's Spots*. The novel developed the story of the "Ku Klux Klan Conspiracy," which overturned the Reconstruction regime in the South. It reached a circulation of a million copies.

"The success of the book," Dixon said, "brought my thoughts back to the lode star on which they had been fixed from my first journey to New York. *The Clansman* must be dramatized and made a living thing in the theater. The printed page would be read by five million people. The play, if successful, would reach 10 million and with an emotional power 10 times as great as in cold type." The play was a success and made $50,000 on its try-out run.

From his first three novels and the play founded on *The Clansman*, Dixon made a comfortable fortune. But, as he put it, he "heard the call of the Goddess of Chance and became a small-fry Wall Street gambler." He invested $350,000 in stocks, mostly United States Steel. In the panic of 1907, he lost every dollar, and in one night his hair turned gray. Dixon was down, but he never knew what it meant to be out.

Dixon is primarily known as the author of *The Birth of a Nation,* the first million dollar movie. *The Birth of a Nation* was based on *The Clansman.* Dixon had offered his screen play to the major movie producers in vain. Finally a new company headed by H. E. Aitken took the play and, after two years and many disappointments, finished the movie. The picture was a phenomenal success. In 10 years it was seen by 100 million people and took in $18 million.

Over 25 years, Dixon wrote 20 novels, nine plays, and five motion pictures. From these he made $1,250,000. (The autobiography was never published. A typed copy is now in the library of Gardner-Webb College, which some years ago received Dixon's personal library.)

But with the crash of 1929, Dixon again lost every dollar he had. Dixon, though, was philosophic about such matters.

"In my relation to material property," he said, "there has always been a screw loose in my make-up. I've always been able to make money but never tried to hold it. When times got hard I've always been able to say to myself: 'Cheer up, old boy, you'll soon be dead!' And what of it? If I should die tomorrow, with my last breath I'd say: 'My love to the world. I have lived a great, beautiful, thrilling adventure called life. The cycle ends. A new one begins. For I shall live again!'"

—*Journal and Sentinel,* Winston-Salem (October 31, 1954)

FRED BEAL

Harry Golden

Fred Beal was unlucky. Whatever he did was wrong, and when he did do the right thing it was at the wrong time. I liked him very much. We corresponded during the past five or six years. He died a few weeks ago. Now he can make no more mistakes. He was involved in that Gastonia strike trouble in the early 1930's. The Chief of Police was killed and Beal and a group of Communists were tried for the killing. Beal had nothing to do with the killing of Chief Aderholt, but when you cannot come into court with clean hands you are in bad shape.

Beal was unlucky. He went to work in a cotton mill in Lawrence, Mass., at the age of 12 or 13—and he was obsessed with the idea of doing something to improve the working conditions and the pay of the textile worker. He let himself get involved with a union which was dominated by Communists. They weren't interested in improving anyone's conditions. They thrive only on trouble. Beal told me an amazing thing—hard to believe, but there was no reason to doubt it—he wasn't saying it for publicity or in any way to exploit his anti-Communism. He told me that William Z. Foster, the Communist leader, directed the whole Gastonia show and the people in the Kremlin insisted on getting weekly reports on the doings in Gastonia. How do you like that? He marks the sparrow's fall. Anyway, Beal, after conviction with the others involved, forfeited the bail and escaped to Russia. After two years in Russia, he was ready to come back and go to jail. I met him when he returned from prison. He told me that during those two years when he watched the Russian workers line up for their black bread every morning he kept saying to himself: "I'm in this trouble because I was fighting for people (in Gastonia) who are eating flap-jacks and bacon this morning." But when he came back with his eyewitness story that the whole Communist set-up was a tragic fake, *no one would listen to him*, except a few true Liberals—the Social Democrats, who then as now are the rocks upon which Communism will eventually be broken.

Beal was unlucky. He became a Communist at the wrong time, and he became an anti-Communist at the wrong time. In 1937 when he came back with his story he couldn't get a publisher to print a pamphlet against the Soviet—he found himself cut off from friends and jobs—not because he had once been a Communist, but because he was now an anti-Communist. He finally wound up getting his story published in the Jewish Daily Forward, the old stalwart Socialist paper—one of the few publications in America which never once took a single backward step in its opposition to Communism from the day after the Russian Revolution to the present time. He came back to North Carolina to do his sentence in the prison. When he came out of jail, the air was right up his alley now—everybody was an anti-Communist, but Beal, as I said before, was born unlucky. Again he was wrong. He was an anti-Communist all right, a man who chose four years in an American jail rather than a Commissar's job in the Soviet, but Beal found out that now the anti-Communists were popular only if they became Republicans to the right of Senator Bricker of Ohio, as part of the redemption process. Beal couldn't do that, and turned down many offers to lecture on the subject. He went back to Lawrence, Mass., to write for an A. F. of L. newspaper. He had tuberculosis which he contracted in the Soviet heaven, and the labor union sent him to a sanitarium. He died a few weeks ago.

He was unlucky. He became a Communist at the wrong time and it resulted in his downfall. He became an anti-Communist at the wrong time when no one would believe his stories of the tragedy of Bolshevism, and finally when everybody went all-out in their feeling against Communism, Beal couldn't take advantage of it and give them anti-Communism in the terms that were demanded. The man who summed it up best was Judge Wilson Warlick of the Superior Court (now a Federal Judge). When Beal applied for the restoration of his citizenship, Judge Warlick said: "Mr. Beal, I read a lot about you, and I give you credit for speaking out about Communism back in the 1930's, but I am sorry that it wasn't popular to do so then. Right now everybody is cussin' Communism and it's popular to do it. I am thinking of you in the 1930's when you came back and I feel you'll make a good American citizen. I wish you luck."

Fred Beal the unlucky is at rest now. I hope he has peace and quiet.

—*The Carolina Israelite*, Charlotte (November, 1954)

LAST OF THE TUSCARORAS

Edenton, Sept. 7.—Frequently have half-breeds died here who claimed descent from Waupomak, early 17th century chief of the Tuscaroras, who wielded a tomahawk ferociously hereabouts until he and his tribe were chased north into New York state. And on Wednesday night Joshua Zachary, 65, who has lived on Ruyder's Lane on the outskirts of town since birth and who has asserted, undenied, that he was absolutely the "last of the Tuscaroras" in North Carolina, died suddenly and was buried with appropriate Indian rites in a nearby graveyard the following day. Zachary peddled small truck about town in a wheelbarrow, and was proud of his Indian blood. The town accepted him at face value.

—*Greensboro Daily News* (September 8, 1940)

BIG TOM'S GREAT-GRANDSON

Bill Sharpe

The Wilsons shake their heads ruefully but indulgently over the antics of the fourth generation. In good season, they say, Ned will come around all right.

But Ned, ten years old, displays no interest in tradition. "I got 43 squirrels this season," he said proudly. "Bears? I don't like bear-hunting. All you do is set around and wait."

Around this mountain community, that is treason, for Ned is not only the son of Ewart Wilson, greatest bear hunter in all the mountain lands. He is the grandson of Dolf Wilson, who killed 113 bears in his day. The only reason Dolf stopped hunting was because he refused to beat the record of his father, Big Tom Wilson, who killed 114. Ned is the great-grandson of Big Tom, already a legendary giant of the Blue Ridges.

It was Big Tom who cleared the Wilson lands and explored this country. Big Tom got into the history books, too, for he was Dr. Elisha Mitchell's guide, and found that noted explorer's body when he fell upon the mountain that now bears his name.

The Wilsons are overlords of 17,000 acres of land on and around Mt. Mitchell and if they were not so well known as bear hunters you could find out that they are farming and timbering folks. But Big Tom set a pattern which sent his name echoing far over the hills into the ears of men everywhere who like to track the mountain brutes. Big Tom was the biggest man in Yancey County, his bear dogs were the fiercest, his shots the most prodigious, and his knowledge of what a mountain bear would most likely do the most complete.

It was said of Big Tom that he could take down his gun and go out and get a bear as easily as his neighbors went into the chicken coop for a frier.

Adolf, his son, now 70, followed, as it were, in the bear tracks of his daddy, but when he had bagged his 113th animal he hung up his gun reverentially. He hoped he would never see his father's mark beat. Those who have hunted with Dolf say he knew every bear on the ranges by its first name.

If anyone beats the record, it will be Ewart, who this year is again leading hunting parties through the Wilson bear lands. There were more animals than ever this year, and folks say that even the bears favor the Wilson tradition by migrating to their timberland. Ewart's dogs are smart like all the Wilson dogs, and Ewart himself is a stout man, who leaves for the mountain slopes before sun-up and won't be back until the sport is all over.

The Wilsons live in a rambling old house by the road which starts there to climb to the peak of Mt. Mitchell. On the floors and walls are the skins of many black bears, and in Mrs. Ewart Wilson's pantries are many jars of canned bear meat.

But to Ned, squirrel is fine eatin', if you cook it right.

—*Tar on My Heels* (1946)

ON WRITING A BOOK WITH DR. SLOOP

LeGette Blythe

In my career as a newspaperman, I have interviewed count-less persons—presidents, panhandlers, pickpockets and princes, bishops and burglars, explorers and opera singers and yoyo champions—the great and the lowly, the good and the bad and the in-betweens. But never have I encountered a character more truly unique than Dr. Mary T. Martin Sloop. No mold shaped her, no die stamped her out.

Until this book brought us together, I had never met her, although all my life I had heard of Crossnore's two Doctors Sloop and their extraordinary accomplishments. I shall never forget that first visit to Crossnore. I reached the Sloop home at eight-thirty one Friday night, expecting to meet a quiet and perhaps even doddering old lady of almost eighty. Instead a vivacious, smiling, chattering little person met me at the door. She wore rimless glasses and behind them her eyes fairly sparkled. Her hair was white, her mouth wide and generous. There was about her an air of unquenchable energy, a contagious vitality. That night she told stories steadily and entertainingly until eleven. The next morning at eight she was at her school office. All day she attended to countless administrative tasks; that evening she made a speech at a dinner of returning business-class graduates; and afterward she square-danced until eleven. This was my doddering old pioneer doctor and educator!

Dr. Sloop always refers to her husband, Dr. Eustace Sloop, as simply "Doctor." He is a tall, exceedingly handsome man with a fine head of white hair, a white mustache, and a clipped white beard. Doctor carries on his medical practice as strenuously today as he did some forty years ago. Her story and his are inseparable; everything they did for Crossnore and the moun-tain people they did together.

The techniques used in getting Dr. Sloop's story varied. Some-times she talked into a tape recorder, at other times I took copious notes. I have been to Crossnore countless times, but my interviews with Dr. Sloop have always been more pleasure than work. I have tried hard to preserve her own words, expressions, and tone. These are her stories, and this is the way she tells them.

Dr. Sloop's work has attracted national attention. She has received special citations and honorary degrees. In 1951 she was named American Mother of the Year. But I do not like to think of her as a special or extraordinary person. She is, rather, one of our last examples of the sturdy, energetic pioneer woman who played such an important role in the settling of America. She is a woman of tremendous faith, both in God and in herself. This combination has proved more than a match for ignorance, poverty, and sickness in the mountains.

But already I embarrass her with fancy words. She is no fancy woman. She is solid, as solid and true as the great mountain people of whom she speaks with such warmth and affection. Nor did she and the Doctor do their great work out of any grim sense of duty. They did it joyously, exuberantly, with a gleam— and often a wink—in their eyes.

It has been a rewarding experience working with her. What is more, it has been great fun.

—Foreword, *Miracle in the Hills* (1953)

AVA'S HOME FOLKS TALK ABOUT HER

Karl Kohrs

"Ava? Why, I've known Ava Gardner since she was knee-high to a duck," said genial N. L. Perkins, veteran Smithfield tobacco auctioneer. "She's a real home-lovin' human being. Remember going out to her Dad's farm one day and there was Ava, barefoot, sweepin' up acorns. She was about seven or so. I said to her Daddy: 'Brother Jonas, is this your baby?' 'Yes, she is,' he says. 'Well,' says I, 'if she was my child, I'd get right on a train and take her out to Hollywood.'"

Folks like Mr. Perkins here in Smithfield (Pop. 6,500) like to talk about Ava Gardner. She's one of their favorite citizens. They remember her as that cute little daughter of J. B. Gardner, who had a tobacco farm at nearby Brogden. Brogden is—literally —a wide place in the road. It has a consolidated school (where Ava was a pupil), a "teacherage" (where the teachers board, and where Ava's mother once was matron), and a general store, run by Mrs. D. L. Creech, Ava's oldest sister.

Ava is the youngest of the six Gardner children—five girls and one boy. Her brother, Jack, and another sister, Mrs. John A. Grimes, live in Smithfield.

"Ava was a Christmas baby," said Mrs. Grimes. "She was born December 24. We were all grown up when Ava came along. She was a lively kid, real cute. She was a healthy child, but

something was always happening to her. When she was about a year old, she got hold of a can of lye. Mother caught up with Ava just as she was putting some of the lye into her mouth." Acting quickly, Mrs. Gardner swabbed Ava's mouth with vinegar, then made her swallow the white of an egg. That saved her life. As the doctor said, five minutes more and Ava might have died.

When Ava was about six, one of her sisters accidentally struck her under the right eye with a hoe. A tiny scar still shows.

At school Ava took her lessons seriously—and that involved her in another mishap. Halfway home from school one day, she realized she had forgotten her books, and ran back to get them. The doors were locked. But one side door, Ava found, had a broken pane. She squeezed through the small open square. A splinter of glass in the frame cut a deep gash in Ava's leg—but she got her books and limped home.

Mishaps or not, Ava liked adventure. She was acrobatic and had a great flair for hanging by her heels.

Mrs. Lucian Allen is the present tenant of the home where Ava was born. The big frame house is on a 200-acre tobacco and cotton farm eight miles from Smithfield. As a child, Ava climbed out on the roof of the porch, was coaxed back inside with candy.

Ava was a great favorite with the boys, but had few "steadies." Said her sisters: "Sometimes when boy friends came to call, Ava would beg us to go to the door and tell them to go home."

About her first "big" high school date—a football star—Ava once said: "I couldn't think of a thing to say—so we just sat."

Hugh C. Talton, store manager in Smithfield, dated Ava in high school. "She was a good sport," he says. "Once we got caught in the rain in my convertible. The top stuck. Ava got soaked. She just laughed."

Teenagers Sarah Hill and Mae Dixon never miss Ava's pictures. Sarah's mother taught Ava in the fifth grade, remembers her as average. Sarah would like to see Ava play more "sympathetic" parts. Mae likes Ava in her present roles.

"I knew Ava's family before she was born," says Dr. W. J. Massey, Jr., "and took care of her teeth when she was a kid. She's still a kid to me. Ava was like any average patient—scared to death."

At school, Ava was the "lone wolf" type—didn't belong to school clubs, wasn't interested in sports. Once she was "drafted" as substitute on the high school girls' basketball team. She shot one basket after another, until the coach took her out of the game—fast. Ava was lobbing the ball into the wrong basket.

Smithfield regards Ava as a home-town girl who made good, and everybody's for her. Smithfield's mayor, Rayford Oliver, says he's proud of Ava as one of the town's leading citizens. "I've known Ava and her family for a long time," he says, "and I think she's a fine person. I'm right proud Ava's from Smithfield."

—*Parade* (January 3, 1954)

SYMPHONY CONDUCTOR

Mary L. Medley

Associated Press stories with a Berlin dateline last week carried a brief account of George Byrd of Anson County, N. C., and Brooklyn—the first American Negro ever to conduct the Berlin Philharmonic Orchestra.

One story gave his origin as an Anson County tenant farm. It was the first concert of the season for the West Berlin orchestra, and Brahms' *Symphony No. 2* was played. He was warmly applauded, accounts said. From chants of the cotton field, banjo picking, and foot shuffling on an Anson County tenant farm to conducting the Berlin Philharmonic is a long journey. The story should be full of interest.

—*Messenger and Intelligencer*, Wadesboro (September 8, 1959)

"ME AND MY OLD MULE"

Larry Powers

One note said: "Me and my old mule is gone."
Another one said: "I am drowned in this pond. My old mule."
Both notes were found near a farm pond in the Delway community Sunday. In 10 feet of water in the pond was found the

body of a Negro man of the community, Mat Augustus Usher, aged 53. Coroner Coleman Carter has ruled the death a suicide. The cause: apparent despondency of the suicide victim over the loss of his mule the previous day.

Sampson Sheriff W. D. Hall received a call at three o'clock Sunday afternoon from James Ezzell of Delway. Ezzell told Hall that an employee of 34 years had apparently drowned himself in a pond. Officers were sent to investigate.

Usher was last seen alive at nine o'clock Sunday when he left his home on foot. Ezzell said the man's mule had died the previous day and that the owner was grieving over the loss.

At two o'clock that afternoon, a note was found lying on a dirt road near the pond. The man's pocketbook containing the second note was discovered on the bank of the pond. Footprints were nearby which indicated that Usher made a running jump into the 10-foot depths of the pond.

—*Sampsonian,* Clinton (March 17, 1960)

INCIDENTS

"The real history of Old Catawba is a history of solitude, of the wilderness, and of the eternal earth, it is the history of millions of men living and dying alone in the wilderness, it is the history of the billion unrecorded and forgotten acts and moments of their lives."

—Thomas Wolfe

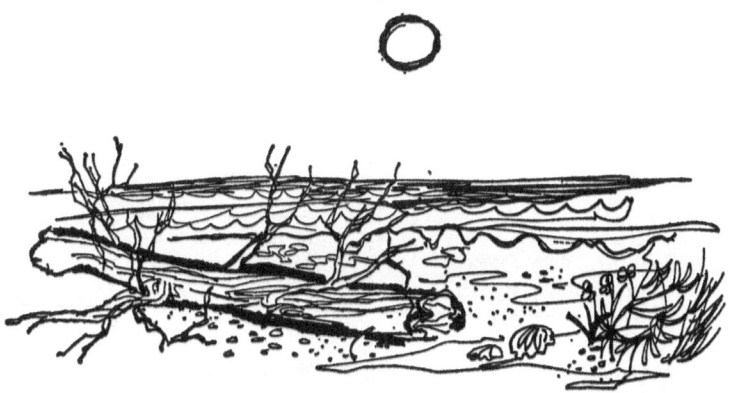

DISCOVERY OF ROANOKE ISLAND
1584

Arthur Barlowe

... wee came to an Island, which they call *Raonoak*, distant
from the harbour by which we entred, seuen leagues: and at
the North end thereof was a village of nine houses, built of
Cedar, and fortified round about with sharpe trees, to keepe out
their enemies, and the entrance into it made like a turne pike
very artificially: when wee came towardes it, standing neere
unto the waters side, the wife of *Granganimo* the kings brother
came running out to meete us very cheerefully and friendly, her
husband was not then in the village; some of her people shee
commanded to drawe out boate on shore for the beating of the
billoe: others she appointed to cary us on their backes to the
dry ground, and others to bring our oares into the house for feare
of stealing. When we were come into the utter roome, hauing
fiue roomes in her house, she caused us to sit downe by a great
fire, and after tooke off our clothes and washed them, and dryed
them againe: some of the women plucked off our stockings and
washed them, some washed our feete in warme water, and shee
her selfe tooke great paines to see all things ordered in the best
maner shee could, making great haste to dresse some meate for
us to eate.

—*Hakluyt's Voyages* (1600)

CULPEPPER'S REBELLION

Richard Benbury Creecy

In 1677 there was a "revolutionary time" in the Albemarle, which section then constituted the chief settlement of Carolina. There was a dual government, or rather a dual usurpation of government. Miller and Culpepper both claimed supremacy. Miller had the best show of authority, being the representative of the duly authorized Governor, by appointment of the Lords Proprietors, who lingered in the West Indies, allured by love, as it was supposed, but professing to be detained by sickness. Miller, his secretary, was sent on ahead to hold the office of Governor by a temporary tenure. He came over to Albemarle with some show of authority and administered the government in an autocratic way. The people respected his authority and obeyed the laws which he enacted for them. He imposed taxes, laid duties upon foreign imports, and ruled by his own free will.

Culpepper, seeing that Miller was usurping power, set up a claim to the Governorship for himself, and soon established a contraband trade with Boston, then a pretentious village in New England. He defied the authority of Miller. He refused to pay the import duties imposed by Miller, and continued to trade with the rich planters of Albermarle Sound and its tributary waters, and was encouraged by them. There was absolute free trade, and Culpepper's profits from the government became greater than Miller's.

This contraband trade was carried on mainly by one Gilliam, who commanded a "skipper" vessel, engaged in the trade with Boston. He was a shrewd fellow, and found a free trade with the farmers of the Albemarle, without the burden of impost duties, was profitable both to the rich planters and to himself. Culpepper winked at this contraband traffic. Gilliam winked back and pursued his business with great diligence.

George Durant, who lived on Little River, was a very wealthy man, and, while a good and upright man, was thrifty in business and successful in the accumulation of wealth. Finding authority disputed, with two men contending for supremacy, and not authorized or caring to solve the trouble, he took sides with that in which he found most profit and favored Culpepper. Favoring Culpepper, he favored Gilliam, and Durant's plantation became Gilliam's headquarters for his illicit trade.

Miller had the largest following, and having gone into office by peaceful methods he had the support of the more conservative classes of the population. Culpepper was a usurper, and made no claim to rightful authority. He was denounced by Miller as a lawless man, and attempts were made to arrest him for treason.

Miller heard that Gilliam was in Little River, pursuing his unlawful business, and that he intended to come round into Pasquotank River and stop at Pembrook (now Cobb's Point) for the purpose of trading. Later he heard that Culpepper was to come round with him in his "skipper." He thought his opportunity had come, and determined to go to Pembrook, board the skipper when she anchored, and arrest Culpepper as a lawless traitor. Relying upon his authority as Chief Magistrate of Carolina, he went to Pembrook and awaited the coming of Culpepper and Gilliam. He did not wait long. The skipper soon arrived and cast anchor in the stream. Miller pushed off in a boat, boarded the skipper, found Culpepper and Gilliam, and demanded their surrender in the name of the Province of Carolina.

Culpepper and Gilliam showed fight, and instead of being arrested by Miller, they overpowered and arrested him, took him ashore and imprisoned him in the jail at Pembrook.

Thus, having Carolina's questionable Governor in durance vile, Culpepper administered his usurped authority for eight years.

What became of Miller in that lawless time, history and tradition is silent, but history tells us that Culpepper was afterwards arrested by order of the Lords Proprietors and taken to England for trial upon the charge of treason.

He was defended by Lord Shaftesbury, the most distinguished jurist of the period, and acquitted upon the ground that there was no organized government in Carolina.

—*Grandfather's Tales of North Carolina History* (1901)

THE CAPTURE OF BLACKBEARD

Captain Charles Johnson

Edward Teach was a *Bristol* Man born, but had sailed some Time out of *Jamaica* in Privateers, in the late *French* War; yet tho' he had often distinguished himself for his uncommon Boldness and personal Courage, he was never raised to any Command, till he went a-pyrating, which I think was at the latter End of the Year 1716. . . .

Teach goes up to the Governor of *North-Carolina*, with about twenty of his Men, surrender to his Majesty's Proclamation, and receive Certificates thereof, from his Excellency; but it did not appear that their Submitting to this Pardon was from any Reformation of Manners, but only to wait a more favourable Opportunity to play the same Game over again; which he soon after effected, with greater Security to himself, and with much better Prospect of Success, having in this Time cultivated a very good Understanding with *Charles Eden*, Esq; the Governor above mentioned.

The first Piece of Service this kind Governor did to *Black-Beard*, was, to give him a Right to the Vessel which he had taken, when he was a pyrating in the great Ship called the *Queen Ann's Revenge*; for which Purpose, a Court of Vice-Admiralty was held at *Bath-Town*; and, tho' *Teach* had never any Commission in his Life, and the Sloop belonging to the *English* Merchants, and taken in Time of Peace; yet was she condemned as a Prize taken from the *Spaniards*, by the said *Teach*. These Proceedings shew that Governors are but Men.

Before he sailed upon his Adventures, he marry'd a young Creature of about sixteen Years of Age, the Governor performing the Ceremony. As it is the Custom to marry here by a Priest, so it is there by a Magistrate; and this, I have been informed, made *Teach's* fourteenth Wife, whereof, about a dozen might be still living. His Behaviour in this State, was something extraordinary; for while his Sloop lay in *Okerecock* Inlet, and he ashore at a Plantation, where his Wife lived, with whom after he had lain all Night, it was his Custom to invite five or six of his brutal Companions to come ashore, and he would force her to prostitute her self to them all, one after another, before his Face....

Captain *Teach*, alias *Black-beard*, passed three or four Months in the River, sometimes lying at Anchor in the Coves, at other Times sailing from one Inlet to another, trading with such Sloops as he met, for the Plunder he had taken, and would often give them Presents for Stores and Provisions took from them; that is, when he happened to be in a giving Humour; at other Times he made bold with them, and took what he liked, without saying, *by your Leave*, knowing well, they dared not send him a Bill for the Payment. He often diverted himself with going ashore among the Planters, where he revelled Night and Day: By these he was well received, but whether out of Love or Fear, I cannot say; sometimes he used them courteously enough, and made them Presents of Rum and Sugar, in Recompence of what he took from them; but, as for Liberties (which 'tis said) he and his Companions often took with the Wives and Daughters of the Planters, I cannot take upon me to say, whether he paid them *ad Valorem*, or no. At other Times he carried it in a lordly Manner towards them, and would lay some of them under Contribution; nay, he often proceeded to bully the Governor, not, that I can discover the least Cause of Quarrel betwixt them, but it seemed only to be done, to shew he dared do it.

The Sloops trading up and down this River, being so frequently pillaged by *Black-beard*, consulted with the Traders, and some of the best of the Planters, what Course to take; they saw plainly it would be in vain to make any Application to the Governor of *North-Carolina*, to whom it properly belonged to find some Redress; so that if they could not be relieved from some other Quarter, *Black-beard* would be like to reign with Impunity, therefore, with as much Secrecy as possible, they sent a Deputation to *Virginia*, to lay the Affair before the Governor of that Colony, and to solicit an armed Force from the Men of War lying there, to take or destroy this Pyrate.

This Governor consulted with the Captains of the two Men of War, *viz.* the *Pearl* and *Lime*, who had lain in St. *James's* River, about ten Months. It was agreed that the Governor should hire a couple of small Sloops, and the Men of War should Man them; this was accordingly done, and the Command of them given to Mr. *Robert Maynard*, first Lieutenant of the *Pearl*, an experienced Officer, and a Gentleman of great Bravery and Resolution, as will appear by his gallant Behaviour in this Expedition. The Sloops were well mann'd and furnished with Ammunition and small Arms, but had no Guns mounted.

About the Time of their going out, the Governor called an Assembly, in which it was resolved to publish a Proclamation, offering certain Rewards to any Person or Persons, who, within a Year after that Time, should take or destroy any Pyrate. . . .

The 17th of *November*, 1718, the Lieutenant sail'd from *Kicquetan*, in *James* River in *Virginia*, and, the 21st in the Evening, came to the Mouth of *Okerecock* Inlet, where he got Sight of the Pyrate. This Expedition was made with all imaginable Secrecy, and the Officer manag'd with all the Prudence that was necessary, stopping all Boats and Vessels he met with, in the River, from going up, and thereby preventing any Intelligence from reaching *Black-Beard*, and receiving at the same time an Account from them all, of the Place where the Pyrate was lurking; but notwithstanding this Caution, *Black-beard* had Information of the Design, from his Excellency of the Province; and his Secretary, Mr. *Knight*, wrote him a Letter, particularly concerning it, intimating, *That he had sent him four of his Men, which were all he could meet with, in or about Town, and so bid him be upon his Guard.* These Men belonged to *Black-beard*, and were sent from *Bath-Town* to *Okerecock* Inlet, where the Sloop lay, which is about 20 Leagues.

Black-beard had heard several Reports, which happened not to be true, and so gave the less Credit to this, nor was he convinced till he saw the Sloops: Whereupon he put his Vessel in a Posture of Defence; he had no more than twenty five Men on Board, tho' he gave out to all the Vessels he spoke with, that he had 40. When he had prepared for Battle, he set down and spent the Night in drinking with the Master of a trading Sloop, who, 'twas thought, had more Business with *Teach*, than he should have had. . . .

They were now closely and warmly engaged, the Lieutenant and twelve Men, against *Black-beard* and fourteen, till the Sea was tinctur'd with Blood round the Vessel; *Black-beard* received a Shot into his Body from the Pistol that Lieutenant *Maynard* discharg'd, yet he stood his Ground, and fought with great Fury, till he received five and twenty Wounds, and five of them by Shot. At length, as he was cocking another Pistol, having fired several before, he fell down dead; by which Time eight more out of the fourteen dropp'd, and all the Rest, much wounded, jump'd over-board, and call'd out for Quarters, which was granted, tho' it was only prolonging their Lives for a few Days. The Sloop *Ranger* came up, and attack'd the Men that remain'd in *Black-beard's* Sloop, with equal Bravery, till they likewise cry'd for Quarters. . . .

The Lieutenant caused *Black-beard's* Head to be severed from his Body, and hung up at the Bolt-Sprit End, then he sailed to *Bath-Town*, to get Relief for his wounded Men.

It must be observed, that in rummaging the Pyrate's Sloop, they found several Letters and written Papers, which discovered the Correspondence betwixt Governor *Eden*, the Secretary and Collector, and also some Traders at *New-York*, and *Black-beard*. . . .

When the Lieutenant came to *Bath-Town*, he made bold to seize in the Governor's Store-House, the sixty Hogsheads of Sugar, and from honest Mr. *Knight*, twenty; which it seems was their Dividend of the Plunder taken in the *French* Ship. . . .

After the wounded Men were pretty well recover'd, the Lieutenant sailed back to the Men of War in *James* River, in *Virginia*, with *Black-beard's* Head still hanging at the Bolt-Sprit End, and fifteen Prisoners, thirteen of whom were hanged. It appearing upon Tryal, that one of them, *viz. Samuel Odell*, was taken out of the trading Sloop, but the Night before the Engagement. . . . The other Person that escaped the Gallows, was one *Israel Hands*, the Master of *Black-beard's* Sloop. . . .

Now that we have given some Account of *Teach's* Life and Action, it will not be amiss, that we speak of his Beard, since it did not a little contribute towards making his Name so terrible in those Parts. . . .

This Beard was black, which he suffered to grow of an extravagant Length; as to Breadth, it came up to his Eyes; he was accustomed to twist it with Ribbons, in small Tails, after the Manner of our Ramilies Wiggs, and turn them about his Ears: In Time of Action, he wore a Sling over his Shoulders, with three brace of Pistols, hanging in Holsters like Bandaliers; and stuck lighted Matches under his Hat, which appearing on each Side of his Face, his Eyes naturally looking fierce and wild, made him altogether such a Figure, that Imagination cannot form an Idea of a Fury, from Hell, to look more frightful. . . .

—*A General History of the Pyrates* (1724)

LOVEFEAST AT SALEM
November, 1771

Adelaide L. Fries

At ten o'clock in the morning of the thirteenth all the Brethren and Sisters in Wachovia, all the members of our congregations and societies, assembled in the new meeting-hall, and after singing "Give us Thy blessing, God our God," Brother Marshall offered the prayer of consecration: "Oh our Lord Jesus Christ, Head of the Church, forgive our sins and give us grace anew to become Thy property. Let Thy presence be deeply felt amongst us. Hear our petition that all gatherings here to be held in Thy name may be aware of Thy presence, that each heart which here shall cry to Thee in need may be graciously heard and richly blessed. ..."

At noon there was a lovefeast at which more than three hundred were present, including the children. Brother Graff presided, and during the service he read from our Text Books the important texts which applied to Wachovia and to Salem:

Nov. 17, 1753, when the first colony of Single Brethren took possession of the little hut at Bethabara: *I know where thou dwellest.*

Feb. 14, 1765, when the site for Salem was chosen: *Let thine eye be open toward this place day and night, even toward the place of which thou hast said, My name shall be there.*

Feb. 19, 1766, when the first eight Brethren moved to Salem: *I will be sanctified in them which come nigh me.*

April 17, 1770, when the foundation stone of the Congregation House was laid: *Sing unto the Lord a new song, and his praise in the congregation of saints.*

Nov. 13, 1771, when the meeting-hall in the Congregation House was consecrated: *The Lord is in his holy temple; let all the earth keep silence before him.*

Then Brother Marshall announced the congregation officers. "Brother Marshall will be general pastor, assisted by Sister Marshall. Brother and Sister Graff will have special oversight of the married people, and for the present will continue to live in Bethabara, serving that congregation and Bethania. Brother Paul Tiersch will be the preacher in Salem. Brother Richard Utley will be the treasurer and business manager of Salem congregation."

This service was closed with a song service, specially arranged, with the ministers, congregation, and choir singing in turn.

—*The Road to Salem* (1944)

THE MECKLENBURG
DECLARATION OF INDEPENDENCE

Hugh Talmage Lefler

The most significant, as well as the most controversial, action of any safety committee, was that of Mecklenburg County in May, 1775. According to a statement written from memory by John McKnitt Alexander in 1800 (because his minutes of the meeting had been burned), a meeting was held in Charlotte on May 20, 1775, which declared the citizens of that county "a free and independent people." According to a June, 1775, newspaper account, a meeting was held in Charlotte on May 31 which adopted a set of Resolves declaring that all commissions granted by the King in the colonies were "null and void" and calling upon the people of Mecklenburg to meet and elect military officers who should hold their powers "independent of Great Britain." Any person accepting office from the Crown was declared to be "an enemy to his country." Governor Martin sent a newspaper account of the Resolves to England and wrote that they "surpass all the horrid and treasonable publications that the inflammatory spirits of this Continent have yet produced." Without a doubt, the spirit of independence was strong in Mecklenburg. The Convention of 1861 placed the date May 20, 1775, on the state flag in honor of the "Mecklenburg Declaration of Independence."

—with Albert Ray Newsome, *North Carolina* (1954)

CAMP MEETING

Guion Griffis Johnson

The excitement of the Great Revival, as of the Great Awakening in New England which preceded it, aroused emotions which were in many instances accompanied by peculiar physical manifestations, commonly known as the "exercises." The sinner "under conviction" often trembled violently, suddenly fell prostrate, remained in a state of coma for varying lengths of time, and finally arose shouting praises to God. Those who had already been converted were also similarly affected. Other exercises frequently seen during the Great Revival were involuntary jerking, dancing, wheeling, laughing, and barking. A person might be affected with several of the different exercises but ordinarily he was subject to only one of them. The Reverend Jesse Lee mentions in his *Memoir* "the wild enthusiasm displayed by a certain female" at a camp meeting which he attended in 1806. "Her exercises were such as to attract the attention of all present, and were of a character novel enough to be sure; for she exhibited at some times the *jerking* exercise, at other times the dancing exercise, and not unfrequently the barking exercise; and taking them all together, made as ridiculous a set of exercises as ever attracted the gaze of the multitude." These exercises were frequently violent enough to bruise and injure the victim and, in some instances, even to cause death.

—*Ante-Bellum North Carolina* (1937)

BURNING OF THE CAPITOL

Hope Summerell Chamberlain

Sometimes improvement is definitely started by the stimulation of a great loss. The Raleigh that we know today only began to come into existence after the old town had been destroyed by a series of fires.

Of these the most serious and the most spectacular was the burning of the old State House in 1831. From Governor Swain's account, given as an eye-witness, we can recall the despair and dismay of this loss.

The fire occurred in broad daylight, the middle of a summer day, June 21st, 1831, and caught from a solder pot which a careless workman took into the loft where he was repairing something about the roof, and there left it, while he went to dinner. During his absence the fire caught and spread unnoticed.

Once before, in 1799, there had been an alarm about fire, a warning given by Andrew Jackson, conveyed to his old friend and former neighbor Colonel Polk, to the effect that it was con-

spired to destroy the State House in that way. It seems that the Secretary of State, Glasgow, holding his office as a respected leader and a Revolutionary officer of repute, had somehow fallen into bad ways, and was issuing fraudulent land warrants. The deception being found out, he was prosecuted, and to prevent conviction he had designed to burn the State House, and with it all evidences of his crime. This plot Jackson discovered, and the State House and its records were saved, while Glasgow fled from justice.

This time, however, the fire was well under way before anyone knew about it, and when the flames appeared they were at the top of the building, and there was not even a ladder at hand long enough to reach the trouble. And so that bright June day, the State House burned leisurely, the black smoke rolled up into the blue sky while the owls and bats and flying squirrels scurried out of the burning dome in panic, and the terrified people of Raleigh ran helplessly to and fro across the Capitol Square. Mr. Hill, Secretary of State, had ample time to save the State papers. A few that were lost at that time were afterwards restored by bequest of Waightstill Avery, from his private collection.

Miss Betsy Geddy, that spirited and gritty maiden lady, rallied all comers to try and move the Canova statue of Washington from beneath the burning roof. The citizens took hold, under her leadership and encouragement, and tried hard, but the marble was very heavy, and there were not hands enough to lift or to move it. There remained nothing to do but to watch it burn. By and by the fire had surrounded it, and it could be seen heated red-hot, glowing like a figure in a fiery furnace. So it shone for a time with unearthly beauty, and suddenly the roof fell in upon it and it broke and crumbled in utter and final ruin. A silence fell on the watching throng, and some little child's voice was heard speaking the sorrow of all: "Poor State House, poor statue, I'm so sorry!"

—History of Wake County (1922)

RATTLE SNAKES

A friend of Ellisville, Warren county, informs us, as a circumstance of very rare occurrence in that section of the country, that a Rattle Snake was killed near that place on the 24th ultimo, measuring three feet 8 inches in length, and six inches round the body. It had eleven rattles and a button. The Rutherfordton Spectator states, on the authority of a gentleman of undoubted veracity, that a Mr. H. Huffstetler, of Rutherford county, killed one of these serpents on his plantation, during the late wheat harvest, of an extraordinary size. The exact dimensions are not given; but it is stated that it took one bushel and a peck of bran to stuff the skin, and that it had *sixty-seven* rattles. A Rattle Snake was killed in the vicinity of Columbus (Geo.) a short time since, which measured in length, 10 feet 8 inches, and 21 inches in circumference.

—*Star*, Raleigh (August 4, 1831)

A METEOR

A meteor of great brightness was observed by several citizens of our village on the morning of Monday the 31st ult. which exploded with a report equalling that of a cannon. The same meteor, it appears, was observed in Fayetteville, and also near Wilmington; how far in other directions we have not yet learned.

The Fayetteville Observer of the 3d inst. says:

On Sunday night last about half-past two o'clock there was a terrific meteoric explosion near this place. Accounts vary about the brilliancy of the light, but the explosion is agreed on all hands to have been the most startling ever known in this vicinity. It resembled the sudden discharge of a park of artillery, and shook the houses even to such a degree as at first to produce the impression that it was the shock of an earthquake. The reverberation of the echo continued several minutes and the effect was majestic beyond description.

The Wilmington Chronicle of the same date gives the following account of this wonderful phenomenon:

Being in the county of Bladen on Sunday night last, about thirty miles in a North-westerly direction from Wilmington, we were startled from sleep between two and three o'clock on Monday morning by a sudden and terrific explosion, as of a heavy, quick clap of thunder, or the near discharge of a large piece ordnance, followed by a rumbling sound of nearly a minute's duration. It aroused the whole household, some of whom distinctly perceived the jar of furniture, &c. Looking out, we found the sky to be clear, and the atmosphere profoundly calm. The conclusion in our mind at once was that a meteor had exploded not very far distant, and this proved to be correct, as we subsequently ascertained from different persons who happened to be out at the time at various places a few miles distant. The meteor first appeared in the North East, and passing over towards the south-west, seemed to fall down near the line of Bladen and Columbus county, and there the explosion occurred. The light emitted by it was about like that of the moon when three or four days old.

It appears from these accounts that this extraordinary meteor could be seen and heard over a circle of some two or three hundred miles.

—*Hillsborough Recorder* (September 11, 1845)

**

As a matter of interest to many of our readers, we copy from the Fayetteville Carolinian and Raleigh Star the following particulars in relation to the Meteor on the morning of the first instant, furnished, it seems, by gentlemen who witnessed the phenomenon.

FROM THE NORTH CAROLINIAN:

On the morning of the 1st of September, I was in my east piazza, about 15 minutes past 2 o'clock, when I saw a large meteor pass with rapidity over my house. I did not see it rise, as my back was to it, and the great light and hissing sound caused me to face round. I learn from several gentlemen, however, who saw it, that it rose from the horizon as well as they could judge, in a northeast direction, emitting a most vivid light, and having a long tail behind it, from which there dropped to the earth along the whole length of its course, a sprinkling of blue flame, apparently of sulphur, which after reaching the ground continued to blaze up probably to the height of 12 inches. When about two-thirds of the way across the firmament, it exploded and spread into millions of little stars or sparks. There were three explosions, apparently, so heavy that they shook my house as though it would fall, causing a rattling of window sashes, and dishes in the pantry. The explosions were followed by a long rumbling sound, as of distant or receding thunder. As near as I can calculate, it must have exploded somewhere over the upper part of the adjoining county of Robeson.

Those who saw it vary in their statements as to the time which expired between the visible explosion and the report which followed, from 2 or 3 to 10 minutes. I thought the time 5 or 6 minutes, but it was probably not so much, as the light was not quite extinguished when the report reached me.

A gentleman at the U. S. Arsenal told me that he plainly smelt the fumes of brimstone on hoisting his window to look out.

Two gentlemen from Randolph county, 70 miles west of this place, told me that the shocks were felt there, and the sound heard, but they did not see the light.

The ball appeared to be about the size of a ten-gallon keg.   C.

From the Raleigh Star:

About two o'clock on the morning of the 1st instant my attention was attracted by the sudden illumination of the southern part of the heavens. The light was brilliant and sufficient to cast a shadow from chairs standing in the room. The streaks of clouds along the sky appeared of a light orange, the heavens generally white, and the floor of the room reddish. The duration of the light was about three seconds. I saw no meteoric ball or globe, but am of opinion one passed about fifty degrees above the heavens, as the light was more brilliant at forty degrees than lower, and the intensity of the light seemed to diminish towards the horizon. My position at first was such that I could not see much over forty degrees above the horizon. If such a globe or ball passed, its course must have been from East North East to West South West, or thereabouts. About three minutes after the light had passed off, a sound faintly audible was heard in the East, which increased in loudness and violence for near ten seconds, when it was so violent as to shake the house to its very basement, though not as severely as I have known thunder: there was a similarity in the sound to thunder. It was a rolling, rumbling, swelling noise, but without the sharp cracking which accompanies sudden bursts of thunder. After the noise had reached its acme, it decreased gradually and slowly till it died away after the full space of a minute's duration. Sound passes at the rate of 1100 ft. per second, or about one mile in five seconds; consequently the meteor (if my calculations be correct) must have been forty miles distant. I saw nothing to justify the opinion that the meteor burst. There was an illustration of the optical illusion of a bluish light succeeding an intense red.

—*Hillsborough Recorder* (September 25, 1845)

GREAT FALL OF FLESH AND BLOOD
EXTRAORDINARY PHENOMENON
IN SAMPSON COUNTY, N.C.

We received on Wednesday last, the following communication from Mr. Clarkson, through Mr. Holland, of Clinton, and take great pleasure in laying the astonishing particulars before our readers:

On the 15th of Feb'y, 1850, there fell within 100 yards of the residence of Thos. M. Clarkson in Sampson county, a shower of Flesh and Blood, about 30 feet wide, and as far as it was traced, about 250 or 300 yards in length. The pieces appeared to be flesh, liver, lights, brains and blood. Some of the blood ran on the leaves, apparently very fresh. Three of his (T. M. C's) children were in it, and ran to their mother, exclaiming "Mother there is meat falling!" Their mother went immediately to see, but the shower was over; but there lay the flesh, &c. Neill Campbell, Esq, living close by, was on the spot shortly after it fell, and pronounced it as above. One of his children was about 150 yards from the shower, and came running to the rest saying he smelt something like blood. During the time it was falling there was a cloud overhead, having a red appearance like a wind cloud. There was no rain.

The above you may rely on, and by Mr. Holland you have pieces of the flesh, which are reduced in size by being kept so long.

Yours, &c,

J. M. C.

The piece which was left with us, has been examined with two of the best microscopes in the place; and the existence of blood well established; but nothing was shown giving any indication of the character of the matter.

It has the smell, both in its dry state, and when macerated in water, of putrid flesh; and there can be scarcely a doubt that it is such.

It is astonishing, and we may say provoking also, that an occurrence of the kind should happen within 13 miles of a village (13 miles southwest of Clinton) of intelligent persons, and no one felt interest enough in it to go and get information about it.

It is three weeks after it occurred before any account of it is sent to the press. An occurrence that is calculated to strike men with awe; and we are told that some persons listened to the relation of it and looked upon it as an idle tale, deeming it impossible that such a thing could have occurred!

The cloud from which it fell is said to have been of a red appearance, which is the color ascribed to the clouds in former cases of this kind.

Although by no means frequent, this is not the first time that such an occurrence has taken place, even in this country. But as yet, the most learned are unable to give any rational conjecture as to the cause of such a singular phenomenon.

—*North Carolinian*, Fayetteville (March 9, 1850)

BEAR KILLED

A week or two ago, a starved out Bear was seen to swim across the river, and land in town at Mr. Jerkim's wharf. Afterwards he was seen early one morning on the steps of the Court House. He was killed in the suburbs of the town, near Jack's Island. Our western friends must not be frightened at the boldness of Bruin, for hunger will break through stone walls. Besides, we frequently have them tame down here.

—*Republican*, New Bern (February 15, 1850)

SNOW

Since our last paper, we have had one of the deepest snows that has ever fallen here. On a level it was full 22 inches deep and in drifted situations it was half thigh deep. In March, 1834, we recollect a storm of snow somewhat similar to this but it was only about a foot deep.

—*Charlotte Journal* (January 8, 1851)

HAIL STORM IN IREDELL

A terrible hail storm visited the neighborhood of Bethany, Iredell county, N. C., on Wednesday of week before last, doing much damage to corn and other crops, and killing poultry. Hail fell and covered the ground to a depth of four or six inches, and high wind prevailed. The extent of the storm was circumscribed within a few miles.

—*Greensboro Times* (September 25, 1858)

A SHOWER OF GRAVEL

Mr. John F. Clodfelter has handed us a specimen of gravel, of which there was a considerable shower fell from a cloud on the plantation of Wm. Knox, Esq., of Iredell county, in October last. It is a fragile gray-colored stone, with large proportion of silex.

—*Carolina Watchman*, Salisbury (December 23, 1864)

CIVIL WAR BALLOON

The Raleigh papers say a large balloon was seen flying over that city on Sunday morning at a moderate speed towards the South. It is described as being well lighted up, not very high, with flags, &c., and at least four persons in it. It is also reported that another was seen on Monday morning or Sunday night.

—*Times*, Greensboro (October 19, 1861)

❧❧❧❧❧❧❧❧❧

NORTH CAROLINA AND THE CIVIL WAR

Frank Holeman

You are going to see a lot in the papers in the next few months about the Civil War. The official celebration of the one hundredth anniversary—"centennial"—of the War Between the States (1861-65) began last week. It will continue for five years. January 19 is Robert E. Lee's birthday, always a time for speeches down South.

Since they're going to make such a to-do over the biggest family fight the U. S. ever had, I want to say a few good words right at the start for my grandfather, Henry Francis Holeman.

He was the only enlisted man in the Confederate army, as far as I can find out. Everybody else's grandfather was at least a captain and most were colonels.

Not only was he a private, he was drafted, off a farm near Oxford, N. C.

"How many boys have you got here?" the "recruiting" officer asked Henry's father. "Three," the old man replied.

"All right, we'll take him," said the officer, pointing at Henry. That's how he got on the road that led all the way to Pennsylvania and a federal prisoner-of-war camp. Along the way, he lost a thumb, and found out there is a lot more to war, victory, defeat, and the Union than the orators will tell you, even today.

The orators like to talk about Abraham Lincoln, U. S. Grant, Lee and Stonewall (Thomas J.) Jackson. Grandpa had one thing in common with Stonewall: They were both Presbyterians. And he had one thing in common with Lee: When the war was over, they both wanted to forget it and get on with the spring plowing.

Grandpa had a real admiration for Gen. Lee, as did most of the other foot soldiers in his outfit. My grandmother, Rosa, whispered to me once, though, that she thought Lincoln was a better man than Jefferson Davis, Lee, Jackson and the whole bunch. She didn't believe in slavery.

The fact is the people of North Carolina really didn't want any part of the war to begin with. There were only 12 plantations in the State with more than 100 slaves. Most people were like my folks, small farmers and tradesmen.

North Carolina didn't secede until May 21, 1861, next to the last of all the 11 Confederate States of America.

"We got into the Union too late to vote for George Washington and out of it too late to vote for Jeff Davis," my history teacher used to point out.

Once in the Confederacy, though, North Carolina furnished more soldiers (134,000) than any other state, and suffered far more casualties (dead and wounded), 20,602 compared to Virginia's 6,947 and South Carolina's 4,760.

The first Confederate soldier killed in action was a North Carolinian, Henry Wyatt, felled at Bethel Church near Yorktown, Va., on June 10, 1861.

On the battlefields at Gettysburg I found another North Carolina monument, a group of heroic figures carved by Gutzon Borglum but now almost hidden by shrubbery.

"One out of four who fell here was a North Carolinian," is the grim reminder chiseled on the base.

But the Tar Heels, in their blundering way, had a terrific impact on the course of the war. By mistake, they shot and killed Stonewall Jackson at Chancellorsville, Va., a couple of months before the decisive battle of Gettysburg. The Lord only knows what would have happened if Jackson had been at Gettysburg with Lee.

No big battles were fought in North Carolina, but the war actually ended there. Gen. Joseph E. Johnston surrendered the last big Confederate force (17,000) to Gen. William T. Sherman near Durham, N. C., on April 26, 1865, two weeks after Lee's surrender to Grant at Appomattox Court House, Va., on April 9.

Sherman took it fairly easy on North Carolina, but he did quarter a troop of Michigan cavalry in the stalls of the library of the State University at Chapel Hill.

The bitterness and suspicion churned up by the war and Reconstruction Era lasted in many parts of the South until World War II, when millions of servicemen from all over the country were thrown together.

When I left home in June, 1940, to seek my fortune in New York, my mother asked anxiously: "Are you sure you want to go? There's nobody up there but Yankees."

I haven't found my fortune yet, but I have found something else that means a lot to me. There are good-hearted people all over the U.S.—North, East, West, and South. I'm mighty glad we're still together. With all due respect, I think grandpa would be, too.

On the way to Augusta, Ga., with President Eisenhower, we used to fly over Raleigh, N.C. I'd look down at the houses and farms and think of Sir Walter Scott's famous lines: "Breathes there a man with soul so dead, Who never to himself hath said: 'This is my own, my native land!' "

That one-state viewpoint has changed now. It happened on the way back from Moscow, via Iceland, with Vice President Nixon in 1959. I looked down at last and saw the beautiful lakes and forests of Maine. The old warmth and pride filled me again.

"This is my own, my native land," I realized suddenly. "The whole wonderful U. S. A."

—New York Daily News (January 17, 1961)

~~~~~~~~~~

YANKEE SOLDIER LIKED IT HERE

Ed Hodges

There was a time when soldiers camped in the fields of this section of the state and wrote letters home telling of rolling red clay countryside and tall long-leaf pine trees that reached up into the sky, swaying in the warm breezes—the like of which they had never seen before.

The soldiers were Yankee troops. The time was 1865. And the place was between Durham and "Raughly, the capital of N.C."

Flushed with the prospects of victory, restless with memories of home and excited over the possibility of being released from the Army, the Yankee troops loitered through sunny summer days and roamed the countryside.

Then, as now, soldiers kept diaries, and one Yankee trooper, Andrew R. Hilborn of Steuben County, N.Y., recorded his daily routine of soldiering in a rustic, simple style that rings of another wartime writer, also simple in style—Ernest Hemingway.

A sample is the April 25 recording:

"This morning we left Raleigh [he had by now learned the correct spelling of the capital] for some place but what place we do not know yet, it was quite warm and dusty. We traveled about

15 miles [west toward Durham] and went into camp a little before sundown in a piece of woods and on a sidehill, a very pleasant place."

The Yankee private was a keen observer of his surroundings and was obviously impressed with his new environment.

"...we have traveled mostly through a timber country since we got in Carolina and it is mostly pine timber and all of it is land that has been cultivated and not many years ago either. It doesn't take but a little while to raise a nice piece of timber in this country, 15 or 16 years for a nice grove. Some of the timber will grow to be as much as 12 or 15 inches through at the stump."

Hilborn was not looking at this growth as a casual observer but as a soldier who found much use for good fire wood. The pine trees that gave North Carolina the name of the Tarheel state were very useful for the invading troops who used it for camp fires and cooking. No growth of trees went unnoticed by a good soldier. It was often their only shelter.

On February 12, Hilborn noted:

"This has been a very nice day and we have been on the march again, but I do not know how far we went. We are now camped in a nice piece of woods made up of scrub oaks and pine and not very thick at that but the worst of all was I had to go a mile and a half or two miles after water to make coffee.

"...our fire wood is mostly pitch pine trails and knots and the air is so full of the smoke that it makes my eyes so sore that I can hardly see and it is impossible to keep clean hands and face, let alone clothes."

The Yankee troops quartered in this section had plenty of time to obtain passes and visit towns and villages in the area. They made only casual raids on "the rebs," sometimes putting up a token defense against some who "were very stubborn."

They visited in homes and had meals, picked the fruit on trees in orchards where the owners had fled and lived off the land.

They burned cotton and wheat and tore up railroads and burned the rolling stock and raided peddler's wagons. Outside of this they left the country to the inhabitants, who were mostly Negroes by this time.

The small-scale fighting was recorded matter-of-factly:

"This day passed without anything special happening except a couple of raids that were made on a couple of peddler's wagons and cleaned out."

Hilborn's North Carolina stay made a vivid impression on him, but like most GI's the most exciting part of his military career was his discharge. He recorded his last day's duty and trip home:

"This morning at 9 o'clock I reported and got my papers and went to the paymaster's office and he said I would have to wait till the afternoon and he thought he would be ready to pay me. At the appointed time I went to the paymaster's office and got my pay and came to Addison on the express train. I got here about sun down."

The leather-covered diary used by Hilborn is pocket size and remarkably preserved for a document nearing the century mark. The notations made in the book are with pencil but the writing is still legible. Each recording is clear and terse. Most of it is written with a casual, off-handed tone.

The "pocket edition" shows little wear for wartime service. It was obviously designed for soldiering. It is a thin volume about six inches deep and fits snugly in most pockets designed by the military.

The leather used is a fine grain material with a flap to cover and close the document. There is a pencil enclosure inside the flap.

The last few pages of the diary are used to jot down home prescriptions for various small infections and diseases. There is also a page devoted to money borrowed and paid.

An address section is on the last page of the book.

Hilborn suggests:

A "good wash for old sores" is "2 oz. copper burned and pulverised. 1 oz. blue viterol pulverised and both put in a quart of rain or soft water, the oftener applied the better."

"To kill lice on cattle and colts," Hilborn recommends, "1 oz. carbolic acid to a gallon of lard. Rub thoroughly on all parts affected."

Various ointments are described along with cures for heaves in horses. Liniment formulas and cough medicine for horses also are listed.

Hilborn's diary is now the property of William H. Hilborn of Phoenix, N. Y., who is a relative of the Yankee trooper.

—Durham Morning Herald (September 26, 1954)

JOHNSTON'S SURRENDER TO SHERMAN

George Lougee

The cause was lost. Out-manned, supplies depleted, and its proud cities facing destruction, the gallant South reluctantly conceded further resistance was futile.

Northern General William Tecumseh Sherman was encamped in a rain-logged Raleigh when on April 14, 1865, he received word from General Joseph Eggleston Johnston at Greensboro that his Southern armies were prepared to lay down arms. Only days earlier Sherman learned at Smithfield of General Robert E. Lee's surrender to General Ulysses Grant at Appomattox Courthouse, Virginia. Elated with the turn of affairs, Sherman agreed to meet with Johnston at a point intermediate between pickets at noon on the 17th. The meeting place selected was Durham's Station, a hamlet of perhaps 200 souls.

Sherman was climbing aboard a train for Durham's Station when he received from Morehead a telegram telling of President Lincoln's assassination in Washington. The shaken general pledged the telegrapher to secrecy. With sadness and apprehension he rode to Durham's Station, a rustic village destined because of the meeting to become a bustling tobacco-manufacturing city.

General Johnston, a native of Farmville, Virginia, and a grandnephew of Patrick Henry, had served in the Black Hawk, Seminole and Mexican wars. He had resigned from the U. S. Army to enter the Confederate service. General Sherman, who like Johnston was a graduate of West Point, was a native of Lancaster, Pennsylvania. Sherman and Johnston had staged what many historians claim was the greatest duel in warfare history.

They were meeting now for the first time at close quarters and with undrawn guns. Johnston, at 58, wore a graying beard and well-groomed mustache. He was neatly dressed in gray uniform coat buttoned to his chin and carried his slight frame with military bearing. The 45-year-old Sherman, a taller man with unruly red hair and straggly beard, in mussed clothing appeared more the fighting private than conquering general.

Following handshaking and introductions, the generals retired to the inside of a small, frame and unpainted dwelling of Lucy Bennett and her four children. Her husband and their father, Lee Lorenzo Bennett, had fallen in battle. Mrs. Bennett and the children retired to one of the two outhouses on the premises to permit privacy for the history-making consultations. While the chieftains conferred, their subordinates outside swapped horses, ran foot races, spun yarns and talked of the future.

As soon as they were alone, Sherman showed Johnston the dispatch announcing Lincoln's assassination. Perspiration came to Johnston's forehead and he made no attempt to conceal his distress. He said with feeling that the murder was a disgrace to the age.

Johnston stated simply that further war on the part of the Confederacy was folly, and that every life sacrificed after the surrender of Lee's army was the highest possible crime. Agreeing that Grant's surrender terms to Lee were honest and fair, Johnston said he desired to embrace in the same general proposition the fate of all Confederate armies in existence. Johnston conceded that slavery was dead. Then he asked for concessions that would enable him to maintain complete control over his followers until they could get back to their homes. Sherman readily agreed to give it consideration.

On April 18, Sherman and Johnston met again at the Bennett house and Johnston satisfied Sherman of his powers to disband all rebel armies. Sherman agreed that Lincoln's proclamation of amnesty of December 8, 1863, was still in effect, enabling every Confederate soldier and officer below the rank of colonel to obtain an absolute pardon by simply laying down his arms and taking the common oath of allegiance. Such a pardon, Sherman understood, would restore them all their rights of citizenship. The side arms, private horses and baggage of the Southern officers also were to go untouched in the surrender terms.

Sherman told Johnston that he would get the memorandum of the surrender terms to new President Andrew Johnson (a native of Raleigh) for official confirmation. An armistice was ordered.

General Grant, who had moved into Raleigh, approved the memorandum and it was forwarded to Washington. Sherman soon learned to his consternation that the memorandum was disapproved without reasons assigned. He received orders to give 48 hours' notice and to resume hostilities at the close of that time. Within an hour a courier was on his way to notify Johnston of the truce suspension.

On the night of April 25, General Johnston asked Sherman for another meeting at the Bennett house at noon on the 26th. Shortly after the generals entered the house Sherman stepped to the door of the dwelling and asked for his saddlebags. A bottle of whisky was taken therefrom and the two leaders renewed their discussion in more sociable manner. Sherman apologetically explained that surrender terms had to be altered. He said that Washington was not recognizing state government in the South and that he could offer no concessions other than those allowed Lee by Grant. Sherman emphasized it was not to his liking.

A historian one day was to write: "If the terms he [Sherman] sketched had been accepted, our country might have been readily united. But the politicians would not have it thus."

Johnston accepted the new arrangements and the two men amicably departed, Sherman once more to report his actions to Washington.

Soon afterward Sherman saw an April 24 copy of a New York newspaper containing military news under the signature of Secretary of State Edwin Stanton. The article gave full report of a March 3 dispatch of instructions from Lincoln to Grant, instructions of which Sherman never had knowledge, and providing the public with what Sherman considered erroneous impressions. Sherman read on. He burned at the report.

"It does seem strange," he commented, "that every barroom loafer in New York can read in the morning journal 'official' matter that is withheld from a general whose command extends from Kentucky to North Carolina.... When an officer pledges the faith of his government he is bound to defend it...."

On April 28, Sherman met with his commanders at Raleigh and completed orders for the future. The next day he left by rail for Wilmington and thence to Washington.

On May 23, in Washington, at a Committee on the Conduct of the War, General Sherman testified in full. He felt content to abide by the judgment of the country on the patriotism and wisdom of his conduct in this connection.

A grand review of the military was staged in Washington on May 24, and Sherman later was placed in charge of Army headquarters at St. Louis.

On May 28, 1884, he wrote from that city his expression of a move to nominate him to the Presidency: "Any senator can step from his chair at the Capitol into the White House and fulfill the office of President with more skill and success than a Grant, Sherman or Sheridan, who were soldiers by education and nature, who filled well their office when the country was in danger, but were not schooled in the practice by which civil communities are and should be governed.... I remember well the experiences of Generals Jackson, Harrison, Taylor, Grant, Hayes and Garfield, all elected because of their military services, and am warned, not encouraged, by their sad experiences. The civilians of the United States should and must buffet with the thankless office, and leave us old soldiers to enjoy the peace we fought for and think we earned."

At an honorary dinner on February 8, 1890, his 70th birthday, Sherman said: "But the way to reform the community is to reform yourselves. But you have to take the world as it is. It is a good world. It is the best we have now. I don't see any who are anxious to depart from it."

Sherman died of the effects of asthma just six days after his next birthday, at his home in New York. At his request his remains were taken to St. Louis, to rest beside those of his wife, Ellen Boyle Ewing Sherman, and "the infant son whose brief span of existence did not bridge the interval of one campaign in the life of his great father."

Johnston was an honorary pallbearer. Standing bare of head in the chilling February air, Johnston, the one-time staunch foe, fell victim to pneumonia. He died of its effects the following month.

—*Durham Morning Herald* (April 9, 1961)

⁂

THE REOPENING OF THE STATE UNIVERSITY

Phillips Russell

In the spring of 1875 word came to Cornelia [Phillips Spencer] that the University trustees had found a way to raise some money and the courts were being liberal. In early March she was able to write June about the exciting outlook. On March 20 a telegram from Kemp P. Battle at Raleigh brought the sudden and tonic news that the legislature had passed a bill permitting the reorganization of the University and even guaranteeing it a measure of support.

This day was her fiftieth birthday; but about that she cared nothing. She ran to her mother with the news. She came back home to walk the floor and wait for the demonstration she was sure would come. Surely the happy villagers would turn out with fife and drum, parade the streets with torches and red fire. An hour, two hours, she waited, watching the streets. At last, no longer able to contain herself, she called to her daughter June, who happened to be at home. She and June collected two children of a neighbor, Susan and Jenny Thompson, and together they started for the campus. On the way they gathered the faithful villager, once the postmaster and University bursar, Andrew G. Mickle. Cornelia marched them all through the Episcopal churchyard and over the broad campus path to the South Building in which hung the college bell and rope. And finding all these silent, she climbed to the belfry and seized the rope. And then she rang and rang and rang. She did more than ring a bell; she rang out an old world of defeat and inertia and rang in a new world of hope and belief. It was an incident that Frank P. Graham, in his speeches as president of the University in the depressed 1930's, used to dwell upon. His report to the trustees in December, 1930, ended with this paragraph:

"In the tragic era, Mrs. Cornelia Phillips Spencer, staunch champion of the public schools and University, received March 20, 1875, a message from the committee in Raleigh that the University was to be opened again. For five years the bell had not rung in Chapel Hill. For five years she had worked and prayed for that day. She climbed the stairs to the belfry and with her own hands rang the bell which has never ceased to ring to this day. The people of North Carolina were on the march again. Under God, we will not turn back now!"

—*The Woman Who Rang the Bell* (1949)

THE TRAVELING CHURCH BUILDING

Ed Koterba

This is the story about the Providence Methodist Church in a small community in North Carolina. Ashley B. Futrell, editor and publisher of the *Washington* (N. C.) *News*, swears it's true. He has affidavits to back up the story. This happened in Swanquarter of Hyde County in 1876.

The congregation had scraped up enough money to start building a house of worship. The Methodists found a good location, a lot owned by a Sam Sadler. But Sadler wouldn't give it up. "I have other plans for the land," the man said. Nobody could change his mind. So the church folks found another plot up the road and started to build.

On September 16, 1876, before the church was completed, a hurricane struck the region. As Editor Futrell describes it: "The winds howled, waters swirled, and the tide had reached such a high level that the unfinished church was taken from its brick foundation and washed away."

The church inched down the gooey road all through the night. The next morning, the rain was still coming down in torrents, and the little church was still moving down the road. It was floating now, and when it came to an intersection, the church struck a general store and bounded across the street. There, according to witnesses, it shimmied and shook and came to a stop.

That little church had settled to earth on the very spot where the congregation wanted to build in the first place!

Next morning, a man—pale and trembling—was waiting at the door of the Hyde County Register of Deeds. That was the owner of the property, Sam Sadler. Then and there, he gave to the church the title to the land.

The little wooden church stands on that spot to this day. On the front, a sign reads: "Providence Methodist Church—The Church Moved by the Hand of God."

—*News and Observer*, Raleigh (April 30, 1961)

THE DAY GOVERNOR AYCOCK CAME

Bernice Kelly Harris

We awaited the Governor's arrival.

All of Poole's Siding were assembled at the schoolhouse. We school girls were thinking less of education than of our importance in the closing exercises. Dressed in our starched white lawns with rosettes of red, white and blue pinned to our berthas, we felt very responsible for the program and a little haughtily sure because the boys wore their rosettes so doubtfully. We were going to wave our colors at the right lines of *Columbia, the Gem of the Ocean,* whatever the boys might fail to do. We were going to render our school song from memory, every word of it.

Mamas stood around in groups on the school ground or strolled down the hill toward the shade. Some remained inside the schoolhouse throughout the wait, to savor the occasion of the Governor's visit as long as possible. Others sat in surreys and buggies to keep an eye on restless children who had to be kept starched and clean and combed till after the Governor had gone.

The little governess from the river road strummed idly on the piano, trying out its tone and singing to herself:

"Coon, coon, coon, I wish my color would fade,
   Coon, coon, coon, I'd like a different shade—"

The Mamas looked at one another, not sure it was a proper song on such a Sunday occasion. They were wondering what the children's Sunday School teacher, Miss Mattie Johns, might think about coon-coon-coon. If they had dreamed that same Sunday School teacher would one day be the wife of the United States Ambassador to Germany, they would have been no more impressed at the thought of Mrs. Dodd in Berlin than at the thought of the gentle Miss Johns they knew in Auburn.

Men stood around outside in shirt sleeves, comparing the progress of their cotton and tobacco and corn. Each time before one took another chew of tobacco, he looked sharply at the road to make sure the Governor was not in sight.

Suddenly there was a flutter of excitement over the waiting groups. Uncle Cana's carriage with the gray horses hitched to it was coming up the hill. Uncle Cana had gone to Auburn over an hour ago to meet the train that was bringing the Governor the twelve miles to Poole's Siding from Raleigh.

The men drew on their coats, did their last pit-too-ee. Women hurried inside, since greeting the Governor was man business, like politics. Teachers lined children up for their part on the program. We girls straightened our rosettes at the exact angle to be waved.

Governor Aycock alighted from Uncle Cana's carriage and was led inside the schoolhouse. Everybody stood in respectful silence as he walked up on the stage.

In our starched white lawns we stood out in front and waved our colors properly when we sang, "Hurrah for the red, white and blue." Then our voices blended in the school song which a teacher had arranged.

> "The academy I love the best
> In all the world is Mt. Moriah.
> Her name is known in East and West
> And North and South, our Mt. Moriah—"

Mamas beamed. Two aunts whispered, nodding their heads. They might have been agreeing that a lot of territory was being covered in that song.

Governor Aycock spoke eloquently about equal opportunity and education for the children of North Carolina. There were tears in the women's eyes at the story of the poor boy who was so eager for an education that he went to school with only green apples for his lunch. The Mamas were wishing they could have fed that little boy.

The men swallowed their emotion and resolved anew that their children were going to have opportunity and education the Governor was talking about if it took their last ounce of strength, their last dollar. It had taken their last dollars many times already, when they had taxed their meager incomes to carry on subscription school. But it was of the future they were thinking now, of longer school terms, of college even.

After the address, little golden-haired Helen Adams, instructed by a teacher who knew about manners and politeness towards Governors, went up on the stage. She handed Governor Aycock a bunch of pink roses from Miss Emily's yard. The Governor bowed his thanks gracefully.

We wondered what he did with Miss Emily's flowers on the train ride back to Raleigh. The pink roses must have been in his way.

—The State (December 26, 1959)

COCK FIGHTING

Margaret Walker Freel

Despite hardships of travel, early settlers would ride fifty miles to see a horse race, or lock up a place of business to witness a cock fight. There was a race track near Murphy, in the Notteley section on the Anderson farm. The well-to-do settlers bred horses for racing purposes.

Cock fighting with birds which had been imported from England and Ireland drew as much attraction as the races. From pioneer times down to the present time, Cherokee County has been famous for its cock fights. Champion cocks are still bred and known by name in this county. Cherokee County carries away prizes at the winter cock fights in the State of Florida, Cuba and elsewhere, where such sports are prevalent at the present time.

The excitement and thrill of the races and fights were not the sole incentive for attendance. There was much wagering and

betting. Cock fighting has been under legal ban for years in North Carolina. However the sport known locally as "rooster fighting" still goes on in secrecy.

—*Our Heritage: The People of Cherokee County* (1956)

AVIATION DAY

Several thousand people visited the state fair grounds yesterday to see the flights by Aviators McCurdy and Ely in Curtiss biplanes, the former making one flight and the latter making two. In making a landing Mr. McCurdy's machine was partially wrecked and the daring aviator had a narrow escape from injury. . . .

The first flight was made about half-past four o'clock by Mr. McCurdy. After circling the field twice, during which he reached the height of about 200 feet and a speed of sixty miles an hour, he made a landing towards the upper end of the field, but owing to the direction of the wind, his machine was forced along the ground on its runners, headed directly towards the crowd. The aviator, seeing that unless something was quickly done there would probably be a terrible accident, veered his machine suddenly. This action prevented the plane from dashing into the crowd, yet it wrecked the machine. Fortunately Mr. McCurdy escaped injury, though his biplane is out of commission for awhile.

The second and third flights were made by Mr. Ely, who made a perfect get-a-way, and after circling the field, one time going outside of the fair grounds, he landed safely each time. He had his machine under complete control at all times, gliding here and there at will, reaching an altitude of 400 feet. At times his speed was more than a mile a minute. The last flight ended shortly before dark.

Other flights will be made this afternoon. The indications this morning for good flights are better than they were yesterday.

—*Raleigh Times* (November 17, 1910)

THE BIG FREEZE OF 1917-18

Dallas Mallison

Perhaps the biggest and longest freeze within the memory of living local residents ... hit the lower Neuse River-Pamlico Sound section the latter part of December, 1917. For ten straight days or more the mercury hovered near the zero mark, and seldom if ever reached as high as freezing limits. Not only was all of lower Neuse River frozen over solid but this also happened in all the broad expanse of Pamlico Sound. Dead fish were scooped up by the thousands by the shivering residents, and whole schools of dead porpoises were swept ashore after the ice had broken up and gone to sea. Both at Oriental and at Vandemere on Bay River, daredevil youths drove model-T Ford cars across the frozen streams and back again, without causing a single break or crack.

Unlike the hurricane of September, 1913, the onset of the big freeze caught the captain [of the Neuse River Lighthouse] on leave at his Pamlico home. Assistant keeper Capt. Jim Miller, an elderly man with an aggravated heart condition, was on duty at the lighthouse.

Quite uneasy about what might be taking place at the lighthouse, Capt. Quidley made hurried preparations to relieve the 65-year-old Miller. At dawn on the morning of the second day of the freeze, he set out on foot for the lighthouse, accompanied by a companion, Tillman Paul of Pamlico. Walking over the frozen bed of the channel of Broad Creek, they pulled a boat loaded with supplies and equipped with wheels the whole three-mile distance to the mouth of the creek. Fearing it was impossible to make the remaining two or three miles to the lighthouse, they secured the boat for the night and returned home.

Again at daybreak he and his companion set out on foot the next morning for the lighthouse, walking over the frozen bed of the stream. Reaching their boat, they found that an "air hole" or break had appeared in the ice between them and the lighthouse, and they were able to row the boat the remaining distance. Before nightfall Paul set out for home, but Quidley remained, to stay out the duration of the freeze.

After several uneventful, lonely, frigid days, the ice began to break up all of a sudden, following a sudden warming of the weather. Water began to appear all around the lighthouse, and the next day Capt. Will Dixon and a companion showed up on a "State" boat. They had started out from Oriental and were trying to make it down the Sound, but found the ice would not let them go further.

Early one morning the mercury shot up rapidly and the ice

really began to break up in earnest and in a hurry. Ice chunks and icebergs, some as much as 25 feet high and as much as 100 feet in width, nearly wrecked the lighthouse as they bore down upon it in their headlong, pell-mell rush to the open sea. Only two of the five main 8-inch steel piling supports remained unbroken and intact. Wobbly and weaving, the unsteady lighthouse was almost ready to topple from its perch and join the ice in its dash to sea. The building almost literally hung suspended in air as the ice let up, disappeared, and the sea became a sea once more.

At the height of the ice breaking up, it was discovered that Capt. Miller had disappeared. After some searching, which almost reached the frantic stage, the elderly gentleman was found in one of the outside toilets, collapsed and suffering from a heart attack. They made a special chair in which to lower him into the boat and Capt. Dixon and his companion made a hurried trip back to Oriental with the sick man to get him to a physician.

It took months to repair the damage done the lighthouse by the freeze. Thousands of tons of fresh rock were brought in by boat to secure again the structure's foundation. Capt. Quidley estimates the total cost of the repair job to have been around $40,000, a much larger sum 40 years ago than it is now.

"I tell you, I surely thought my time had come when those big icebergs were breaking against the walls of the lighthouse," Cap'n Tom declared. "It felt like one earthquake after another was hitting us, and I thought the very next minute would be our last. I don't think old Capt. Miller could have stood it alone, and even I was glad that Capt. Dixon and his friend came in to be with us those last few days. It was hell on earth, believe me. Last winter the folks were talking about how cold and unbearable the cold weather was. My boy, let me tell you, last winter was baby stuff compared to that freeze of 1917-18. If anything could be worse than a hurricane, that was it!"

—*North Carolina Folklore* (December, 1958)

GERMAN SUB IN WORLD WAR II

Louis T. Moore

Reports that unidentified submarines may have been prowling along North Carolina's coast remind Wilmington residents of a night during 1943, a night when there was a sudden blackout, and when many war planes roared over the city en route to the ocean.

During the days that followed, there were many rumors flying around, rumors that a German sub had surfaced off Kure's Beach and had fired shells at the Dow chemical plant there. The rumors never were verified at that time. Since then, it has been learned that the sub did surface and that it did fire five rounds onto North Carolina soil.

The incident was revealed by A. B. Love, Jr., Wilmington native, who at the time was a chemist at the Ethyl-Dow plant at Kure's Beach and who later continued his connection with the Dow organization at Ludington, Michigan. The Kure's Beach plant is not in operation now. Love wrote about it in a letter to his father, who has since died.

When he was acquainted with the facts which had been brought to light, the report of the attack was declared to be "substantially true" by Louis Hanson, of Wilmington, Commander of the Coast Guard Auxiliary here at that time. The letter from son to father started with the query, "Do you remember the air raid alert we had in 1943 at 3 A.M. on a Saturday?"

"Well, we had always wondered what it was all about and thought there must have been some reason for it. Mr. W. L. Tisdale, who is from Midland, and who was in charge of plant protection at Ethyl-Dow during the war, was in a watch repair shop in Midland the other day and noticed a picture of a submarine on the wall. The shop is run by a former Army flier and Tisdale asked him about the picture.

"To make a long story short, it developed that the Army flier had been stationed at Elizabeth City, N. C., near the line between

Virginia and North Carolina, in the upper section of our State. His squadron had direct orders from Washington to fly a 24-hour patrol over the plant at Kure Beach. (He told all this to Tisdale without knowing the latter had been at the Ethyl-Dow plant when the incident occurred.)

"On the night of the alarm, the flier was on patrol around our operation and they spotted a submarine about five miles off-shore firing at the plant. The Army man said that five shots were fired but that they were long and to the right so they would have fallen on the Cape Fear River side of the peninsula, or possibly in Brunswick County, across the river.

"The submarine spotted the plane and submerged before they could get to it, but the next day, with the help of surface boats, they discovered the submarine and sank it. That was the submarine he had the picture of. Mr. Cantwell, former manager of the plant, says the story undoubtedly is true because the officer in charge of the Army guards around the plant told him the alert was the real thing but refused to give him any details."

Because it was making material used in the manufacture of high octane gasoline, the Ethyl-Dow plant probably had the highest priority as a target of any installation in the Wilmington area, persons familiar with the war-time situation declare today.

When informed of the letter, Hanson, then a lieutenant in the Coast Guard, recalled the alert which many other Wilmingtonians and residents of the nearby beaches remember as the most sensational one of the war here. Every light in New Hanover County, including those at the busy shipyard (where 243 mammoth cargo carriers were constructed in about four years' time), was ordered extinguished and all traffic was halted during the period.

Hanson was in charge of the Auxiliary's participation in the alarm. During the night, he and his party, including artillerymen from Camp Davis, spent four hours aboard a small boat in Masonboro Inlet, just south of Wrightsville Beach. A silhouette, believed to be the superstructure of a submarine, was sighted in the darkness and the artillery officer called on batteries, hidden at Wrightsville Sound, to open fire on the target. No hits were scored and the suspected craft later disappeared.

After Hanson entered active service as district director of the Coast Guard Auxiliary, he met a Lieutenant Murphy. They talked of the earlier days of the war along the Carolina coast and Lieutenant Murphy mentioned the fact that he had been on patrol off the New Hanover County coast. They recalled the night of the extensive alarm and the CGA's active participation and the lieutenant informed Hanson that the submarine was sunk the following day. Hanson is authority for the statement that this was but one of several instances in which the Coast Guard Auxiliary aided in guarding the coast line during the height of the Nazi U-Boat activity in World War II.

Operation of oil tankers along the coast was extremely hazardous. A number of such craft were sunk by the Germans and on several occasions seamen were rescued and brought to the ports of Southport and Wilmington. On one occasion a dozen or more sailors, severely burned from ignited gasoline, were brought to the local hospitals and treated for their injuries.

Despite the fact that operations at the Ethyl-Dow plant were suspended in December of 1945, this operation, erected at a cost of millions of dollars, continues to be one of the most attractive exhibits which tourists and visitors inspect. The buildings cover several acres of ground, and are located closer to the Cape Fear River than to the ocean.

Ocean water was pumped into the plant and when processed was disposed of in the river nearby. The plant had an initial capacity of 500,000 pounds of ethylene-dibromide per month by treating the sea water to liberate its bromide and convert the latter to the desired product by reaction with ethylene gas, a derivative of grain alcohol. Between 25,000 and 50,000 gallons of water were treated every minute, with the plant operating on a 24-hour basis. The sea water remained in the treating process for only ten minutes, and then was dumped into the Cape Fear River, to be carried far out of the reach of the intake.

—*News and Observer*, Raleigh (February 27, 1955)

THE WRECK OF THE *CARROLL A. DEERING*

David Stick

Of the hundreds of ships which have been lost in the Grave-yard of the Atlantic, none has commanded more attention than the five-masted schooner *Carroll A. Deering*, which fetched up on Diamond Shoals in the darkness of a stormy winter night in 1921.

At sunset, January 30, there was no sign of the *Deering* or any other vessel on the shoals; just the ocean rollers, coming in from two directions, crashing together above the Diamond's sand bars, dropping more sand to form new shoals and move the old ones. But at dawn the next morning, January 31, there was something else out there on the Diamond, a schooner, tall and stately, sails set on her five masts, abandoned by her crew, with no sign then or later as to what had happened to the men who once sailed on her. The *Carroll A. Deering*—Ghostship of The Diamond.

There have been rumors aplenty; repeated rumors of mutiny and murder and piracy. Hardly a year passes that some new theory is not advanced, new clues supposedly uncovered. But what happened to the crew of the *Carroll A. Deering* remains as much a mystery today as it was January 31, 1921, and with the following facts at hand you are welcome to draw your own conclusion.

The *Deering* was launched in 1919 at Bath, Maine, the last of many large schooners constructed for the G. G. Deering Company. Named for the owner's son, she was described as "a tremendous sailing ship," measuring 255 feet in length, 44.3 feet across the beam, and registered as being 1,879 tons.

Under command of Captain F. Merritt, the five-master sailed from Boston in September, 1920, bound for Buenos Aires. When off the Delaware Capes, Captain Merritt became ill, so he put in at Lewes, Delaware, and was relieved of his command by a veteran retired shipmaster, Captain W. T. Wormwell.

The *Deering* then proceeded to South America, apparently making several calls there, and leaving Rio de Janeiro on December 2, 1920, en route home to Norfolk, Virginia. She carried no cargo and made one stop on the return journey, at Barbados in the West Indies.

At 6:30 A.M., January 31, 1921, Surfman C. P. Brady, on lookout duty at the Cape Hatteras Coast Guard Station, sighted a five-masted schooner "with all sails set" on Diamond Shoals. At the time the wind was from the southwest, the sea was rough, the tide, strong.

In two boats, lifesavers from four stations—Big Kinnakeet, Cape Hatteras, Creeds Hill, and Hatteras Inlet—put to sea, reaching the vicinity of the stranded vessel in midmorning.

In his official report Keeper C. R. Hooper of Big Kinnakeet Station stated that she was "driven high up on the shoal...in a boiling bed of breakers...with all sails standing, as if she had been abandoned in a hurry." Keeper J. C. Gaskill of Creeds Hill reported that "she had been stripped of all life-boats and no sign of life on board...crew had apparently left in own boats, as ladder was hanging over side."

Because of the breakers surrounding the vessel the lifesavers could get no closer than one-quarter of a mile to the schooner, and at that distance they were unable to make out her name.

The next day the sea continued rough and the Coast Guard cutter *Seminole* was dispatched to the scene from Wilmington; and the day after that the cutter *Manning* and the wrecking tug *Rescue* joined the *Seminole* from Norfolk. Not until February 4, however—four full days after the five-master was first discovered aground—was it possible to board the schooner. Waves had been breaking over her deck, and when the wreckers reached her, water filled her hold. Her seams were so badly ripped apart that there was no hope of floating the vessel. Her steering gear was disabled, charts were scattered about the master's bathroom, and food was set out in the galley and on the stove.

Subsequently the wreckers removed what they could from the vessel, and following a severe storm three weeks later she was dynamited. Her large stern section presumably is still there, but the smaller bow part later drifted south, eventually stranding on the beach at Ocracoke where it is still visible at times.

So much for the facts; now for the theories, rumors, and speculation.

Mutiny—Investigation revealed that Captain Wormwell had confided to a friend in Barbados that he was ill, and that he had no faith in his crew, especially his first mate. It was further reported that the vessel had passed Cape Lookout Light Vessel the day before she stranded, and that a crewman (not the Captain) had shouted through a megaphone that the vessel had lost her anchors in a storm off Cape Fear and needed assistance. This led to the conclusion in some quarters that "Old Man" Wormwell had been murdered by the mate or other crewmen, but it offers no explanation of what happened to the survivors.

Piracy—Several other ships disappeared at sea at about the same time (though thousands have disappeared off the Atlantic coast with no trace in years gone by) and there were reports that they had been captured by Russian pirates. At about this time a resident of Buxton claimed he had found a bottle on the beach with a note inside indicating that pirates had boarded the *Deering* and murdered the crew. It was later reliably determined that the man who reported finding the message had written it himself.

Abandoned at Sea—The most frequently voiced opinion—and the one given most credence by the Coast Guard and other agencies which investigated—was that the *Deering* had encountered a storm off the lower Carolina coast, drifting toward Diamond Shoals in a disabled state, and that her eleven crewmen, certain that she would strand on treacherous Diamond, had abandoned her in panic, drifting to sea and certain death in their open boats.

Mutiny, piracy, abandonment by the crew. Take your choice. And if you ever get to Ocracoke examine the remnants of her bow, as thousands of others have, so that you too may become an authority on the fate of the five-master *Carroll A. Deering*.

—*Graveyard of the Atlantic* (1952)

THE ZIPPER STORY

Carl Goerch

It may sound funny to you and to me, but it was almost tragic to the people who were involved in the incident.

It happened in the State Theater in Raleigh.

There's a certain gentleman in Raleigh (we'll call him Mr. Brown for the sake of convenience) who weighs well over 200 pounds. One night last week he went home to supper and found that his wife had prepared backbone and dumplings—a dish of which he is particularly fond. So he sat down at the table and gorged himself until he could hold no more.

Then he suggested that they go to the State Theater and see a picture. Mrs. Brown was agreeable, so down town they went.

They found seats at about the center of the theater and after they had settled themselves comfortably, proceeded to enjoy the picture. Mr. Brown began to feel that his belt was too tight.

Inasmuch as the theater was dark, he didn't hesitate to unloosen it. But even then he didn't feel exactly right: there was still too much pressure around his middle.

He had on a pair of trousers with zippers down the front, so he reached down and ran the zipper-jigger down a few inches. After that he felt fine, and gave a huge sigh of relief as he prepared to enjoy the picture.

Everything went along fine for ten or fifteen minutes, and then a lady, sitting on the same aisle, about three or four seats away, decided that she had seen all she wanted of the show and got ready to leave. The people sitting next to her obligingly rose in order to make way for her. When she approached Mr. Brown, he, too, rose to his feet. And then he suddenly remembered that his zipper was unfastened, so he reached down hurriedly to pull up the jigger.

When he did, he caught the lady's dress in the zipper and couldn't work the thing up or down to save his life.

She felt a tug at her dress and turned around to give him a hard look. She felt another tug, whereupon she leaned forward and hissed: "What are you trying to do?"

That attracted Mrs. Brown's attention. She turned to her husband and whispered hoarsely: "John, what are you trying to do to the lady?"

"Not a thing," whispered back John.

"He is, too," said the lady. "He's tugging at my dress."

Mrs. Brown half-way rose from her seat. "Turn her loose this instant!" she commanded. "Whatever in the world has come over you?"

"I can't turn her loose!" protested Mr. Brown.

"Why not?"

"Her dress is caught in my pants."

Mrs. Brown gasped, and so did the other lady. People sitting behind them were beginning to get impatient and there were cries of "Sit down!" and "Down in front!"

Mr. Brown began to perspire freely. He tugged at that zipper for all he was worth, but the more he tugged, the more firmly the lady's dress became entangled in its meshes.

"What are you-all trying to do?" asked a gentleman sitting directly behind Mr. Brown.

"Her dress is caught in my pants!" hissed Brown.

"Good Lord!" said the man behind, and after that he didn't say another word.

"Do something!" insisted the lady.

"I'm doing all I can!" growled Mr. Brown, "but it's getting worse and worse all the time."

By that time everybody in the neighborhood was taking a keen and unholy interest in the proceedings.

"We'll have to go out in the lobby," finally said Mr. Brown.

"Together?" she asked.

"You're darned right—together," he told her. "Think I'm going to take off my pants and let you walk off with them?"

She agreed that there was nothing else to do but act upon his suggestion. Moving slowly toward the end of the aisle, she led Mr. Brown along with her.

Then they started toward the lobby. It was the side of her dress that had been caught in the zipper and so, while she was able to walk along all right, taking rather short steps, Mr. Brown had to go sideways, something like a crab on the beach. Folks sitting on the aisle almost fell out of their seats as they saw what was taking place. Their eyes followed Mr. Brown and the lady as they waltzed in the direction of the lobby.

By the time they got there, both of them were so mad that they couldn't see straight. One of the ushers—after the situation had been explained to him—took them into a little sideroom, where Mr. Brown took out his knife and proceeded to do some effective work with it.

At last the lady was free. She shook down her dress, shook herself all over, gave Mr. Brown a final dirty look and sailed majestically out of the theater.

Mr. Brown returned to his seat, where he had to listen to Mrs. Brown's whisperings and also to the chuckles emanating from all the seats in his immediate neighborhood. He sat through the rest of the show with his belt tightly fastened and with the zipper pulled all the way up, but the damage had already been done and he really didn't get much pleasure out of the picture.

If anybody wants a pair of pants with zipper attachments, I can tell him where he can get them at a very reasonable price. He'll have to be a rather fat man, however.

—Down Home (1943)

PAUL GREEN'S *THE LOST COLONY*

Inglis Fletcher

We drove from Edenton to Manteo and Fort Raleigh, where we saw *The Lost Colony* for the first time of this season. It was a splendid performance. It moved with precision and ease. The new performers in the cast did not stand out as new faces or new voices, but they were an integral part of the whole tragic story, which is a tribute to the work of the actors and the directors.

Seeing *The Lost Colony* always constitutes an adventure. Sometimes I have tried to analyze the feeling one has in listening to Paul Green's fine play. Deep emotions are stirred as the life of those courageous people unfolds. The words are rhythmical, almost Shakespearian. Again, one thinks of Greek tragedy, as the play marches on to its inevitable doom. But the Shakespearian form prevails, with its comedy close to tragedy, and the tragedy moving to heroic proportions.

The people of the play are not actors. They are Devon folk, set out on a great venture, as their earlier kinfolk set out on an heroic undertaking under Sir Richard Grenville in that first colony, when a hundred and seven men of Devon and Cornwall came to Roanoke Island, and for a year struggled to establish a colony in the New World, for the glory of Elizabeth and England.

These men and women of *The Lost Colony* had no thought of being history's children. They were intent on gaining a foothold in the New World, adding their share to halt the power of Philip of Spain, in America. The shadow of Spain lay over them, and who knows but that shadow became the hurricane that finally engulfed them?

The value of having the play on the spot where the events took place is beyond question. The earth itself becomes a part of the play and the action on the stage.

The setting is well thought out, well executed, unobtrusive; like the actors and the music, it is all so well integrated that it is the living part of the whole. These were heroic people, yet I doubt if a man or woman felt heroic. Time has given them that stamp, raised them to what the Elizabethans called "Equestrian proportions."

The effect of the drama of *The Lost Colony* upon the audience is different from that of any play I have ever seen. Many people have seen it many times. Sometimes I think the audience knows the play as thoroughly as the actors who speak the lines. This, too, is Elizabethan, where vigorous prompting often came from men seated in the pit.

The audience is frank to praise or criticize each change that is made in lines or in stage business. Each successive change has its partisans.

I belong to the group who think that the earlier ending was the best. After some years I still remember watching that little group of defeated men and women walking off into the unknown, in silence. People all about sat quietly, tears streaming down their cheeks. Their emotions were stirred to the depths, watching a little group of defeated folk walking away.

They thought they were marching into the forest. We know they were marching into history. That moment of silence was great drama.

Now they march away on a triumphant note of music and song. Perhaps that is better. Perhaps that is what was in the hearts and souls of those staunch Devon folk. Who knows? But somehow I feel that their going was stark tragedy, and that they moved off silently, in despair, knowing that the deep forest held no hope for them.

This play, this *Lost Colony*, is so important in history that I wish that every youth in the country could see it. The lesson is so obvious. Our nation was not built out of easy living. It was not a gift. It was the struggle of devoted, stalwart people.

—*Chowan Herald,* Edenton (August 19, 1948)

LUMBEE INDIANS ON THE WARPATH

Even in this tension-ridden year of 1958 no one expected to read or hear about Indians taking to the warpath in North Carolina.

But such was the case last weekend.

Reports from Maxton say that several hundred armed Indians of the Lumbee tribe, provoked by recent cross-burnings in their area, broke up a night-time rally of a dozen or more Ku Klux Klansmen with gunfire.

Riding to the "rescue" of the Klansmen in the tradition of U.S. cavalrymen going to the relief of a besieged wagon train in the old West, were squads of sheriff's deputies and State Highway patrolmen. Their arrival and use of tear gas ended the Indian-Klan encounter.

Adding a light note to the deplorable incident was a telegram signed "George Armstrong Custer" extending "deepest sympathies" to the Klansmen. (Custer, be it remembered, was defeated by the Sioux at the Battle of the Little Big Horn.)

Reports said the armed Klansmen, one of whom was robed, did not return the fire of the Indians who used thousands of rounds themselves. Only four persons were wounded, none seriously, evidence that the Indians are poor marksmen or they were simply seeking to scare off the Klansmen. The latter seems to have been the case, for most of the Indians fired into the air.

The violence climaxed a week of rumblings and tensions in Robeson County, where some 30,000 proud Lumbee Indians live. The trouble stems from racial bias, the Klan having issued warnings against racial mixing after an Indian family moved into a white neighborhood and an Indian woman dated a white man.

The first real Klan activity in that area since the organization was broken up by authorities in 1952, the entire episode was disgraceful—a mark on the good name of North Carolina in the field of race relations.

The Sheriff of Robeson County has announced his intention of seeking indictment of Klansmen on charges of inciting a riot. They contend for the right to assemble peaceably, but they leaned on weak legal reeds when they assembled with weapons in their hands.

There is no place for the Klan in North Carolina, or elsewhere for that matter. Its purpose is intimidation and clearly they sought to scare the Lumbee Indians.

As for the Indians, they appear to have acted in concert, a matter which requires leadership. The Klansmen say the Lumbees trespassed on private property, and damaged property. Whatever their provocation, the Indians did not have the legal right to resort to violence, which is a solution for nothing.

The "battle" of Robeson County calls for a thorough probe by proper authorities with legal action where indicated. . . .

—*Asheville Citizen* (January 21, 1958)

ODDMENTS AND
OBSERVATIONS

"Fortunately, there is present now in North Carolina the self-criticism which is always essential to progress at home."

—JONATHAN DANIELS

TOBACCO FOR SIR WALTER'S COLONISTS

Thomas Hariot

There is an herbe which is sowed a parte by it selfe & is called
by the inhabitants *vppówoc:* In the West Indies it hath diuers
names, according to the seuerall places & countries where it grow-
eth and is vsed: The Spaniardes generally call it *Tobacco.* The
leaues thereof being dried and brought into powder: they vse to
take the fume or smoke thereof by sucking it through pipes made
of claie into their stomacke and heade; from whence it purgeth
superfluous fleame & other grosse humors, openeth all the pores
& passages of the body: by which meanes the vse thereof, not
only preserueth the body from obstructions; but also if any be,
so that they haue not beene of too long continuance, in short
time breaketh them: wherby their bodies are notably preserued
in health, & know not many greeuous diseases wherewithall wee
in England are oftentimes afflicted.

This *Vppówoc* is of so precious estimation amongest thē, that they thinke their gods are maruelously delighted therwith: Wherupon sometime they make hallowed fires & cast some of the pouder therein for a sacrifice: being in a storme vppon the waters, to pacifie their gods, they cast some vp into the aire and into the water: so a weare for fish being newly set vp, they cast some therein and into the aire: also after an escape of danger, they cast some into the aire likewise: but all done with strange gestures, stamping, somtime dauncing, clapping of hands, holding vp of hands, & staring vp into the heauēs, vttering therewithal and chattering strange words & noises.

We our selues during the time we were there vsed to suck it after their maner, as also since our returne, & haue found manie rare and wonderful experiments of the vertues thereof; of which the relation woulde require a volume by it selfe: the vse of it by so manie of late, men & women of great calling as else, and some learned Phisitions also, is sufficient witnes.

—*A Brief and True Report* (1588)

MORAVIAN MUSIC

Chester Davis

Of all their traditions the Moravian love of music is, perhaps, the oldest and the deepest seated.

In 1501 the Brethren of Bohemia published the first Protestant Hymnal. From the very beginning these people enjoyed song and encouraged congregational singing.

In Salem, as in other areas, this small church has had a marked impact on Protestantism generally. Martin Luther, for example, lifted large chunks of the Moravian Hymnal of 1501. John Wesley, the founder of Methodism, translated many of the Moravian hymns from German into English and, in so doing, brought a new warmth into English hymn singing.

The classical period of music—the period of Haydn, Mozart and Beethoven—bracketed the years 1750-1800. Actually, however, the great works of those masters came within a limited period late in the century. But the groundwork for those few years was laid throughout the 18th century.

The Moravians came to America out of the heart of that period. Their musicians knew and worked with the leading musicians of that time. John Antes, a Moravian violinist and a composer, for example, knew Haydn and played in ensembles with him.

Music was as much a part of the Moravians' religious life as prayer. Children entered life listening to the *Wiegenlieder* or cradle hymns. And the final notes of life were those of the trombones—the "last trumpet" in the "Going Home" of the Moravians—played from the belfry of the church.

In the morning and again in the evening Moravian families gathered about the table and recited "the daily words." They read the daily text, usually a Psalm, and then sang the words of the hymn dedicated to that particular day. They sang as they worked. There were hymns for the Sisters at their spinning wheels, for threshers and for those who plowed the fields. When the Moravians had "one for the road" they raised their voices (rather than cups) in *Reislieder* or traveling hymns. At harvest time men came into the fields with horns and oboes to play hymns of thanksgiving for the bounty of God. The Lovefeasts were times of worship, fellowship and song. In the Moravian towns there was music from dawn to dusk, and in the night the watchman made his rounds, blowing out blasts on his pierced conch and chanting "The Song of the Hours."

This trait was unusual in Colonial America. For in the 18th century the Puritans and the stern doctrines of Calvinism frowned on almost all forms of musical expression. Where the Moravians used music to glorify God, the Puritans suspected that music—particularly instrumental music—was of the devil.

By 1746 the Moravians in Bethlehem were using an organ to accompany them in their singing. Most Moravian music called for instrumental accompaniment. These people were the first to bring instruments in any quantity and variety to America. They also were the first to use a variety of instruments in their church services.

They used trombones much as other churches used bells. Their trombone choirs (soprano, tenor, alto and bass) were unknown elsewhere in America. The choirs gathered to announce births, deaths, weddings, the arrival of distinguished guests and all manner of community affairs.

The French horn was another favorite. In their churches men accompanied the singers on trumpets, flutes, bassoons, oboes, clarinets and even on the improbable zink. The zink, a medieval trumpet with a mouthpiece of ox-horn, was last used in some of the compositions of Johann Sebastian Bach. Yet in 1805, at least 100 years after the zink became extinct elsewhere, the Moravians in Salem ordered a pair specially made.

Along with the organ the Moravians in America used the piano, the harpsichord (a piano-like instrument in which strings are plucked by quills), the clavichord (here the strings are hammered with metal mallets), and the harp.

They were just as versatile when it came to stringed instruments, favoring the "fiholine," cello and viola.

When the minister broke into song—and that he often did out of pure inspiration—the organist was expected to pick up the tune thread of the correct hymn (there were four hundred or so for the minister to choose from) and do that in precisely the correct key. That sort of antiphonal music is a Moravian tradition, possibly dating back to the days when the church choir was separated, the men singing from one side of the altar and the women from the other. It helps explain how the massed bands at the Easter Sunrise Service will pick up a tune and then pass it back and forth, one band answering the other.

Musical skills run deep in these people. In most churches, for example, the congregation sings only the melody line while the choir tends to the harmony. Even today in a Moravian church it isn't unusual to hear the entire congregation sing a hymn in well-handled four-part harmony.

In Europe, during the time when music was largely limited to the church, institutions known as the *Collegia Musica* were formed. These were the symphony orchestras of the time and they brought music—most of it secular music—to the people. A *Collegium Musicum* was established in Bethlehem before 1744. Salem organized its orchestra shortly after 1780. Other cities—Philadelphia, Charleston, New York and Boston—had occasional concerts before 1740. But these were played by troupes of traveling musicians.

In the Moravian settlements these home-grown orchestras played regularly. The *Collegium Musicum* of Bethlehem probably was the first symphony orchestra in the United States (Charleston disputes that claim) while that in Salem was the third or fourth. And these early orchestras showed discernment in what they played.

Haydn, for example, published his great oratorio *The Creation* in 1800. In 1811 *The Creation* was played for the first time in America at Bethlehem. The oratorio was played in the South, again for the first time, in Salem in 1829.

The curious thing about their musical tradition is that it existed in the absence of full-time professional musicians. The finest of the Moravian musicians were ministers and very busy men indeed. Gottlieb Schober, for example, was an organist in Salem and the community's musical director. At one time or another in his busy life, Brother Schober was a weaver, tanner, schoolteacher, storekeeper, postmaster, lawyer, and supervisor of the beggars who visited the village.

These musical ministers wrote music in much the same spirit ministers of other faiths wrote sermons.

Christian Gregor (1723-1801) was the first of the 18th century Moravian composers. He also was one of the most prolific. Gregor invented the Moravian anthem, usually a text from the Psalms set to music.

Jeremiah Dencke (1725-1795) was the first of the American Moravian composers. Of the Americans, Johann Friedrich Peter (1746-1813) probably was the most talented. Peter came to America in 1769. After some years in the Pennsylvania settlements he came to Salem in 1780 as musical director. There he organized the *Collegium Musicum,* composed a number of anthems (including one to celebrate the completion of the new church at Bethabara) and, for the only time in his life, wrote six pieces of secular music.

Moravian composers often were tempted by secular music but they rarely yielded to the temptation. Violinist John Antes, for example, once wrote three trios for strings. Because they were not sacred music, he published them under the alias "Giovanni A-T-S, Dillettante Americano."

In all, there were some thirty-seven Moravian composers. Those in Europe—men like J. F. Freydt, John Antes, J. C. Geisler and Christian Latrobe—worked in the circle that surrounded Handel, Mozart and Haydn.

The American composers—such as the Peter brothers, Bishop Johannes Herbst, Dencke, Bishop Jacob Van Vleck, Johann Christian Bechler, David Moritz Michael, and Peter Wolle—wrote within the classical tradition. But they wrote in a separating stream.

That is significant. For the real importance of this early Moravian music lies in the fact that it was a part of America: good music that was often written and always played by Americans and, that, in a time which musicologists have tended to consider as being barren of any more talented expression than *Yankee Doodle.*

—*Hidden Seed and Harvest: A History of the Moravians* (1959)

GERMAN IN OLD ROWAN

James S. Brawley

These German immigrants for the most part lived to themselves and spoke their native language. They obtained pastors, teachers and books directly from Germany. In fact, an interest in books was characteristic of the Germans in Rowan, because from old records one can see that they expended surprisingly large amounts of money for the importation of books. It was not until 1787 that a German pastor, Paul Henkel, delivered an English sermon from a pulpit of a German church.

—*The Rowan Story* (1953)

GAELIC IN THE SAND HILLS

Malcolm Fowler

Gaelic lasted through several generations of the Scotch settlers and descendents throughout the Sand Hills: As late as the 20th century, old Scotchmen would meet and carry on a friendly conversation in Gaelic. Children would stop their play and listen fearfully at the sound of short, snappy syllables and deep tones which sounded as though a severe bodily encounter between the conversing parties appeared imminent. The language was sometimes understood by individuals who never spoke it. One Sand Hills lady would occasionally have a caller spend a day in conversation during which the visitor would never speak an English word—and the hostess never speak a word in Gaelic!

At Barbecue Church it was customary with a number of the earlier pastors to preach two sermons each Sunday of appointment there, one in English during the forenoon, and one in Gaelic in the afternoon. The Reverend John C. Sinclair was the last of these "speakers of the auld tongue" to maintain this practice, his service ending there about the time of the outbreak of the most uncivil "Civil War." At these early services where the mother tongue was used in sermon and hymn, it has been said that even the babies seemed to cry in Gaelic.

—in John A. Oates, *The Story of Fayetteville and the Upper Cape Fear* (1950)

"BUNCOMBE"

Richard Walser

A word whose meaning is known to everyone is *buncombe*. It is a respectable word, though the average person would probably think it slang. It does not, however, become slang till it is shortened to *bunk*.

If one greeted a friend with some such statement as "This morning is deleterious to my health, for these miasmic atmospheric conditions cause my olfactory organs to scent odors which disturb my psyche"—well, we would just know he was putting on airs without really trying to say anything. The friend probably would reply, "Uh, that's just bunk." And he would be right.

How did that fancy kind of language get to be *buncombe?*

The word is one of the few in the English language to have a definite North Carolina origin.

Today, down highway 64 beyond Plymouth in Washington County, is the little town of Roper. Nearby an official highway marker informs the motorist that Buncombe Hall once stood one mile north. During Revolutionary times, the estate was the home of Edward Buncombe, Colonel of the 5th North Carolina Regiment of the Continental Line. In 1778 the Colonel was captured at the Battle of Germantown and shortly thereafter died a prisoner of the British. He was one of North Carolina's heroes of the Revolution.

When a new county in the western part of the state was created in 1792, it was named Buncombe County to honor the memory of the gallant Colonel. Asheville is the county seat of this beautiful mountain region.

So far, so good. Buncombe is an eminently proud name. But several decades later, in the 16th Congress (1819-21), a local politician from Buncombe County was Representative of North Carolina in Washington, D. C. He was a glib and garrulous talker, and doubtless it was his very trivial and high-sounding verbiage which found favor with the word-loving mountain voters of the day. One morning he rose to his feet in the Congress and spoke on a political matter in a manner dear to himself and to his Buncombe County folk back home. As soon as he began, his meaningless language flowed mellifluously. The mountain voters would have been thrilled with his twaddling oratory. Not so his Congressional colleagues in the House of Representatives. Soon the members began to leave the hall, and eventually the speaker found himself with few listeners. He was not downcast. He finished what he had to say.

Later, when he was asked his reason for displaying such a torrent of palaver, he replied, "I was not speaking to the House, but to Buncombe."

Then came the comment: "And buncombe your talk certainly was."

The word stuck.

First *buncombe* was used to mean any "insincere speechmaking intended merely to please political constituents." Then it was identified with any hokum—any nonsensical and meaningless language. And finally the word was shortened to *bunk*.

So this story is all *bunk?* Not at all. It is quite true. With his chatter, Congressman Felix Walker brought disrespect on the old Colonel and the great county named for him, but he had added a new and useful common noun to the English language.

—From manuscript (1954)

THE DRUNKARD'S TREE

The
Sin of
DRUNKENNESS
Expels Reason, drowns
Memory, & distempers the Body,
Defaces Beauty, diminishes Strength,
Corrupts the Blood, inflames the Liver,
Weakens the Brain, turns men into walking
Hospitals, causes internal, external, & incurable
Wounds; is a Witch to the Senses, a Devil
To the Soul, a Thief to the Purse, the
Beggar's companion, a Wife's woe,
And Children's sorrow; makes
Man become a Beast, and
A self murderer, who
Drinks to others'
good health and
robs himself of
his own! nor
is this all;
It exposes to the
Divine

☞DISPLEASURE HERE!
and hereafter to
ETERNAL DESTRUCTION

Such are
some   of
the evils spring-
ing from the root of

DRUNKENNESS!

—*Star*, Raleigh (June 17, 1830)

SNUFF AND THE LADIES OF MONROE

A correspondent of the Wadesborough *Argus*, who dates from Monroe, N. C., says: Among the many vices of our country, and useless and pernicious habits, I deem that of eating snuff not the least;—and so destructive is it to both the beauty and health of the ladies of our country, I think the power of the Press should be brought to bear against it: and every other moral engine that will have a tendency to effectually suppress it. The ladies of Monroe and its vicinity, have made a move in the matter; and I think their example is worthy of imitation. An Anti-Snuff Society has been formed by them, and the following is their pledge:—

Believing, as we do, that the practice of taking snuff has become an excessive and dangerous habit, destructive to beauty, pernicious and ruinous to health: Therefore, we do pledge ourselves as ladies, to abstain entirely from the use of it, and in every prudent way exert our influence in persuading others to abandon its use.

Susannah A. Covington
Mary Jane McCollum
Eliza Doster
Rosa May
S. A. E. Farrer
Jane Ray
Martha Heart
L. A. Pistol
T. Farrer
Margaret Trott

Mary C. Webster
Emeline A. Doster
Caroline Cuthbertson
Nancy Jane Covington
C. J. Holmes
J. Parker
Arabella Heart
M. J. Austin
Martha Medlin
F. A. McLearty

April, 1849

—*Charlotte Journal* (May 25, 1849)

LUCKY DISCOVERY

A gentleman of our city, says the Norfolk American, who has just returned from Currituck, N. C., informs us, that a large quantity of ancient coin, composed chiefly of quadrangular silver pieces, gold half joes and doubloons, was ploughed up last Friday morning, on the plantation of Mr. Benjamin Dye, a brother of the gentleman of that name in Norfolk. The total value is supposed to be at least five or six thousand dollars. Our informant states that search is supposed to have been previously made on the same plantation for money, as large holes now remain in different places, which it is thought were made in a hunt for the hidden treasure.

—*Patriot and Flag*, Greensboro (May 29, 1857)

SALT MARSH PONIES

It is known to comparatively few, especially of the younger people of this part of the State, that there is a section of country in North Carolina where *Ponies* are reared. The passengers of the *unfortunate* "Post Boy," a list of whom were published in this paper last week, in their voyage from Newbern to Beaufort, saw many of these ponies feeding in their pastures on the salt marshes of the mainland, and on the marshes of the sand bar which stretches along our coast, separating the waters of the sounds from those of the ocean. Many of these marshes afford very extensive pasturage of the best kind for cattle, winter and summer; and those of them best adapted to the purpose are used for *pony pastures*, and on them the inhabitants of that part of the State, raise what they call the "Marsh Grass" or "Bank Pony" —a species of small horse, native to the soil; for we were told they had been reared there since the time the memory of man runneth not to the contrary; and tradition says that Sir Walter Raleigh's men found them there, and that that great man imported the Stock into England, whether as curiosity or for crossing with the English stocks, we are not informed.

The pure blood marsh pony is small, though considerably above the average size of those of the Shetland variety, sometimes seen in this country. They differ in color and vary also in size. In winter, their hair is long and shaggy; but in summer, short and sleek. They are tough, hardy and durable, far beyond the fine bloods of the country, generally; and some of the most perfect models of the Horse have been found among them. They are nearly all "natural pacers," and cannot often be excelled as saddle horses—carrying the rider with surprising ease and comfort—carrying him handsomely and speedily, day after day.

We have heard of a physician in one of the Eastern counties who did a large and extensive practice for five years on one of these ponies, using no other horse, and afterwards sold him for a very large price. The only care this horse required after a hard day's work, was to be turned loose on the common to shift for himself. He was always ready for service next morning. During all that time his owner never fed him a ear of corn or a blade of fodder.

Many of them will not eat corn, and there is a risk to run in attempting by starvation, to teach them to feed on the provender usually fed to other horses. The slender feeding they require when taken beyond the reach of their native pastures, if allowed to graze on the common, makes them the cheapest horse known. At home, they require, and receive, nothing beyond what they can gather from the marshes. In former times they were lightly esteemed; but of late years, a first rate pony will readily command from $150 to $200. They are used either in harness or under the saddle; but are not, we think, depended on for heavy work.

There are two days in each year when the owners of ponies visit the pastures and have what they call "pony pennings." —These are very public days, and large numbers of people usually attend them. The objects in view are, either to brand the colts which have been dropped during the Spring, or to take away such of the horses as the owners may wish to use or sell.— Last Saturday (May 15th) was one of these days, and the 15th of July is the other. These are days of excitement and fun, as well as of business. It is said to be rare sport to catch and confine the ponies. Foaled and reared on the sand banks and marshes at some distance from the habitation of man, they are as wild as mountain goats; and to capture them requires skill, courage, and strength.

The first thing necessary to be done to catch them, is to build a strong pen on a point of land jutting out into the water, leaving the land side open so that the ponies can run into it. Mounted drivers are then sent through the pasture to drive up the herd, while the people who have assembled on the occasion arrange themselves in two rows leading from the pen like the wings of a bird net. After a while the yelling of the drivers and the cracking of their long whips are heard in the distance; and soon the ponies are seen tearing through the tall grass. The people at the pen remain quiet, and in due time the drove rush into the pen, when, so far as that goes, they are secure. The two wings come together, and the pen is then closed up on all sides. The ponies are trembling with fright and pack themselves so closely together in one end that it is no uncommon thing to see one pressed up above the rest and floundering on the backs of the herd.

But to catch them, one by one, and bring them out, is said to be the work of difficulty and daring. It requires a strong and fearless man to do this successfully. The mode is to enter the pen and catch them by the head or around the neck, and by physical strength overcome them and lead them out. (We think a better plan could be adopted.) The man and horse struggling amidst the herd, is sometimes on top, and then under the rest —all of them rushing, rearing and jumping in the wildest confusion, so that spectators are alarmed for safety of the man. But having once overcome one of them and secured him with a bridle or halter, he is submissive and yields without further resistance. In a few weeks they become tame and confiding, and are then ready for service.

—*Carolina Watchman*, Salisbury (May 18, 1858)

GAS AND SHADE TREES

A number of towns in North Carolina have within the last two years introduced gas into their streets, and among them is Greensboro. With us the experiment has, in some respects, been very unfortunate. The pipes were very carelessly laid in the streets, leaking the gas in all parts of the town. As a sad consequence of these leaks nearly half of the beautiful shade trees on the side walks nearest the pipes have died or are dying. Much feeling exists upon the subject, and if any remedy can be suggested, it would be of very great relief both to our citizens and the Gas Company; or else we fear the pipes will be torn up from the streets.

—*Times*, Greensboro (July 14, 1860)

CONFEDERATE ARITHMETIC

L. Johnson

A Confederate soldier captured 8 Yankees each day for 9 successive days; how many did he capture in all?

*

7 Confederate soldiers captured 21 Yankees and divided them equally between them; how many did each one have?

*

An army of 15,000 men has provisions for 12 months. If 3,000 more be added to this army, how long will the same stock of provisions supply the whole number, without any change of rations?

*

A man has a capital of $15,250; he invests 15 per cent of it in Confederate bonds; how much does he keep?

*

If one Confederate soldier can whip 7 Yankees, how many soldiers can whip 49 Yankees?

*

If 32 soldiers eat 896 pounds of beef in a week, how many pounds will 175 soldiers eat in a week?

*

If one Confederate soldier kill 90 Yankees, how many Yankees can 10 Confederate soldiers kill?

—*An Elementary Arithmetic*, Raleigh (1864)

EARLY "TAR HEELS"

"*gallant Colonel R. of S. C.*"

The following occurred December, 1864, when Hoke's division was sent out on a reconnaissance upon the Darby Town road. Kirkland's N. C. brigade (of as true metal as men are made of) was passing us to take position on our left, and greeted us with "Rice-birds," "Sand-lappers!" "Hagood's foot cavalry!" etc. One of our men cried out, "Go it, *tar-heels!*" This title the North-Carolina troops were justly proud of, it having been given them at the battle of Manassas, where a general remarked, "That regiment of North-Carolinians must have tar on their heels to make them stick as they do." To this retort of "Go it *tar-heels!*" one of Kirkland's men replied: "Yes, we are tar-heels, and tar *sticks*;"

and "Yes," shouted back another of the South-Carolina rice-birds, "when the fire gets hot, the *tar runs.*"

—*The Land We Love* (August, 1866)

CORN BEER

Maria Massey Barringer

Take a pint of corn, boil it until soft, and add to it a gallon of water sweetened with a pint of brown sugar. Cork it tightly and set it in a warm place, and put into it a *small quantity* of yeast if the weather is cold. In warm weather omit the yeast. Add a few roots of bruised ginger, and a few sliced lemons. The same corn will answer for a year.

When you pour out a pitcherful of beer, put in one of sweetened water.

—*Dixie Cookery* (1867)

YAPON

Mary Ann Mason

This is a shrub, growing on the sand-banks of the coast of North Carolina. It is cut in August, boughs and leaves, into small portions, then laid in the sun till partially dried, when it is placed in a heated brick oven, and thoroughly dried and browned.

It is now ready for use, and is prepared thus:

Boil a large handful of the yapon in a quart of water for fifteen minutes, then remove it to your teapot, and drink it with sugar and cream.

The flavor is very pleasant,—very much like black tea.

—*The Young Housewife's Counsellor and Friend* (1875)

SOUSE MEAT

Boil head and feet of hog. When thoroughly done, remove the bones, and mash well. Season with salt, pepper and vinegar. When congealed, slice and serve in vinegar.

—*Old-Time Recipes, Nu-Wray Inn*, Burnsville (undated)

TAR HEEL COW

Bill Nye

There is no place in the United States, so far as I know, where the cow is more versatile or ambidextrous, if I may be allowed the use of a term that is far above my station in life, than here in the mountains of North Carolina, where the obese 'possum and the anonymous distiller have their homes.

Not only is the Tar Heel cow the author of a pale but athletic style of butter, but in her leisure hours she aids in tilling the perpendicular farm on the hillside, or draws the products to market. In this way she contrives to put in her time to the best advantage, and when she dies, it casts a gloom over the community in which she has resided.

The life of a North Carolina cow is indeed fraught with various changes and saturated with a zeal which is praiseworthy in the extreme. From the sunny days when she gambols through the beautiful valleys, inserting her black, retroussé and perspiration-dotted nose into the blue grass from ear to ear, until at life's close, when every part and portion of her overworked system is turned into food, raiment or overcoat buttons, the life of the Tar Heel cow is one of intense activity.

Her girlhood is short, and almost before we have deemed her emancipated from calfhood herself, we find her in the capacity of a mother. With the cares of maternity other demands are quickly made upon her. She is obliged to ostracize herself from society, and enter into the prosaic details of producing small, pallid globules of butter, the very pallor of which so thoroughly belies its lusty strength.

The butter she turns out rapidly until it begins to be worth something, when she suddenly suspends publication and begins to haul wood to market. In this great work she is assisted by the pearl-gray or ecru-colored jackass of the tepid South. This animal has been referred to in the newspapers throughout the country, and yet he never ceases to be an object of the greatest interest.

Jackasses in the South are of two kinds, viz., male and female. Much as has been said of the jackass pro and con, I do not remember ever to have seen the above statement in print before, and yet it is as trite as it is incontrovertible. In the Rocky Mountains we call this animal the burro. There he packs bacon, flour and salt to the miners. The miners eat the bacon and flour, and with the salt they are enabled to successfully salt the mines.

The burro has a low, contralto voice which ought to have some machine oil on it. The voice of this animal is not unpleasant if he would pull some of the pathos out of it and make it more joyous.

Here the jackass at times becomes a co-worker with the cow in hauling tobacco and other necessaries of life into town, but he goes no further in the matter of assistance. He compels her to tread the cheese press alone and contributes nothing whatever in the way of assistance for the butter industry.

The North Carolina cow is frequently seen here driven double or single by means of a small rope line attached to a tall, emaciated gentleman, who is generally clothed with the divine right of suffrage, to which he adds a small pair of ear-bobs during the holidays.

The cow is attached to each shaft and a small singletree, or swingletree, by means of a broad strap harness. She also wears a breeching, in which respect she frequently has the advantage of her escort.

I think I have never witnessed a sadder sight than that of a new milch cow, torn away from home and friends and kindred dear, descending a steep mountain road at a rapid rate and striving in her poor, weak manner to keep out of the way of a small Jackson democratic wagon loaded with a big hogshead full of tobacco. It seems to me so totally foreign to the nature of the cow to enter into the tobacco traffic, a line of business for which she can have no sympathy and in which she certainly can feel very little interest.

Tobacco of the very finest kind is produced here, and is used mainly for smoking purposes. It is the highest-priced tobacco produced in this country. A tobacco broker here yesterday showed me a large quantity of what he called export tobacco. It looks very much like other tobacco while growing.

He says that foreigners use a great deal of this kind. I am learning all about the tobacco industry while here, and as fast as I get hold of any new facts I will communicate them to the press. The newspapers of this country have done much for me, not only by publishing many pleasant things about me, but by refraining from publishing other things about me, and so I am glad to be able, now and then, to repay this kindness by furnishing information and facts for which I have no use myself, but which may be of incalculable value to the press.

As I write these lines I am informed that the snow is twenty-six inches deep here and four feet deep at High Point in this state. People who did not bring in their pomegranates last evening are bitterly bewailing their thoughtlessness today.

A great many people come here from various parts of the

world, for the climate. When they have remained here for one winter, however, they decide to leave it where it is.

It is said that the climate here is very much like that of Turin. But I did not intend to go to Turin even before I heard about that.

Please send my paper to the same address, and if some one who knows a good remedy for chilblains will contribute it to the Sabbath *Globe*, I shall watch for it with great interest. Yours as here 2 4.

P. S. I should have said relative to the cows of this state that if the owners would work their butter more and their cows less, they would confer a great boon on the consumer of both.

—*Bill Nye's Sparks* (1891)

❧❧❧❧❧❧❧❧

STARTING OFF TO SCHOOL

John Charles McNeill

This, being the first of September, is a heavy-hearted time for the children of the world, anyhow for the country children. The golden summer, rich in liberty, is gone, in all things except its heats, and now must book-sack and dinner basket be taken from the shelf and the "scholars" must go to school.

A blessed thing about the faculty of memory is that it involuntarily lets grow dim whatever was unhappy and keeps bright all else in degree. No man but recalls his school days with unalloyed pleasure and sighs to re-live them. The school patron who attends the Friday afternoon exercises and "speaks to the children" warns them in foreboding terms that these are their happiest days and that they had better make the most of them.

He thinks he is speaking truly and sincerely. But the poor homesick boy gathers that life must be a right hard task. His small keen griefs are uppermost then. Dearer to him than dreams of glory is physical freedom; and school is captivity. When chalk dust floats in the murmurous air and time is sleepy-footed, he sees from his window the hunters go by and his heart almost breaks. He sees no sense in it all. Why should he know where Afghanistan is, or that *John* is a noun, or that Alfred was king, or that 8 times 7 are 56? The steps toward knowledge are so short and slow that he never gets a panorama view. He feels himself unjustly treated when he is whipped for poor spelling. School to him is an undeserved punishment. A little boy, loitering at the gate and being urged off to school by his mother, sobbed, "Mama, what does the teacher pay you?" Her reply presented a problem to his mind which he did not solve for months.

He soon learns to go early to get the half an hour of play before books; but the bell to him is not a chime; it is a knell. The ten-minute recesses he fills with riotous life, nipped in the bud. The noon intermission of an hour and a half is the heaven of his desire, shut off in the glare of its glory. Then till 4 o'clock there remains only an inquisition. He knows the route that the sunbeams must travel. If they should reach the point he has marked for "school's out," and school is not turned out, he feels rebellion grow big in his breast.

The only hour of unmarred joy the day brings him is when he sets out on the tramp home. There is nothing till tomorrow, thank heaven! He may saunter slowly as he pleases. If he lingers to dam the brook and turn it into a new channel, nobody suffers for it. He may turn his wild imaginings to their wings, may fancy himself in palaces, in senates, red and rough with battle, the center about which the universe revolves, world-watched, feared, envied, and loved. For at that age every mind is richly creative; every child is an exuberant poet. If he flushes a flock of turkeys or a covey of quail, if a fox looks at him a moment and steals away into the wood, the thrill runs through him that has run through a thousand of his hunter ancestors. Perchance he picks up a few of his father's sheep and cattle and herds them home. In any event, that hour is a rose without a thorn, and memory needs not to work it over.

Then, when he gets a little older, new pleasures and jealousies will crowd his path. He will find where the purplest fox-grapes and the blackest—there are degrees in blackness—muscadines hang, and will gather them for the girls. When we are become men, unless there has been a careful record of the emotional experience, we are sure to set the date of love's young dream years later than it should be set. There is many a child of eight deeply in love, sometimes with a contemporary, but oftener with a woman of twenty. Those who have forgotten the details of their childhood will scout this as preposterous; but it is all the same true, and boys of eight who read these lines will blush.

As soon as he gets in love he interprets life in its tender terms. Not yet understanding the end of knowledge, he applies himself to his books that he may win praise and impress her for whom he sighs. Here begins a consuming desire, "the last infirmity of noble mind," the quest for fame; and the motive then is the motive that impels him all his life to "scorn delights and live laborious days." A flogging is now a mental anguish, where it was but a physical terror; the study hour is a coveted imprisonment, when he may stare above his book at her curly head; and playtime discovers the strangest paradox in life—that love breeds war. If his sweetheart is on the ground, he is quick to quarrel and eager to fight. Women, from five years to ninety, love a fighter, as all other female animals do, and he knows this, as all other male animals do, without being told.

So now is a dreary day only for the tot that racks along behind his elder sister, clinging to her hand and choking with sobs. Poor kid! He ought to enjoy a longer lease of freedom. He is too tender for rules and duties, and too recently from heaven for earthly endeavor. But thousands of them will be on the way this morning, and they will never forget whether the teachers are kind or unkind. They will be glad to cuddle in their mothers' arms tonight and lisp into their ears the history of the first hour of school: how many scholars there were; all the teachers said and did; who are their desk-mates; whether they were turned back or set forward; a hundred nothings to which their mothers will listen with smiling interest. Much more than March 4 is this inauguration day; and all the grown folks, returning from their vacations and buckling down again in the chase for the dollar, should, each of them, chuck some gloomy-faced toddler under the chin and cheer him up.

—Select Prose (1936)

COSMOPOLITANISM

Isaac Erwin Avery

You notice that Charlotte people are going to Europe. For a long time they did most of their sightseeing in New York, but ten or fifteen years ago a resident spent three months in Germany and came back speaking broken English, and in recent years another resident returned from England, saying, "I seen the Queen." Since then the exodus to Europe has been steady, and it is singular that as travel increases there is less talk in Mecklenburg of the wonders of the foreign lands. The grand trip has become a matter-of-fact, every-day sort of a proposition, and the village query, "What did you see while you were gone?" seldom has birth here. But the injection of a be-travelled cosmopolitan element into the community is already doing good. It strikes a blow at conceit, narrowness and the provincialism that is satisfied to sit eternally in a small area and judge surely and dogmatically the world and the things of the world. Every man who is not a fool is a better citizen after he goes far enough from his bailiwick to realize his smallness and utter ignorance.

—Idle Comments (1905)

RETURN

Thomas Wolfe

(Note by the Editor of the Asheville Citizen-Times: In the fall of 1929 a book "Look Homeward, Angel," by Thomas Wolfe, a native of Asheville, was published. Asheville was its setting and it aroused controversy and feeling. After a time people discussed the book in a calmer mood, but the career of Mr. Wolfe has been watched with interest. Mr. Wolfe returned home recently for his first visit since the publication of his initial book which was followed by "Of Time and the River," "From Death to Morning" and numerous short stories in magazines. He was asked, while here, to write an article describing his feeling at being home again after so long an absence. The following piece, written just before his departure for New York, is the result. As a youth, Mr. Wolfe was a carrier boy for The Asheville Citizen, this being mentioned to clarify certain references in the following article which Mr. Wolfe has entitled, "Return.")

I have been seven years from home, but now I have come back again. And what is there to say?

Time passes, and puts halters to debate. There is too much to say, there is so much to say that must be spoken; there is so much to say that never can be told,—we say it in the impassioned solitudes of youth, and of ten thousand nights and days of absence and return. But in the end, the answer to it all is time and silence: this answers all; and after this, there is no more to say.

So has it been with me. For there has been a time when I would wake just at the first blue-grey of dawn to feel the shoulder strap again upon my arm, the canvas bag, the blocked sheet and the final shot beneath the oak tree on the lawn before the lawyer's great white house—to know my route was ended and that work was done, and that morning had come back again— so thinking, feeling, and remembering, then that I was far away, and that I had been long from home.

Then all old things would come again—both brick and wall, and step and hedge, the way a street sloped or a tree was standing, the way a gate hung or a house was set, the very cinders of a rutted alley way—such things as these would come again, leaf, blade, and stone, and door. So much more door than any other one could ever be—like all things that belong to men—the essence of all doors that ever were because it is his own, the door that he has passed a thousand times—all things like these would come again, the whole atomic pattern of my native earth,

my town, my childhood and my youth, with all the faces, all lives and histories of long ago—and all forgotten weathers of man's memory would come again, there in the darkness in some foreign land, would come so poignant, swift and vivid in the whiteness of their blazing panoply that I could feel my foot upon the street again, my hand upon the rail, the strap upon my shoulder, the whole sensuous unit of my native earth with an intensity that I had never known before. And I could taste it, feel it, smell it, live it through again, hard to the hilt of exile, as I was born perhaps to live all things and moments, hard to the hilt, and carrying on that furious and impassioned argument of youth and solitude, contending fiercely with a thousand disputants, would think: "I have a thing that I must tell them: I'll go home again, I'll meet them and I'll say my piece: I will lay bare my purposes, strip down the vision of my life until its bare soul's nakedness, tell my people what it is to try to shape and spin a living thing out of the entrails of man's life, and what he visions, why he does it—oh, some day I will go back and reveal my plan until no man living in the world can doubt it—I will show them utterly:—"

—And I have come back now: I have come home again, and there is nothing more that I can say.—All arguments are ended: saying nothing, all is said then: all is known: I am home.

Where are the words I thought that I must say, the arguments I thought that I should make, the debates and demonstrations that so often, in those years of absence, memory, wandering, youth, and new discovery I had so hotly made to solitude, and to the ghostly audience of an absent fellowship, the thousand things that I would prove and show when I returned—where are they now?

For now I have come home again—and what is there to say? I think that there is nothing—save the silence of our speech. I think that there is nothing—save the knowledge of our glance. I think that there is nothing—save the silent and unspoken conscience in us now that needs no speech but silence, because we know what we know, we have what we have, we are what we are.

So what is there to say?

———

"You've put on weight since I last saw you."

"Yes, but you are just the same."

"Have you seen Bob yet? He's been looking for you."

"No, he came by the house last night, but I wasn't there. I'm seeing him today."

"Sam Reed was asking about you. ... Here's Jim now."

... "Come on boys! Here he is! We've got him now! He's on the spot! Let's pin him down and make him own up! ... Wasn't that Whit Nelson you had in mind when you told about the night he bought up all the gold fish down at Wood's? ... What's that he wrote, Ed, about the time you slept all night in Reagan's hearse and woke up scared to death next morning when you found out where you were?"

... "Why, Lord, he got the facts right, but the figures were all wrong! I slept all night in Reagan's hearse, all right, but you and Jim were with me, too—and you were worse scared when you woke up in the morning than I was! That's all I objected to, he should have put that in!"

... "And what was that you said, Paul, when he told of how you used to take the grass widow from Paducah down to Riverside on Thursday night and buy her popcorn? ... Come on, now ... you can't back out on us: you know you said it—tell him what you said."

... "Why, hell, I only said she wasn't forty-four, the way HE said, but forty-eight, and that instead of two gold teeth the way HE had it, she had three. And two of them were on the side, with a great big bright one in the middle—not one above and one below the way HE told about it. And it wasn't popcorn that I bought 'her,' but a bag of peanuts. I just wanted him to get it straight, that's all!"

"Come on, now! Own up! You had us all in mind! We've got you on the spot.... Confess! ... Look at his face! He don't know what to say! ...

... "Hell, son, there's nothing that you have to say. We all understand. There were some folks around here when that first book of yours came out who thought you'd written up the town and put them in the book: and some of them were mad about it for a while. But that's all forgotten now. So much has happened since those days that anything you said was mild. You stayed away too long. We're glad that you've come home."

And there is nothing more to say.

———

... "You'll find things changed though. It's not the place you used to know.... I guess you'll find it changed a lot.... Your father's marble shop was on this corner.... Do you remember the old wooden steps? ... The draymen sitting on the steps? ... The tombstones and the angel on the porch? ... Your father standing there a thousand times ... the old fire department and the city hall ... the city market and the calaboose ... the fountain and the street cars coming in upon the quarter hour....

We've put buses in since the time you went away.... Have you been through the tunnel yet?... It's all changed so much you wouldn't know the place."

Change? There is no change. These surfaces have altered and these shapes are new.... There is a wrinkle by the eye we did not have before; a furrow in the cheek; a kind of worn humor in the grin about the lip, a look plain, steady, naked, touched with care, that twenty did not know—our hue is rougher and our groove more deep—time passes, WE have grown older, much water and some blood has gone beneath the bridge since then: I think we know each other better—but, oh brothers, friends, and comrades of this mortal dust—we have not changed!

... For here again, again, I turn into the street, finding again the place where corners meet, looking again to see if time is there. And all of it is as it has always been: again, again, I turn, and find again the things that I have always known: the cool sweet magic of starred mountain night, the huge attentiveness of dark, the slope, the street, the trees, the living silence of the houses waiting, and the fact that April has come back again. ... And again, again, in the old house I feel beneath my tread the creak of the old stair, the worn rail, the white-washed walls, the feel of darkness and the house asleep, and think, "I was a child here; here the stairs, and here was darkness; this was I, and here is Time."

These things will never change. Some things will never change: the groove in deeper, but the leaf, the bud, the wheel, the blade, and April will come back again.

The wheel will turn, the immortal wheel of life will turn, but it will never change. Here, from this little universe of time and place, from this small core and adyt of my being where once, hill-born and bound, a child, I lay at night, and heard the whistles wailing to the west, the thunder of great wheels along the river's edge, and wrought my vision from these hills of the great undiscovered earth and my America—here, now, forevermore, shaped here in this small world, and in the proud and flaming spirit of a boy, new children have come after us, as we: as we, the boy's

face in the morning yet, and mountain night, and starlight, darkness, and the month of April, and the boy's straight eye: again,
again, the thudding press, the aching shoulder, and the canvas
bag; the lean arm and the rifled throw again, that whacked the
blocked and folded sheet against the shacks of Niggertown.

... These things, or such as these, will come again; so too,
the high heart and the proud and flaming vision of a child—to
do the best that may be in him, shaped from this earth, as we,
and patterned by this scheme, to wreak with all his might, with
humbleness and pride, to strike here from his native rock, I pray,
the waters of our thirst, to get here from his native earth, his
vision of this earth and this America, to hear again, as we, the
wheel, the whistle, and the trolley bell, so too, as we, to go out
from these hills and find and shape the great America of our
discovery; so, too, as we, who writes these words, to know again
the everlasting legend of man's youth—flight, quest, and wandering—exile and return.

—*Asheville Citizen-Times* (May 16, 1937)

POST OFFICE MURALS

James Boyd

Last Tuesday as we approached the post office on the way to
get our mail, and have a look at the new mural painting on the
wall, it was possible to guess that something was afoot inside.
A knot of people stood around the entrance walk, looking in
through the door and smiling and whispering to each other.
While we tried to catch what they were saying, two colored
women hustled out the door; the door, as it swung, let out a
piece of a roar and cut it off again and the two colored women
kept right down Broad Street, looking mighty uneasy in their
minds.

We had caught a glimpse of a familiar Model T across the street and were therefore prepared for some of what we saw but not for all of it. It was Mr. Hugh Dave MacWhirr, all right, in his retired Army overcoat and a kind of bear hunter's cap with earflaps that he sometimes wears in cold weather, but as we came in the lobby it looked like Mr. MacWhirr was about to assault our popular and widely esteemed postmaster, Mr. Frank Buchan. In fact, Mr. MacWhirr appeared to have Mr. Buchan by the collar.

Luckily before we became involved in the apparent affray, we were able to make out that Mr. MacWhirr actually only had Mr. Buchan by the coat lapel and that his attitude was only one of earnest confabulation. As we withdrew to the other side of the lobby, Mr. MacWhirr was saying:

"Frank, I have knowed you since you was a shirt-tailed boy." Here he shook Mr. Buchan for emphasis. "Why, dog my whiskers, I have knowed you since your daddy was a shirt-tailed boy, or would have if you had been there to be knowed at that date." He pulled on Mr. Buchan's lapel as though it was a bell cord. "Now, come out, boy, and state your opinion."

Mr. Buchan ruffled up the short hairs on the back of his neck. "Mr. Mac," he said, "I declare, I don't know about such things."

"You taken on city ways since you moved to Southern Pines, but you were born and bred in Manly, ain't that so?"

"Of course it's so, and I'm proud of it," Mr. Buchan said.

"Well, then," Mr. MacWhirr said, "don't you know mules?"

"I hope so," Mr. Buchan said. "As much as a white man can."

"Don't you know hosses?"

"Well, some," Mr. Buchan said. "Not like mules, though."

"Don't you know fox dogs?"

"A little," Mr. Buchan said. "Neighborhood dogs, that is, not ordered like the Boyds'."

"Neighborhood dogs is what I mean," Mr. MacWhirr said. "And don't you know Negroes?"

"Yes," Mr. Buchan said, "I really believe I know a little about them."

"Then," Mr. MacWhirr said, "state your opinion."

"But I don't know about Art," Mr. Buchan said.

"But you know about Negroes and mules and hosses and dogs, and this Art is about Negroes and mules and hosses and dogs; therefore, you know about this Art." Mr. MacWhirr turned Mr. Buchan loose. "He won't say," he murmured to himself. "Naturally, he won't say. Who ever heard a postmaster talk against the government? Even when it done this." He waved his long hand at the new mural on the wall which depicts a fox-hunting scene of Negroes and animals in a clearing. "But I'll say. I'll say this: that I've hired many a Negro in my time but, scarce as hands are, not one of them fellows on the wall could ever get board and a pallet in the shed out of me."

"Is that a fact?" Mr. Buchan said.

"They ain't stout enough to make a hand or smart enough for a yard boy," Mr. MacWhirr said. "And I'll tell you more. I've sold many a horse in my day—"

"That's what I've heard tell," Mr. Buchan said.

Mr. MacWhirr looked at the mural again. "Them hosses there I could not guarantee to sell to a Yankee golf player even. If they are hosses," he added, "and they are bound to be, because they're too big for salamanders and too small for the beasts in the Book of Revelation."

"What about the dogs, Mr. Hugh Dave?" Mr. Buchan said.

"I am coming to the dogs," Mr. MacWhirr replied. "When I was a child I was carried to see a rich uncle on my mother's side in Kinston. The scheme was my mother's, but it did not pan out. He taken a look at me and left his money to a foundling home. All I recollect of the visit is that he had two dogs similar to them up there on the wall. They was made of lead and used to prop open the front doors in the summertime." Mr. MacWhirr took Mr. Buchan's collar again. "If the government wants scrap," he said, "they should melt down their lead dogs instead of putting them on post office walls."

"Mr. Mac," Mr. Buchan said, "you are always against the government."

"Why, of course," Mr. MacWhirr said, "that is the first duty of a citizen." He reflected, rocking Mr. Buchan slowly by his

lapel. "A democracy is a large body of folks against the government. That's what a democracy is and that's what's good about
it; in fact, it's about the only thing that is good about it. In a
democracy, the government gets throwed out just a mite faster
than it turns addled."

"This government has not been thrown out," Mr. Buchan said.

"And maybe it won't be," Mr. Hugh Dave said, "but it will
have to change its ways." He pointed to the mural. "If my fellow man is suffering for lack of clothes and rations, I am willing
to be taxed for his relief."

"I'm glad you go that far," Mr. Buchan said.

"But it's all the far I do go," Mr. MacWhirr said. "When I
have paid the tax, I have done all the government should ask.
I am not obligated to let him paint up the buildings I have also
paid for."

Mr. MacWhirr started to expectorate on the floor, recalled
himself and swallowed. "It is enough to have to support my
brother," he said, "without also having to be swarmed at by
iron dogs, mule-eared salamanders and washed-out high-yellows
whenever I go to mail a letter."

"Well, Mr. Hugh Dave," Mr. Buchan said, "every man is entitled to an opinion."

"That is a fact," Mr. MacWhirr said. "And what is yours, son?"
He paused.

Mr. Buchan smiled and nodded and was about to speak when
he noticed that a representative of the press was in the lobby.

"Well, Mr. Hugh Dave," he said, "come back and see us any
time."

—*Mr. Hugh Dave MacWhirr* (1943)

TAKE ONE CRISP FALL MORNING

John McKnight

A shuddersome thing has happened in the twenty years I've been away from my native North Carolina.

The length of the State, from the misty blue heights of the Great Smokies in the west to the pocosin land of the tidal east, good Tar Heels shake their heads despondently and tell me, "No'th Ca'lina cookin' ain't what it used to be."

I'm told, moreover, that the plaint is general throughout the storied Southland. A Southern contributor to *The Saturday Evening Post* not long ago spoke his mind sharply on the degradation of an ancient art—and escaped the tar-and-feathering that probably would have been his lot one or two score years past. More recently, the food editor of *The Atlanta Constitution*, perhaps the South's most influential newspaper, came right out and said that new-fangled ways had upset the candied yam cart: while today's diet below the Mason and Dixon line may be more healthful, she observed, it isn't Southern.

Perhaps an inferiority complex bred of this self-criticism accounts for the fact that the London restaurateur who wrote some months ago asking North Carolina's favorite dish and the recipe therefor, so that he might feature it on his menu, has not yet—as far as I know—received an answer.

The London Boniface addressed his letter, quite properly, to the State News Bureau. Desiring advice on the delicate inquiry, the bureau released it to the Press. Controversy rose, and raged for weeks. Every Tar Heel appeared to have his own idea as to the proudest achievement, past or present, of the State's cuisine. And hardly two of them agreed.

Nominations ranged from the humble pan-fried "chitterlings" (hog tripe: the word is locally pronounced chit'lings; the dish is especially favored of our darker brethren) through angel food (angel cake) to "hushpuppies" (cornmeal pats fried crisp in deep hot fat and eaten with meat or fish, so called supposedly because hunters use them to quiet hungry, keening hounds).

Well, if the State News Bureau can't make up its mind among the proliferating suggestions, I can. So I'll answer the Londoner's letter. Here goes.

Selection of the Old North State's top culinary achievement is indeed, it may be said at the outset, difficult, more difficult than with some other States.

The very mention of Maine brings to mind its lobster. Massachusetts is no less famed for succulent clams steamed in seaweed, and for clam chowder in the grand tradition. Pennsylvania is especially proud of its scrapple (bits of meat with herbs and Indian meal boiled, moulded, sliced and fried) and its lusty pepper-pot soup.

In the South, and almost everywhere the barnyard fowl is esteemed, fried chicken Maryland enhances the renown of the State for which it is named. Scarcely less well known is Virginia's nutty, aromatic Smithfield ham. Hoppin' John—peas stewed with bacon and red pepper, and served with rice—is considered by fanciers to be most artfully prepared in South Carolina, which is also proud of its fat waterfowl gorged on wild rice. Georgia is traditionally the home of Brunswick stew, the thick, savory hunter's pottage of chicken, pork, rabbit, squirrel, tomatoes, fresh maize, other vegetables. Florida offers, along with fine citrus fruit, the varied fish of the Gulf stream, of which pompano and yellowtail are especially favored. Louisiana's jambalaya is one of the countless gustatory delights in that ancient French-Spanish state. And so across the continent. . . .

But it is hard to pick out one delicacy as truly representative of North Carolina because—"the most Northern of the Southern states, the most Southern of the Northern"—its taste is catholic. It relishes the cookery of every state and of every land.

In the year since I returned from feasting at the sophisticated tables of the Old World, I have eaten my way from one end to the other of the 600-mile length of this first of the thirteen colonies to declare its independence of George III (acting alone, at the Mecklenburg County court-house, 20 May 1775).

I have smacked my lips over black-eyed peas boiled with home-cured bacon or hog jowl, and over tender winter turnip greens cooked quickly in very little water and served with broiled spare-ribs or boiled pork neck-bones. I have feasted on "shelly" beans (the tender pods cooked together with the just-forming seeds) steamed with the hock of hickory-cured, well-aged ham, and served along with young boiled maize, tomatoes and sliced onions. I have been awakened in the morning by the nose-tingling aroma of thick slices of that same ham sizzling alongside plump new-laid eggs.

In several expeditions to the coast (in one of which I bagged four plump Canadian geese, than which there is no finer eating), I have eaten oysters fresh from the nearby sound, off the shell or steamed or roasted; I have relished cold, boiled shrimp ranging in size from "peewees" to jumbos the size of small lobsters; I have eaten thick savory stew of hard-shelled crabs, to be taken from the shallow waters of inlets as fast as you can toss over your line with the hunk of pork tied to it; I have eaten fillets of bluefish, cooked golden under the broiler, pan-baked mackerel and sea trout, shad roe with lemon butter.

I have eaten thick, juicy steaks from North Carolina's own fast-increasing herds that rival the best of the West or Argentina or Scotland; I have regaled myself on the crisp fried chicken and the deep-dish, crusty chicken pie that are the proudest accomplishments of so many Tar Heel housewives (few of whom have cooks any more, in this labor-short state); I have revelled in flocculent spoonbread, that *soufflé* of Indian meal that rises so gloriously above its humble ingredients: I have....

I have said enough. To say more is unduly to twist the knife in the flesh of my English readers. But it will be perceived that I have done well by the inner man since my return home, and that I take no part with the mourners at the bier of Southern cooking. They just don't know the right places. It will be perceived, also, that I speak with some authority when I undertake to nominate, for the benefit of that London restaurateur, the Old North State's finest dish.

It is none of those I have named. It is young pig, pit-barbecued in the open air.

The recipe? Well, you may take your choice of dozens.

There is as much argument among Tar Heels over the finer points of barbecuing pig as there is, say, among New Yorkers over the proper proportions of Martinis or among Englishmen over the right degree of rareness of the joint or among Frenchmen over the respective merits of the wines of two great years.

A native of New Jersey, new to North Carolina, stood about one brisk morning, when advice to the *maestro* encharged with the barbecue was flowing as freely as the bourbon-and-branch-water that is an inevitable concomitant, and at last observed:

"Whatever your illiteracy figures" [and they are not something we North Carolinians pride ourselves on], "I'm sure there's nobody in North Carolina who couldn't write a book about barbecuing a pig."

Nevertheless, I have no hesitancy about offering my own recipe to the London innkeeper. It may objected that it borrows certain subtleties from the preparation of the *lechón asado* that is the standard Christmas dish of Cuba and some other Latin countries. To that extent, it may not be wholly North Carolinian. But as we say in these parts, you can go farther and do worse.

Take one crisp fall, winter, or spring morning. Build fire of oak, hickory, or other hardwood. Alongside it, dig shallow pit.

Lay metal bars close together over pit. As fire burns down, shovel small coals and ashes into pit.

Take one small pig (seventy-five pounds or less: the smaller—as you know, if you are up on your Charles Lamb—the better). Scrub carefully with water and bicarbonate of soda. Rub inside and out with salt, mashed garlic, pepper, lime juice, vinegar.

Place pig prayerfully on the metal bars. Cook slowly three to five hours, renewing coals and hot ashes as needed, until underside browns. Turn, and cook another two or three hours. Throughout, mop pig frequently with sauce made of vinegar and hot peppers. Mop inner man as frequently with bourbon-and-branch.

When skin (of pig) crackles and whole is golden brown, remove from fire, tear apart, and eat without benefit of cutlery—accompanying with cole slaw and black coffee (or beer) if you can find time for them.

How mine London host is going to get his pig, in that austerity-ridden land where only recently a *soupçon* of pork has been restored to sausage, I do not know. But that's *his* problem.

—*Wine and Food*, London, reprinted
in *The State* (September 20, 1952)

THE EARTH-BORN GOOBER PEA

W. C. Burton

Poets have sung in praise of wine
And bread and fruit on which they dine;
And many a lyrical, lusty eater
Has set his love of meat to meter.

Some bards there be, perchance, who'd stoop
To odes to oatmeal, sonnets to soup,
But I'll lift voice and verse to utter
Paeans in praise of peanut butter.

Rich, brown blend of nuts nutritious,
The tidbit tasty, dollop delicious;
Diet on which the youngster thrives,
Sustainer of men with absent wives,
Substitute supper, breakfast, lunch,
Facile feast on which millions munch.

Handy snack for the midnight snacker,
Spread on bread or soda cracker—
O cream of the earth-born goober pea,
A heavenly manna you are to me.

There, friends and poetry lovers, is a sincere and full-throated tribute. It is also an old debt lovingly paid.

I am a man with simple tastes, frequently recurring fondness for food and little liking for the complicated, messy work of whipping up things with various ingredients in pots and pans. There are times when playing the self-styled chef can be fun, but when I get the impulse to bite into something good to eat I want to do so without delay. Then, no ritual with victuals for me.

Therefore I have frequent recourse to the peanut butter jar. It is probably the simplest, most satisfactory culinary practice in use today; the peanut butter, something to spread it on, a knife to spread it with, and you're in business. Nothing to wash except the knife—and possibly, your teeth.

When I was a kid I thought peanut butter was about the best-tasting food in the world. When I got old enough to know right from wrong I found out I was right. I love the stuff. I never tire of it. It perks up my palate just as it did when I was in knee pants.

At my house we buy the large, economical family-size jar and when it gets down to within six inches of the bottom—as it soon does—I rush right over to the grocer and replenish the supply. Yes, sir, at our place, if we haven't got more than six inches of peanut butter left, famine looms.

If peanut butter had to be wrested from poor, defenseless little fish in far-away waters and shipped over several thousand miles of ocean, it would cost more than caviar. And I would pay it. Because it is the product of a plant pod grown in abundance, dug from our own section of Dixie, made up without much bother or expense and you can get a big jar for half a buck, we may fail to appreciate its virtues. It is savory, filling and nourishing. It is a lovely umber unguent for the human tongue and a benediction to the bread-basket.

A few overly meticulous masticators complain that peanut butter sticks to the roof of the mouth. Modern processing has just about eliminated this mild objection, but it never hampered my enjoyment anyway. What I say is: if it sticks to me, I'll stick to it.

At the beginning of this piece I suggested that I owe a debt to peanut butter. I do. It has saved my life. Or, at least, it has saved me from the ravages of aggravated galloping malnutrition. During a period in which the United States Army very recklessly paid all my personal expenses and kept me in clothes, shelter, and some sort of diet, peanut butter was often the most pleasant and dependable portion of the latter.

Anyone who has been a regular patron of any army mess hall can tell you that the menu was not always comparable to the blue-plate special at Antoine's. But we always had tons of peanut butter. Sometimes, when the bill of fare offered braised brisket of G. I. beef or C rations Rockefeller, I would consume four courses of peanut butter on bread, daintily use my mess kit for a finger bowl and go my way content. I was often thousands of miles from home but never more than a hundred yards from a pail of peanut butter. It created a bond, I can tell you.

Nowadays children and women often sully their peanut butter with jelly or some such gook. Ernest Hamlin Baker, the *Time* magazine cover artist, who is a friend and fellow peanut-butter enthusiast, favors a half-and-half sandwich (which he invented) with cream cheese as the other ingredient. It's very good, too, but by instinct and training I am a straight peanut-butter man.

In a nutshell, I'm nuts about peanut butter.

—*Greensboro Daily News* (May 22, 1955)

OCTOBER

Sam Ragan

Poets and lovers traditionally have a special affinity for spring —April not only being the cruellest month but one also to stir the fancy.

Yet the month that has even more power to move the sensitive and cause the stirring of the soul in restless and unnamed longings is October. Though it is the time of the year's dying, it is the flaming death of Icarus. And it is not a death that slows the feet, but quickens the step.

Knowing October, though, is a special thing, and requires a special contemplation. No one knows October who has not walked old fields and felt the loneliness of man. No one knows the month who has not felt the tug of lost longings that slowly stir in October's haze.

For October, though its skies are blue and bland, does not have the deceptiveness of April by day. But there is no languor in the nights. The clean, bright moon does not reveal the uneasiness that lies forever with man. For man may cloak himself in the flaming frenzy of living, but in truth he lives and dies alone.

That is the October meaning of those who walk old fields and woods.

—*News and Observer*, Raleigh (October 13, 1957)

A RECIPE FOR A HAPPY CHRISTMAS

Clarence Poe

Would you like to have this year the happiest Christmas of your life?

Of course you will start first with your family, friends, and kinfolk. Then you may accept the wisdom of One wiser than any of them, Who said, "It is more blessed to give than to receive." You may also need to read Christ's test of every soul at the Last Judgment: "For I was an hungred, and ye gave me meat: I was thirsty, and ye gave me drink: I was a stranger, and ye took me in: Naked, and ye clothed me: I was sick, and ye visited me: I was in prison, and ye came unto me."

The next thing to do, therefore, is to remember all such unfortunate people. It may be by an appropriate gift or a cheering visit. It may be by a letter or even a postcard.

In any case, why not list all the persons you know in any of these classes—and then give first consideration to those persons not likely to be remembered by anybody unless you remember them?

Some person you know may have made a mistake and now pays a heavy penalty in prison—what a lift it might give him to know that he had not been utterly forgotten and disowned! Then there are people sick with any physical or mental illness at home or in any hospital. There are others growing old. Then all little children of whom the Master said, "Of such is the kingdom of heaven," and much more recently someone has said, "We cannot always make some grownup person happy every day, but it is possible every day to make some child happy."

Finally, when many worthy and faithful people of other races and creeds may mistakenly think that all their group are hated or scorned, might it not mean much to them for you to find some way to express friendliness where they had expected indifference or ill will?

—*Progressive Farmer* (December, 1958)

SLEEPING PORCHES, LIGHTNING RODS, BAY WINDOWS

Zoe Kincaid Brockman

Reading the stories and viewing the pictures of new homes in and around Gastonia as carried as a feature in my favorite newspaper, it belatedly occurs to me to wonder what became of sleeping porches.

In my day of assisting in planning a house, sleeping porches were all the rage and a householder who didn't have one could scarce hold up his head. With my family, we had to plan for space for all the people who would be living in the house and there wasn't any money for extras. But the plan did provide for the adding of a sleeping porch, and that was my dream for many years until it suddenly occurred to me that dreamers can be pretty silly. "See here, my girl," I sternly addressed Zoey, "you have got all the house you're ever going to have, and if you keep a roof on it and pay taxes you'll be lucky." And so I no longer visualized a sleeping porch at the back of the upper room.

In my childhood, very many people had lightning rods; in fact, practically every other house bristled with them. But we didn't have lightning rods on our house and, somehow, I began to associate lightning rods with the rich. People with money had lightning rods, and people without fat bank accounts didn't.

Another thing I especially admired and greatly yearned for was a bay window. And, again, I associated bay windows with pots of money. If you had a lot of money you had a bay window on the front of the house nicely draped with red velvet with matching ball fringe. The bay window was usually complete with a table holding an ornate lamp, a potted fern, and/or sundry knick-knacks. And often, when my friends with bay windows (in their houses, of course) had parties, the punch bowl, cutglass and sparkling like diamonds, was often placed on the table in the window recess. To me, it seemed the epitome of luxury.

Bay windows are playing a return engagement, I note, and

picture windows appeared on the scene some time ago. But, unless I owned a lovely wilderness, something approximating Walden, I wouldn't care for a picture window, the mission of which is to frame beauty, not the bustling highway. And so, never having achieved lightning rods, a sleeping porch, nor bay window, I'm quite content to let picture windows lie where they fall. Me, I can do without one.

I quite understand the sentiments of the woman who recently came into a little money. "I'm gonna investigate this money in a house and nobody can talk me into doin' nothin' else with it."

It's pretty smart, I suppose, to investigate money in a house. But a house really rides you from that day forward. You're the horse, and the house is the rider. Anytime you think you might be able to have your living room furniture covered anew, the plumbing comes down with the cramps, something pops loose in the basement, or bricks in the chimney simply turn loose of their mortar. It's never anything that can be seen with the naked eye. The money doesn't go for having walls freshened, latching onto new draw curtains, or brightening up a bit here and there. It goes, in large wads, for repairing something that has to be repaired but doesn't show after it's done. But one would be, I suppose, pretty lost and lonely living in one room in somebody else's house. So it's likely that people will continue to investigate their money in houses and hope for the best.

—Unguarded Moments (1959)

ATOMIC PEANUT

The atomic age for agriculture is here. A new peanut variety developed through irradiation of seed is making its debut in the Carolinas-Virginia area this spring. What's more, agricultural scientists across the nation are now busy using the atom in an effort to bring about major improvements in other crops.

The new "atomic" peanut, known as N.C.4x, was developed at North Carolina State College. While it looks and tastes like an ordinary roasting-type goober, it has several advantages for farmers—thicker hulls to protect the kernels, more resistance to leafspot diseases, yields that compare favorably with leading varieties now used, and a higher proportion of jumbo-sized nuts that bring a premium on the market.

Dr. Walton C. Gregory bred N.C.4x. A few years back he took 50 lbs. of ordinary peanut seed to Oak Ridge, Tenn., and exposed them to high-powered atomic rays. The dosage used was 37 times stronger than would be required to kill a man. As the rays passed through the nuts, they "shook up" the genes, the elements in the seed that determine hereditary characteristics. When planted later, the irradiated seed produced almost every conceivable type of growth.

Strange plants produced: Some plants grew only three inches high; others spread vines out three to five feet. On some plants the leaves were solid white; on others, variegated white and green; on still others, the usual dark green. The experimental field also produced nuts of varying sizes, shapes, and colors—some white, some almost red, but most the usual flesh color. Some kernels were small and round like the Spanish-type nuts put up salted in cellophane bags, while others were three times the size of jumbos—almost as large as pullet eggs.

Altogether some 11,000 mutations or genetic changes were recorded, all at the same time in a single field. From the millions of plants observed, Dr. Gregory and Dr. W. E. Cooper started many new breeding lines, some of which are expected to pay off in even better varieties in the future. One possibility is a larger, erect plant of luxuriant growth that will yield more hay and can be harvested more easily.

Peanuts were used in this pioneering experiment because they are self-pollinating and normally show very little genetic variation from one generation to the next. But scientists are confident that, within limits, they can use the same procedure to improve other crops.

Flue-cured tobacco seed, for example, is being irradiated by

North Carolina State to try to develop black-shank resistance in old-line varieties that are outstanding for quality. It is also irradiating soybean seed with the aim of coming up with an earlier-maturing bean. Elsewhere, small grains and horticultural crops are being tested.

Dr. Gregory's work with the peanut represents one of the first times that an improved strain of any living thing has been developed through atomic research. A real milestone in fundamental genetics, it is being cited as an outstanding example of how atomic energy can be used to help rather than destroy mankind. Now that the precedent has been set, even greater results can be expected.

—P C A Farming (March-April, 1959)

THE LEAF OF GALAX
AND THE HABIT OF PYROLA

Jonathan Williams

Iwauchuwa in Japan; *Shortia galacifolia* in Transylvania and Oconee counties in the Southern Appalachians—the most legendary of our plants. Mr. Donald Culross Peattie is the custodian of the whole story. He has told it so beautifully in *Green Laurels* and in *The Great Smokies and the Blue Ridge* that it would be of no point for me to elaborate on his work. Suffice it, that a brief entry, dated December 8, 1788, in the journal of André Michaux was the beginning of a hundred years of investigation and search for the plant by Asa Gray, Charles Sprague Sargent, and other conspicuous American botanists. Michaux simply noted: "...I came across a new bush *(arbuste)* with notched leaves that was rampant on the mountainside not far from the river." He was at the headwaters of the Keowee (Kiwi, as he wrote it), below the confluence of the Horsepasture and Toxaway rivers as they have dropped from the ridge of the Balsam Mountains and levelled off above the present settlements of Tamassee and Jocassee in Oconee County, South Carolina. Today it is not difficult to find colonies of the plant under kalmia and rhododendron in woods along the river.

There is another colony of plants further downriver these days, after the Keowee becomes the Savannah, there at Aiken/Augusta where Thermonuclear Pale Face works at the instruments of his salvation. It seems questionable which species will outlast the other. But, disregarding this moral and ecological matter which seems to favor the shortia, let it be realized that the America of André Michaux and William Bartram has been long lost to the predators and that there will be no Sunday after the war for humane men. It is interesting that Bartram's grave is now unknown, though a two-day search in the environs of Philadelphia located for me the remains of his father, John. The stone is in the Quaker graveyard in Upper Darby, Pennsylvania, and the inscription reads: Approximate Grave of John Bartram. . . .

I spent a hundred days the summer of 1961 hiking the Appalachian Trail from Springer Mountain, Georgia, to Bear Mountain, New York, to try to make my own peace with the rivers and the fields we have polluted and infected. It is so apparent, what Henry James said in *The American Scene*, that nobody has *cared enough* for the land. Simply that: it has been despised and our own nature has become somehow despicable. Man is a symbiot. There are places in the bald meadows of the Smokies where the bluets are windy clouds, and the eye that reflects them is uncommonly lovely.

I could not find a sacred grove, even in the Pennsylvania forest that Gifford Pinchot has named for André and François Michaux. The trees were there, yet I could not find the citizens. Sacred for whom? to whom? The flawless boles of tulip poplars can be measured variously and board feet by the hundred provide no wonder. I wondered whether the name of the god had not perhaps been drowned in the song of the wood thrush?

Mr. John Stewart Collis has suggested that "sin" is *separation*, whose contrary is *atonement*, at-one-ment. One can go to Jocassee and atone for a lot in the deprived landscape by visiting Michaux's handsome little plant. We are not lacking for prophets to tell us to do so. Edward Dahlberg writes in *The Sorrows of Priapus:* "The difference between a civilized and a detestable nation is in its votive fruits, spices, and animals. The Philistines, to appease the God of Israel, returned the stolen Ark with golden replicas of mice and hemorrhoids. Aaron had an oracular Rod upon which almonds budded, and Perseus named the city Mycene after a woody mushroom. Lucretius mentions the marjoram young suitors smeared on the door-posts of damsels. Solomon sang of the myrrh and sloes on the locks of the bridal door; Jesus ached for the alabaster of fragrant ointment the Pharisee denied him. 'Would to God that all the Lord's People were Prophets,' said Moses who sighed for men whose souls smelled of frankincense and orchard fruits."

Dr. Charles Wilkins Short, the doctor-botanist of Kentucky, for whom Asa Gray named the plant, must have been such.

—From manuscript (1961)

INTERVIEW WITH PAUL GREEN

Interviewer: Do you feel that the North Carolina background still remains an undeveloped area in so far as fiction goes?

Mr. Green: Well, what do you mean by North Carolina background? Do you mean North Carolina life? North Carolina customs—superstitions, religious beliefs, folk song, folk music—all that rich up-boiling raw material of human action? You mean history maybe. Well, let's speak of history a bit.

From the point of view of numbers and quantity the area has not been undeveloped in fiction. William S. Powell, Librarian for the North Carolina collection at the University here, edited a book some years ago covering North Carolina fiction from 1734 to 1957. I recommend it to you. As you look through that book you may well be astonished at the amount of historical fiction that has been created in this state. I can rattle off a few names at random. We can go back to Judge Robert Strange long before the Civil War, and then believe it or not to Harriet Beecher Stowe who wrote a tale called *Dred* which deals with an ante-bellum plantation in Chowan County. And then there was Judge Tourgee—the judges seemed to go in for this kind of fiction—up in the Piedmont and mountain region. And O. Henry used some North Carolina historical material in his stories—not much but some. And Mary Johnston of Virginia wrote about the Lost Colony of Roanoke—and so on up to recent and present times—with James Boyd, Janet Gray, Gerald Johnson, Tom Wicker, Ovid Pierce, Tom Pridgen, Inglis Fletcher, LeGette Blythe, and Manly Wellman, to mention a few names. The roll call could be even longer.

Some of this writing has been good. Perhaps the best of it was the work of James Boyd. I make another recommendation to you —read his *Drums, Marching On,* and *Long Hunt.*

Yes, North Carolina has done pretty well by herself in historical writing, that is, as I say, so far as quantity goes.

No, she has not neglected herself.

Interviewer: Do you feel that North Carolina has been neglected in fiction?

Mr. Green: That's pretty much the same question as before. Maybe I can answer a little differently and to some purpose. If you mean North Carolina has been neglected in fiction—and that includes the historical—as a great literary art, then no doubt the answer would have to be yes. Let's keep our thinking in a transitive-verb sense and consider the neglect as of her own doing rather than of her being done to.

North Carolina certainly has neglected herself in fiction as an art just as she has neglected herself in all the arts, in all the sciences, in all the great philosophies. She has never done her part in, well, culture. We've never had a first-rate composer, never a first-rate poet, never a first-rate scientist that I know of, never a first-rate philosopher, a first-rate sculptor, painter, dramatist, and so on. We've had one first-rate lyric poet-novelist, or auto-biographer, in Thomas Wolfe. He wasn't really a novelist. He was a soaring, singing voice, singing of man, singing of America—with some progression in time and space in what he wrote, progression as he himself as an artistic behemoth made progress plunging on down the days and years. He cut a great surging swath through the world, stated himself in a great cascade and jet fountain of words, and we ought to be thankful and feel thankful for that wonderful manifestation of the human spirit—youthful, I say, and un-grown-up spirit. He wasn't a story-teller and didn't have to be. He sang of man, yes, and that man was himself, Thomas Wolfe.

But as I say he was an exception, and he had to get away from North Carolina to be free to do his stuff. At least he thought he did, felt he did. The climate wasn't right here for him. In fact the climate has never been right in North Carolina for what without apology I call culture. And you have to have climate, the right climate for plants to grow in.

Take the matter of practices and tendencies and persuasions and fashions and customs which occur in every area of human interest and concern and on every level of endeavor. They appear only in the climate proper to them. They have their hour and day and, like the plants of the earth, the flowers about us, they fade away under the frosts and beatings of the storms of the world's opinion and taste. Then they are succeeded by others which have their day too and change or die. But it is wonderful to think that even in such matters as these, in their living and their dying, the process of creation goes on—that is, the perishing is never totally so, for some influence, some residue of power more often bene-ficent than not is always left behind in the ashes or in the ruins.

Climate, climate is what we are talking about.

Why do these things come? Why do they go? A mystery—in the main a mystery except to say that man must be up and doing, has to be building, changing, searching, creating, bettering himself, moving on.

Yes, creating is the word here and now and at any time. Excuse my long-windedness but all this means something to me. It's my bread and meat, my staff of life, the breath of my being.

Sometimes the process seems like the wind or like the weather. It bloweth where it listeth, and it will rain when it will rain. But to repeat—and you can't repeat this sort of thing too much— creation must be at work. Get the conditions right and life appears —whatever the galaxy, whatever the stellar system. The fact that we are here on earth in the yes-saying present, this immediate living moment, proves it. We are no exception and cannot be. We are the norm, and how wonderful it will be, how exciting when in days not far off other living creatures are discovered to have their existence in the regions of the endless and timeless universe. Well, then, get the conditions right, get the weather right, and the living plant appears and grows.

With your indulgence I will continue for a bit more.

So if the climate and the weather are right for art and drama, then art and drama will tend to appear. A suction to existence is created, and existence must come. A reach is put forth and the grasp is made. Build a birdhouse, say, and soon you see a bird active about its door. No house, no bird—at least not that particular bird. Or set up a pulpit in the green woods and the chances are that some morning you will come unawares on a St. Francis occupying that pulpit and expounding the nature of the universe and his hopes for salvation to the ants, the rabbits, and the bees.

But in order for such things to happen, for such purposes and intents to come to pass, men must work at them. And the tougher the job, the harder the work. It's not as easy to grow artists, painters, sculptors, composers, playwrights, as it is to grow nature's sprouts, of course, or make a box or a pulpit. Human beings have wills, they have appetites and feelings, and in creating beauty, in creating any human thing, whether a gadget or a thrust to glory, the human will, the wish, the urge must be there and be there in plenty.

So for art, for literature to flourish the right climate is necessary. They don't just happen. Here we differ from nature's vital automatism. We must want these things, we must wish for them, yearn to bring them to pass. And go beyond that—get busy and active in working for them.

And so if you mean the state of North Carolina has been

neglected by other people as a subject matter for art, well, I would say that's not the point, not at all. The point is that we've neglected ourselves. Any kind of lack that North Carolina has had in the arts, in literature, she has had through her own niggardly, lazy, poor-white point of view about these subjects. So the answer is yes, she has neglected herself! And that's the important thing to remember—self-neglect.

Interviewer: Do you feel that being a Southerner has its advantages for writing?

Mr. Green: Yes, I think so, if raw experience is the first need, and maybe it is—experience linked with imagination. And here I hurry to say that there can be both kinds of experience, the actual kind and the imaginative kind. Some of our writers have held an aesthetic credo that in order to write about an experience one must have had that experience. Of course this is nonsense. If Dostoevski wanted to write about murder in *Crime and Punishment* he didn't have to go out and kill two old women in order to do it. And he wrote horrifyingly well. No, the purpose of the imagination is to be able to experience and see and feel by proxy as it were.

So perhaps the South has had more of both kinds of these experiences than any other part of the country. Let us enumerate a bit. She has experienced more hate, more anger, more prejudice than any other part of the country. There have been more sin, a greater sense of guilt, more frustration, and maybe more spiritual hunger in the South than in any other part of this country. The South is the only part of the nation that has suffered the humiliation of a military defeat. We've been occupied. This hill here where I live was occupied by Sherman's soldiers. The University of North Carolina up there a mile away from here was occupied by these same soldiers. People love to tell the old story that Sherman's horses were housed in the lower rooms of what is now the Carolina Playmakers Theatre. At least we've made progress in that particular.

Yes. We had the carpetbaggers later and the hate of the carpetbaggers. We had the Ku Klux Klan here. For instance, my uncle started the Ku Klux Klan down in Harnett County where I was brought up as a boy. At least he was one of the leaders in it. And one night he and his companions waited on a young Negro man named Reuben. Now Reuben had been talking sassy, they said, and they were going to set him straight. When they got to his cabin he called out from inside that he would kill anybody that tried to break in. Well, Heck Gaskins was in front of my Uncle Heck. (They were both named Heck.) So when Heck Gaskins smashed in the door Reuben killed him with an axe. And my Uncle Heck pulled out his pistol and shot Reuben down, shot him six times. And he left him dying there on the floor, he thought. But Reuben didn't die. He later crawled off into a ditch, and there a Negro girl who loved him found him, hid him, and nursed him finally back to health. Well, fifty years later as a little boy I often cut wheat in the fields with Reuben, who by then was an old man and I called him Uncle Reuben. But he was still tough and wiry. And over the years he and Uncle Heck had become the best of friends. In fact I think they loved each other better than brothers. When they would meet they would hug and almost kiss. (Uncle Heck was a postmaster down in Wilmington and would sometimes come up and visit us.)

Well, this sort of thing happened all over the South—this shooting, this killing, this cruelty, and then the repentance and the forgiveness and love that followed. Instances like Uncle Heck and Uncle Reuben could be multiplied thousands of times. I know of half a dozen myself. So it is perhaps true that in the South we've had more love too, more friendship between the Negro and the white. This feeling is something wonderful to behold. It was. It still is. But I wouldn't recommend your shooting anybody in order to produce a wonderful friendship later.

So the material out of which art, out of which writing and music and drama and philosophy and sculpture and painting can be made, is here. I keep saying the same thing. We are full of the drip of human tears. And I hasten to add we also have lots of laughter—enough—with the sparkling eyes of humor and fun.

All we need here is to get rolling and keep rolling, use what we have, and if we do that, well, we might very well participate in the great literary, artistic, and therefore cultural birth in this country. We've had sporadic people like Wolfe, Faulkner, Eudora Welty, Tennessee Williams, Red Warren down here, but they're not enough—and the slant they have on things is not enough. No sir, not enough. Here in North Carolina we've got a population equal to that of Norway. Call the roll of the great literary figures of Norway and you'll know what I mean by comparison.

Interviewer: Do you feel that recent developments have borne out the wisdom of the Supreme Court decision concerning integration?

Mr. Green: Right after the Supreme Court decision I talked to a number of people. I especially talked to a neighbor of mine, a poet come out of the slabs of the sunburnt West. I said to him, "Let us take a stand on this matter. Let us get out a statement, we writers of North Carolina, let's speak up!"

His reply was a good deep chuckle, a musical chuckle, and the added words, "Hell, let'm fight. Let'm all fight. People got to bleed," he said, "kill each other." And he added, "Anyhow I'm busy."

Well, like old Archimedes more or less, he was drawing his figures in a tub of sand. Archimedes, you remember, invented all kinds of things. He discovered specific gravity, for instance. One day the Roman soldiers captured his town, and the philosopher felt a shadow behind him, and he said, to the soldier there, "Stand out of the light, you are bothering me." It made this soldier mad, and what did he do but up and kill Archimedes with his spear. I told this to my poet friend. I said to him, "Don't you see him? That soldier?"

"Well," he said, "I don't see him and I got 'lectric light anyhow. He's not making any shadow."

"But he's there," I said, "in the room with that spear. He's right behind you."

"No," said my poet friend. "No, he's not there. Anyhow I'm not worried."

And I kept saying, "Don't you see him?" And he kept chuckling and working and saying he didn't see him.

Wisdom of the Supreme Court decision you say?

Well, after all we can't escape questions of right and wrong, can we? In spite of the psychiatrists we can't. I remember talking to the President of the United States once as a humble citizen, and he said you couldn't settle things today on the basis of right and wrong.

I said, "Well then, Mr. President, how do you settle them? On what basis do you act?" And he laughed and said, "On the basis of expediency. I try to see what works. That's the best I can do." Even while he was talking I was thinking of what George Washington said in his Farewell Address, of what Thomas Jefferson said, of what Abraham Lincoln said, of what Woodrow Wilson said—about a nation. You remember Washington said in his Farewell Address that a nation was like a man, that it should have some code of honor like a man, its obligations were sacred, its word was its bond, and so on. So here was the President of the United States saying you can't do business that way. Well I decided not to vote for him next time, and I voted for the other man. But it wasn't any improvement.

So, as I say, we can't escape this question of right and wrong. At least I don't think we can. Was the Supreme Court right? Yes, it was right. I think so. Then you ask me if the events that followed justified their action. It's not a question of what the events justified. If you measure that way then you're back in the business of expediency again, and by what judgment do you judge the results?

So when you ask me "Have the events borne out the wisdom of the Supreme Court's action?" I have to answer that events are not always the result of wisdom. Plenty of events that followed this decision were crazy as heck, prejudiced, sour, and full of ignorance and darkness. A lot of them happened in Louisiana, in Mississippi, in Georgia, and a lot of them happened in this state too. As an example—I remember being in Paris one time and getting the morning paper and there spread on the front page of this French newspaper in a big wide picture was a scene of harassment and hate in Charlotte, North Carolina. A little Negro schoolgirl named Dorothy Counts, as I remember, was walking a straight path toward me in the picture, carrying her school books close against her, staring ahead of her, staring at the future, and behind her came a spitting, jeering crowd of ignorant and misled young white students, North Carolina boys and girls.

Later to my expostulation one of my friends answered with the same old bromide, "Those nine foolish women on the Supreme Court bench—if they'd kept their mouths shut this sort of thing wouldn't have happened." You see he was saying that the events were proving the wrongness of the Supreme Court's judgment. No, all that was being proved was the wrongness of the happening in Charlotte.

And here I could sing a doleful little refrain out of an old Negro folk song—"And he never said a mumbling word, not a word—" the governor I mean.

When Jesus said "Suffer little children to come unto me and forbid them not, for of such is the Kingdom of God," he didn't say let the brown ones stay back and the black ones stay still farther back and bring on the white ones first. When Charlie Aycock in 1904 said, "I want to educate all the people," somebody said, "Mercy 'pon us, you mean *all?*" He said, "I mean all." Back in those days in eastern North Carolina and on up in the Piedmont too there was a lot of growling as the poor whites snapped their grimy overall suspenders and spat tobacco juice through their spraddled dirty teeth and said, "Many a good plowhand is gonna be ruint by this bizness."

I went over and talked to this businessman governor of ours and pleaded with him to take leadership and help the state forward in a generous program of unprejudiced progress. If he would only speak out—show us the way, I said. He shook his head, "No, Paul, no," he said, "it won't do for me to step out in front like that. I believe the way you do,"—he said this twice—"but I have to play it this way, play it quiet."

Weary—weary is the story.

"Well, Governor," I said, "if quietness is what you want—there's nothing quieter than the grave. I hear tell there's no life in that place, none at all."

"But I've got to go slow," he said, rising to dismiss me.

"How slow?" I said, accepting the dismissal.

Think of it—the Negro has been here in North Carolina for

more than three hundred years—ever since the state began down there in Currituck Peninsula in 1660. During that long stretch of time some twelve to thirteen million Negroes have lived and died here. How many of them ever reached their full potential as thriving, creative human beings? Very, very few.

I do some farming now and then, and I employ a number of Negroes—plowing, cutting trees, cleaning out the forest, piling brush, cleaning up the newgrounds, reforesting old fields, and so on. And what a wonderful untrained, undeveloped talent there is among them! Some of them of course are not worth killing, and if their brains were dynamite they wouldn't have enough to make them sneeze. But that sort of judgment applies to all colors and kinds of human beings—to your folks and mine too, maybe. And I do know that many of these laborers would go far in the world if they had the proper chance—yes, most of them would go far. You remember that Thomas Jefferson said—speaking out of the very heart of our democratic heritage—that the purpose of a state, a nation is to help the talents of its people to grow into full and beneficent flowering—talents which nature sowed as plentifully among the poor as among the rich. Some of these workmen who help me, for instance, have terrific voices. One was out here working yesterday. What a voice he had! The normal pitch of his conversation was around B-flat below low-C. Here was another Chaliapin, another Lawrence Tibbett, another Cesare Siepi—I mean a possible one. He could have been a star in the Metropolitan Opera, he could have thrilled thousands perhaps. You and I might have bought his hi-fi records. But he never will, we never will. No chance came to him. Why? Because of his color. And you could multiply this in instance after instance. Out of these thirteen million human beings have we had a great poet, a great scientist, a great lawyer, statesman, and so on? No. Who are we robbing? Ourselves. Not only them but ourselves—everybody. A state, a nation, a world is only as strong as the citizens are strong in it. If one-third of our people here in North Carolina are weakened, handicapped because of our social point of view and practices, then North Carolina is just so much weakened in proportion. Can you have a fine football team with one-third of the members sick? Can you have a strong railroad bridge with one-third of the piers defective?

In economics and engineering we know these things, these laws of stresses and strains. We accept them without question. And the truth is, the same sort of laws hold good in social relationships.

A businessman from Kinston was here recently speaking out for the old-timey point of view. "My Lord, Mr. Green," he said, "in our city we have built the Negroes" (he pronounced it differently) "a four-hundred-thousand dollar school building."

"Yes, and I'm darned tired of being taxed to put up buildings for the Negroes," I replied. "I want them to be able to build for themselves. I want them to be able to own good property and pay their proper proportion of taxes."

And here I'm reminded of our recent governor again and of his energetic hunt for new industry for the state. If the over a million Negroes in North Carolina could get good wages, were businessmen, merchants, leading lawyers, leading real estate men, were big contractors, owned farms, neither he nor anyone else would have to go hunting for industry.

Right at this moment there are some three or four hundred Negro boys and girls in this town of Chapel Hill with bright eager minds—minds that only need a chance for training—for development. But they will never get their due training, will never go to college, they will never realize their full potential bcause they haven't got the money with which to go away to college. But they could stay here and get an education, they could work on the weekends, get self-help jobs, they could even borrow from the loan fund here at the University—if prejudice would get out of the way. I'd be glad to sign the note of any number of them—sign to the limit the University would allow. The comptroller recently told me that the University loan fund had built up to several hundred thousand dollars. "It is not being used enough," he said.

True, we have a small number of Negro students here now, some thirty-six, the President of the Consolidated University told me the other day—thirty-six in an enrollment of more than eight thousand! So what a stupid thing—when we deny a person his human rights because of his color! What a betrayal and mockery we make of our heritage, our democracy—of the vision of Washington, Jefferson, Franklin, Hamilton, Madison, and of those later witnesses to the truth—Emerson, Whitman, Abraham Lincoln, and Woodrow Wilson—when human beings have to sue for what already belongs to them by natural right. The Negro race is a talented race, and every time we kick them down we kick ourselves down in a most vital spot.

Of course we are making progress but slow, too slow. The confidence of the world has been shaken in us. I know. For some years ago I traveled around the globe, talking and lecturing and meeting with people over matters of art and democracy in the United States. And I was hurt and even discouraged to find how much antagonism, even animosity had developed, in the countries of Asia especially, against us. In the numerous countries I went not a single voice expressed dislike for our philosophy of government—our theory of democracy, nay, everywhere there was uniform admiration for that, but there was no admiration for what we the living had done to that philosophy, to that democracy. So I came back home determined to work harder than ever, to speak out when I could to promote what little bit of truth I could in the workings of our system.

Our leaders just don't lead. Some kind of conspiracy goes on. Some illusion that deludes us. Take, for instance, the young President's inaugural speech. He said, as I remember, and I quote, "Our freedom comes from God." Well, you and I know darned well it doesn't. We have to dig for it, we have to cherish it, be responsible to it. The president before him, good man that he was and a smiling one, talked a great deal about "freedom with justice." Never did he define that freedom or that justice—tell us what they were. Our present President carries on the refrain of freedom and justice too, freedom and justice—speaking a lot about the "free peoples of the world." What does he mean by these terms? For instance again, does he mean freedom for the oil companies to exploit Venezuela? Or freedom for the American sugar companies to exploit the peons in Cuba?

In Russia there is a tremendous lot of talk about freedom too.

For the first time in that country everybody is free to have an education, they say. For the first time there Marxism is free to flourish—and so on. So let's have some straight talk here, some honest definitions of these terms and quit whiffing them about like a "bird" in a badminton game.

Interviewer: Do you feel that certain themes lend themselves to adaptation to the movies?

Mr. Green: Any human theme lends itself naturally to the movies—just as any human theme lends itself to poetry, to music, to sculpture, to drama. Because each of these mediums is a universal medium, that is, it can deal with any kind of human experience, actual or imagined. The motion picture medium—the camera with the all-seeing eye and the all-hearing ear—is a universal medium for art. So I wouldn't say that there are any certain themes, I wouldn't select that way. I would simply say all themes lend themselves for use in the motion picture medium. The movies are of course first an eye medium and the voice dialogue part should always be more of a buttress and an accompaniment for this seeing. Now the stage, the theatre is an ear medium mainly, and the eye stuff on the stage, the pantomime, the movement, the action of the body should be an accompaniment for the ear. Of course you can have an extreme in either direction. In the case of Charlie Chaplin—he is a first-rate motion picture actor and most of his action is designated for the eye—he is a wonderful pantomimist. An exceptional word man, that is a dramatist for the ear, was Paul Claudel, the French poet and diplomat. I recommend one of his plays to you especially, entitled *The Tidings Brought to Mary*. The radio of course is completely an ear medium. The television now is much the same as the motion picture, with a smaller screen only.

But whether it be stage, radio, television or motion picture, the subject matter in these mediums is human nature—man, man in his universe, man hoping, struggling, aspiring, moving on, creating, going yonder as I said before. The sorrowful thing about these mediums is that they have been bastardized mainly for the purpose of money-making—for the sale of cheap and easy entertainment, the luxury of easement from pain and the pleasure of enjoyment—in our beloved country they have.

I suppose there's no nation in the world that puts out more violence for its people to sop up as entertainment than we do. It's understandable if we consider the money-making craze which has become—to those same millions of people I referred to in Asia —which to them has become the mark of our nature. Yes, these mediums sell violence in terms of violence. I've written a lot for the movies, quarreled with the producers, and I know from the inside their greedy, ignorant, cynical point of view.

Not too long ago I was in a movie house over in Durham. I got in there under false pretense, I suppose. Anyhow on the screen the little while I was in there I saw a picture of Pretty Boy Floyd with a machine gun mowing down innocent by-standing human beings. Yes, I saw it shown in cold blood and people with a lot of little boys and girls in the audience, sitting there, lapping it up, and feeling the urge to imitate. And in answer to my protest to the manager later he said, "Oh, Pretty Boy is not so bad." "But my goodness," I said, "he's in there murdering people." "Well, after all," said this manager of the Durham theatre, "the American public likes this sort of thing. It is a kind of escape for them." "Escape from what?" I yelled. And he smiled and made no answer as he turned to take some teen-ager's eager tickets. My Lord, what a business! Talk about traitors to your country—the Rosenbergs and Sobels!

And the stuff we get on our television screens could hardly be worse. As I recently wrote for a magazine—"It out-carnals old St. Paul's vision of carnality in its debauchery of lust and pain."

It is a complicated matter I grant you. For pain actually is our guide to survival. We live by way of pain. Without the warning and protection of pain we could hardly exist. If you step on a red-hot coal it burns you. You instantly jerk your foot away and therefore keep your foot from being crippled.

What hurts us we tend to stay away from, and what pleases us, gives us joy, makes us forget pain, that we go after, we hunger for it, we reach for it.

So anything that has to do with pain, with violence, gets an immediate attention, even if a natural one, a childish reaction out of us. And the same thing is true of physical comforts and joys. These two phases, pain and pleasure, are basic, are primary with us. They have to be. But art, literature, the real thing lies not in these, in depicting these, in purveying these, but in getting beyond these, for this is the area of appetite, and here of course in the flowery meads of appetite these hucksters who control the mediums mentioned above find they can make the most money easily, get the easiest reaction out of the public. And so they and their stock holders and we their public spinelessly accept the spoils and the ruin of all spiritual and cultural taste that go with this acceptance.

Thus the neurotic materialism in these United States continues its wild and unchecked flourishing. That is the great enemy to art, to beauty, to true science, to true philosophy—materialism.

And what hypocrites we are! We know better. Our rational selves are not fooled. "Oh, but everybody's doing it," they say. And even though we say that, we are not fooled. We know there is no moral safety in numbers. Our reason, our knowledge tells us that, and that reason is the king of ourselves. He sits on his throne inside each of us there behind our skull peering out at the world gravely, steadily with wisdom. We don't fool him. He is a spirit there, this judge, this appraiser, this person. Yes, he is reason essentialized.

And that man of reason, he's the man the artist wants to reach, must reach as an artist, a true one. For that man is once more himself there—kings identical.

Now this seer, this thinker, this creative spirit which resides in each of us does not decry violence, pleasure, pain as such. No, he realizes their nature, their place, in living existence. But he does not make them goals and ends in themselves. He approves of pain, of violence if they are suffered, endured, produced in the service of values more important than they. Taking to himself the pain of death, the violence of crucifixion, the martyr proves his devotion and proves it finally for the ideals he believes in.

But violence for the sake of violence whether under the guise of art or not is evil.

Let me be more specific even in repetition. Take the violence of Jesus on the cross, nailed up there, the hole under his short rib, his head to one side, breathing out his life and the blood drip-drapping from him on the ground. Well, the violence he was subjected to only has reality in the ideals that he defended through this violence. What a tremendous subject for tragedy! But his tragic might has been diminished in proportion to the divinity the preachers and the churchly folks have wished upon him.

Interviewer: Do you feel that Southern writing is in danger of becoming sociological?

Mr. Green: I don't know what you mean by sociological—not exactly. I suppose you have in mind some ideology or idiom or pedagogical point of view which would mean practical benefits and betterments for everyday living. Sociological means society, doesn't it? And society means human beings and human beings maybe mean brotherhood or enemies, with all levels of relationship in between. The sociologists here at Chapel Hill have come through with tremendous visions—multitudinous visions. We have the work here of Howard Odum, Rupert Vance, Guy and Guion Johnson, Gordon Blackwell, Harriet Herring, Katherine Jocher, George Simpson—a lot of wonderful sociologists. There are sociologists all over the place, in fact they've developed a language of their own. Sometimes I hardly know just what they're talking about, what they're after—except I guess they're after what all of us are after as I said, better living for all—more friendship, more industry, more health, more taxes, better roads, longer life, more smiles—a happier world. So, if our writing is in danger of becoming an advocate of that sort of thing, what's wrong with it? Or if you mean our writing might be in danger of becoming loaded and laden with a message, a preachment? Is that what you mean?

Interviewer: No, I meant more of a didactic tone to it.

Mr. Green: Yes, that's what I say—preaching. Let's look at that word, didactic. I guess it means to lead toward some goal or across some difficulty, or leading out and onward. It comes from the Latin. Education means to lead out. I guess a writer can't help being didactic more or less. That's the question, whether the more or whether the less. You've got to teach something.

You've got to stand for something. Now if a writer has a thesis, a preachment, a favorite cause and he lets this thesis, this preachment swallow up his characters, distort his story line, breed its own climate and atmosphere apart from the needs of the characters, from the demands of the story-line—then this is didacticism overdone. But if it is like some of the great work of Paul Claudel or some of the things of Shakespeare and nearly all of Aeschylus and Sophocles—why, man, those things are loaded with didacticism. That is, they are loaded with some meaning for the spectator, for the reader. They have an attitude toward life, they have an attitude toward evil, toward good. And they say something about man's purpose on this earth.

I agree with Schiller, the German writer of the eighteenth century. Schiller once said that people were accusing him of copying Voltaire, Voltaire the didactic writer. But he said something like this—"The purpose of art, of literature is to give joy, exhilaration, illumination to man. And the greatest literature must have some sort of moral attitude. It must take a stand for something. Now in a drama, the greatest joy for man is the resolvement by the protagonist, by the characters involved of a moral dilemma." Let the audience see this protagonist struggling to solve this dilemma, and when he solves it or when he loses his life in trying to solve it —the satisfaction of that man 'sitting behind your skull I spoke of a while ago is the fuller, the richer.

Now the trouble with so much of our Southern writing—the most highly thought of writing at the present—is that it has no moral attitude. It is a great turmoil of passion and feeling, a whole spew of human statement pouring out, and the favorite sources of this pouring out seem to be perverts, idiots, cranksided, deformed, and unhealthy people.

Interviewer: Do you feel that the South has passed its so-called renaissance in writing?

Mr. Green: Renaissance is a word by way of the Latin again which means a rebirth. The truth is we haven't had the birth in the first place yet. But I think the birth is preparing. As I say it's a matter of climate and I believe we are working some at creating it.

And who knows, we may be brewing up a terrific thunderstorm around here, and the lightning flashes of genius, and forked lightning at that, may soon break across the sky.

—Adapted from *The Rebel*, East Carolina College
(Winter, Spring, 1960)

GOOD INTENTIONS

Weimar Jones

The fellow who coined that old saying about good intentions paving roads was indulging in understatement. Good intentions also can get you in trouble.

We've found that true on *The Press*. Often we've felt it our duty to publish a news story or an editorial that we expected to raise the roof—and got no reaction whatever. On the other hand, the very next week, we'll carry something that appears quite innocent and is published with the best intentions—and it does raise the roof!

That's true, too, in personal relations, as I had unpleasantly brought home to me only the other night.

Mrs. Jones and I were visiting friends.

In the course of the evening, our hostess displayed two objects (I haven't the faintest idea of their name, but I'd guess they were a sort of cross between a tray and a plate) and commented that here were gifts they really were proud of.

I must be a sympathetic sort of soul, because, when someone is enthusiastic about something, I try to be enthusiastic, too. In this case, I wasn't to be outdone.

I arose and went closer so I could get a better look. The hostess was beaming, and so I beamed. She said they were beautiful, and I agreed. I went further. I said they were about the nicest things of the kind I'd ever seen. I think I even went so far as to use a word I rarely use, because I don't like it; I think I said they were "lovely."

I should have caught the warning signals beamed towards me by Mrs. Jones. I should have sensed the waves of embarrassment she was radiating. But I didn't. I went right on "mirating" till I finally got around to saying they were "lovely."

Well, that was all my wife could take.

"You've said enough," she remarked, drily. "Those are the Christmas presents *we* gave them, you know."

—*My Affair with a Weekly* (1960)

FOLKLORE

"Folklore is that complex of knowledge (beliefs, customs, magic, sayings, songs, tales, traditions, and so on) which has been created by the spontaneous play of naive imaginations upon common human experience, transmitted by word of mouth or action, and preserved without dependence upon written or printed record."

—Arthur Palmer Hudson

THE WHITE DOE

Isabel G. Murphy

The story of the White Doe is founded on historical fact and, although mythical in substance, its connection with the disappearance of the Roanoke Colony is of historical interest and descriptive of the American Indians' belief in witchcraft and sorcery. . . .

When the colonists who had established a settlement on Roanoke Island were forced to desert Fort Raleigh, they are supposed to have joined Manteo's tribe of Croatoans who had befriended them during their struggles to hold their settlement, offering them refuge from attacking Indians and helping them in other ways. Few, if any, are thought to have survived. The legend of the White Doe relates the events which might have happened during the time of Virginia Dare's life among the Indians who had adopted her.

The fair-skinned Virginia, whose lovely English complexion and golden hair had set her apart from the dark savages, must have been regarded by them as a child of the gods and, as she grew to young womanhood, was eagerly courted by the Indian braves. The legend of Virginia Dare gives the babe of Roanoke the Indian name of Winona-Ska, "first-born white daughter."

The young Indian braves were not alone in their admiration for the fair Winona. The old eyes of the tribe's chief magician, Chico, began to brighten when they looked at her and to turn with longing toward the white maiden. He became increasingly jealous of Okisco, who had won her affection, and, when it was apparent to old Chico that his wooing had failed, he decided to work a spell of bewitchment upon her.

Mussel-shell pearls were believed to contain the spirits of

Naiads imprisoned because of disobedience to the sea king. They could only be released from their prison if dipped in magic water, and upon such benefactors they bestowed the powers of enchantment contained in the pearls. Naiads were nymphs believed to live in and give life and perpetuity to lakes, rivers, springs and fountains. There was, according to legend, a spring of magic water on Roanoke Island where the Naiads gathered to hold their revels, and one who bathed in it had the power to undo evil spells.

Old Chico gathered mussel-shell pearls and made a necklace which he placed around Winona's neck and which he believed, with the powers received from the Naiads, would bewitch her. With this in mind he invited her to go with him across the water to Roanoke Island to gather grapes, knowing that when she stepped on land the magic necklace would work its spell. As the young woman stepped from the canoe, a White Doe bounded up the slope of the Roanoke shore and disappeared into the forest.

The lovely animal continued to roam the woods and dunes of the island, safe from hunters whose arrows fell harmlessly beside her.

The report of a White Doe on Roanoke Island simultaneous with the disappearance of the white maiden caused the Indians to suspect the magic powers of the old magician, and the young brave Okisco sought a rival magician for means of undoing the evil spell.

In the meantime Wingina, the king of Roanoke, invited all the neighboring tribes to a harvest celebration determined that the elusive White Doe should provide the feast. The Croatoans would not come, believing the White Doe to be their Winona. Okisco, however, under the rival magician's direction, had perfected the ritual required for the magic arrow that was to pierce the heart of the White Doe and restore the maiden to him.

King Wingina desired the honor of bringing down the White Doe, as did Wanchese, who believed in the powers of the silver arrow given him by Queen Elizabeth upon his visit to England.

Fleeing before the pursuing hunters, the White Doe came at last to bay at the place of her people's settlement, and there the magic arrow of Okisco and the silver one of Wanchese met in the heart of the Doe, the magic arrow transforming her to her rightful human form, and the silver one inflicting a mortal wound. Wanchese, frightened at the transformation he had witnessed, fled, leaving Okisco to bury his beloved Winona near the place of her birth.

Legend has it that her spirit, taking the form of the White Doe, still roams the dunes and woods of the region and can be seen on moonlight nights bounding away into the shadowy forest, leaving tiny hoofprints in the sands to mark the path of her going.

—*Surfside News* (August 16, 1959)

CURRITUCK COUNTY TROUBLES

Evelyn L. Griffin

Belief in witchcraft has existed in Currituck, according to Hathoway's Register, where we find the following:

"Presentiment is made to the Grand jury that Susannah Evans of the precinct of Coratuck in the County of Albemarle did devilishly and maliciously bewitch and afflict with mortal paynes, the body of Deborah Bourthier whereby said Deborah departed this life."

A jury was impaneled and sworn in: Mr. Robert Wallis, James Farlow, Wm. Erly, Frances Beasley, James Ward, John Worley, John Watkins, Zack Keeton, Robt. Loury, William Simson, William Luftman, Hugh Pritchard, Cornelius Jones, Richard Stamp, Rich Madron and Cornelius Fitz Patrick.

They listened to the following depositions of Thomas Bourthier:

"It sayeth that on 24th July 1703 ye deponents household was in perfect health, excepting one person: ye same day at eve. I called one Tho. Walker, a servant, but he could not come. He continues disabled to this day. The next morning Walker's wife came from John Evan's house to nurse her husband—within an hour or two my wife was taken with a pain in her foot so extreme that she cried out. After 24 hours, this pain ceased but she was tormented in her bowels until her death about a month later. While she was sick, she cried out against John Evans' wife, saying she was an evil woman, and that she Deborah, suffered these great pains and would surely die because of her. My wife desired me to have Susannah Evans searched and examined to prevent her doing more mischief. Before my wife died John Evans came for me to meet his wife at Mr. Thomas Vander Mullens before Mr. Richd Cominfort. His wife was not willing to have such reports made against her. I readily went to acquaint what my wife says. There John Evans and his wife did abuse and threaten me."

Verdict: "Wee of ye jury find no bill and ye person Ignoramus. It is ordered that ye said Susannah Evans be acquitted."

—*The Currituck Record* (1954)

~~~~~~~~~~

WITCHCRAFT TRIAL IN UNION COUNTY

There is a curiously mediaeval touch to the tragedy of Rev. William Richardson, one of Union's noted preachers.

The Rev. Richardson was subject to melancholia, induced, perhaps, by the suffering of his people in Scotland and the turmoil in the colonies. In one of these fits of depression he committed suicide. Family and friends, fearful of the harm his act would do to those who admired him, kept secret the manner of his death.

This air of mystery started tongue wagging, and finally the beautiful widow was openly accused of having caused her husband's death through witchcraft.

Her relatives were resentful and demanded that the matter be brought to trial. In this superstitious manner, perhaps a survival of custom in the old country:

That the corpse of the dead be exhumed and the accused one

required to touch it, when, if guilty, blood would immediately gush forth.

This gruesome "trial" was held. The body was disinterred, and before the assembled congregation Mrs. Richardson was put to the test but not a drop of blood appeared.

Wrote Lily Doyle Dunlap: " 'Tis said that one man crushed her hand into the forehead in his eagerness to see the blood flow."

And to make the story even more remarkably like a scenario: In the assembly was George Dunlap, a young man, who was so moved by the young widow's travail, that he followed her home and offered her his protection and love. They soon were married.

A nephew and namesake of the preacher was William Richardson Davie. He was reared for the ministry, but instead became a general in the Revolution, third governor of North Carolina, founder of the University, and envoy to France.

—*The State* (December 1, 1956)

OLD DAN TUCKER

Old Dan Tucker was a fine old man,
He washed his face in the frying pan,
On Christmas morning he got drunk,
And fell in the fire and kicked up a chunk.
  Get out of the way, old Dan Tucker,
  You come too late to get your supper.

Old Dan Tucker ate raw eel
And combed his hair with a wagon wheel,
He gave his neighbors the squarest deal
And died with toothache in his heel.
  Get out of the way, old Dan Tucker,
  You come too late to get your supper.

That old ballad has been a favorite, especially in the realm of so-called hillbilly music, for two centuries or more, and the assumption has been that Dan Tucker was a creation of some songwriter's imagination.

But Old Dan lacked a great deal of being a mythological character. He was a lively, healthy and "fearless man of brawn and muscle," whose boyhood and young manhood were spent in Bath, North Carolina's oldest town.

Dan Tucker was born in London, England, in 1714. In 1720, when he was six years old, he came to America with his parents who settled in the little town of Bath. Twenty years after coming to this state he married Margaret DeVane, a beautiful girl of French descent, and with his bride migrated westward to what is Randolph County.

This section was then a wilderness thickly inhabited by wild animals, rattlesnakes and bloodthirsty Indians. But Tucker, who believed in predestination, was unafraid. "What is to be, will be, and I won't die before my time," he often said.

On the spot where the little settlement of Spero now stands, Dan Tucker built his first shelter. It was a lean-to made of pine poles banked and roofed with pine and cedar boughs. The bed also was made of a heap of boughs. Here he and his bride lived until he could hew logs and build a cabin. The cracks of the cabin were chinked with a mixture of clay and dried moss, softened with water; the chimney was made of rocks and sticks plastered with mud. As he had no nails, the boards were attached to the walls and roof with wooden pegs driven into round holes which he bored with an auger. The only tools he had with which to construct his home were an axe, two iron wedges, a hatchet, hammer, auger, gimlet and drawing knife. This cabin was built near a spring of clear mountain water and was three miles from the nearest neighbor and a hundred miles from any store. It was here on an open fireplace that Margaret Tucker cooked the wild game Dan brought in from the woods, the fish he caught in the streams, and the corn bread made from meal they brought with them from Bath. Their total supply of cooking utensils consisted of a twelve-inch spider, a frying pan, and a three-legged iron skillet.

Dan owned a horse and wagon, but as there were few roads and nowhere to go, the wagon was of little use. He cleared a plot of ground and planted his corn, his only farming implements being a homemade plow, a hoe and pick. His hunting equipment consisted of a gun, hunting knife, pocket knife, and a steel tomahawk.

Dan was a hunter and trapper as well as a farmer. The skins and furs from the animals he shot and trapped brought him in a fair income. Once a year he saddled his horse, took his stock of furs and skins and carried them to the store a hundred miles away.

Tucker was noted for his honesty, thrift, good humor and love for his fellow man. He never borrowed but was ever willing to lend; he always gave a square deal, and when the neighbors called him eccentric and made up funny songs about him, he laughed and sang the songs with them, enjoying a joke even on himself.

As the years went by, the hunting trails became wagon roads and other pioneers came and settled in Tucker's territory until a dozen or more cabins sprouted up like overgrown mushrooms in the forests. It was these neighbors who laughed at Dan's rigid thrift and peculiarities, made up the funny songs about his behavior, and composed the Old Dan Tucker song. On account of his thrift they accused him of washing his face in the frying pan and combing his hair with a wagon wheel. He often visited his neighbors in the evening but would never sponge upon them by eating a meal. By so doing, there came into being the line of verse that he came too late to get his supper.

Dan Tucker lived to be a hundred years old. It is said that his death was caused by a stone. One day while plowing his corn, he stepped on a sharp rock that imbedded itself deeply into his bare heel. Sitting down on a log, he cut out the stone and bruised flesh with his pocket knife, then continued plowing. Three days later he died of lockjaw.

The neighbors gave old Dan a gay and noisy burial, which was what he would have enjoyed. The wake was filled with food, song, dance, and drink, lamentations and eulogies. Stories were told of his kindness, his thrift, honesty and eccentricities. It was at this time that his most enthusiastic friend burst forth with the eulogistic lines

> *He gave his neighbor the squarest deal*
> *And died with toothache in his heel.*

No, Dan Tucker is no myth. He once lived on Carolina soil, loving the blue of her skies and the strength and beauty of her hills. He was buried somewhere near the little village of Spero.

—Unsigned, *The State* (April 28, 1951)

THE CASE OF PETER DROMGOOLE

Millie Johnson

> Yasser—das de rock; en dis is de place
> Mars Louis en ter man, face ter face,
> Stood in de moonlight en shoot at one ner—
> Fer de sake of Miss Fannie—das wut fer.

"De rock" referred to in the poem is what University of North Carolina students and alumni now know as Dromgoole Rock. The duel described by the old Negro slave had become a tradition by the time L. B. Hamberlin wrote his poem in the *Carolina Magazine,* three pages in length, in 1892.

The scene is a peak, a half mile east of the peaceful university village of Chapel Hill, known as Piney Prospect. Piney Prospect tops the neighboring ridges by several hundred feet. From there a magnificent view of the lowlands east can be had. The enemy—

were this the glorious age of knighthood—could be seen ap-
proaching long before he could get within striking distance of
Gimghoul Castle.

Here a lover was sought and wooed. Here a duel was fought
and a lover killed. Here a lover was buried. In those days no
Gimghoul Castle adorned Piney Prospect. Only tall slender pines
greeted lovers as they wandered there.

Every pleasant Sunday afternoon, or practically any afternoon,
Gimghoul Castle has many visitors. They circle around the castle
in an admiring tour of inspection. They sneak near to the castle
walls and try to peep through the windows at the fantastic
tapestries and ornaments and statues. If spied by guardians who
now dwell in the spacious halls of the castle, they are quickly
ordered behind the "keep out" sign.

They then go to the brow of the hill and take various shares
of rapture from the purple-misted valleys and ridges. Walking
back around the castle they come upon the Dromgoole Rock,
over which hovers Chapel Hill's most romantic legend. If they
have not heard its history, they may wonder why it is encircled
with a well-kept hedge of box woods.

The stains adorning the rock may look like iron to scientists,
but they are continuously pointed out by others as the drops of
blood of a lover who was killed in a duel there. Not even the rain
and snow nor the frost of more than a century have been able
to wash them away. They only grow deeper into the huge stone
piece.

Peter Dromgoole was a reckless young man from Brunswick
County, Virginia. He entered the university in 1833 but did not
matriculate. He was fond of card playing and wild company.
One day he took offense at a remark of one of his instructors and
refused to submit to further examination. A few days later he
disappeared; rumors circulated in the university village that he
had been killed in a duel at midnight following the annual commencement ball and his body carefully concealed on Piney
Prospect.

The story of the duel is associated with a pretty maid by the
name of Miss Fannie. Peter and the young man, also a suitor of

Miss Fannie, met at midnight on the top of Piney Prospect. Both were madly in love with Miss Fannie. Words were exchanged and it was agreed that a duel would be fought. The winner would have the hand of fair Miss Fannie.

An old slave overheard the conversation and rushed to the nearby home of Miss Fannie who, clad only in her nightgown and ballroom slippers, rushed to the moonlit hill of Piney Prospect.

> But des es we come ter de tu'n er de hill,
> De pistols fire; Miss Fannie stop still.
> I look behin', fo' God I 'clar
> I never see nuthin' lak was there.

> Her shawl had drapt off, en her long black hair
> Wus loose wid runnin', I reckon, en there
> She stood—one han' on her heart en de ter
> One holdin' her temple—des lak dis yer.

> En her eyes was shut, en her putty head
> Was dropt on her bres', en 'er streak 'er red
> Was tricklin' down on her snow-white gown
> Right fum twixt her lips, clar down ter de groun'.

> De gent'emens move fum de awful place
> En dar was Mars Louis—de moon in his face.
> Young Miss never move, en she ain't say a word.
> Des a long, long sigh was all I heard.

Peter Dromgoole, the legend asserts, was buried under the rounded rock on the top of the peak. Afterwards Miss Fannie was never the same.

> Arter dat, hit seems lak she drif' away,
> Not die—des driftin', day arter day—
> Ter what her lover hed gone befo'
> En her gittin' silent, mo' and mo'.

She's go ter de spring jes back of de hill,
En look in de water—a smilin' still,
Des lak w'en she hear Mars Louis say
He love her befo' dat awful day.

Den she sigh, en come fer de rock down yan,
Whar he uster set en hol'e her han';
En she blush er sittin' dar all alone,
Des lak he kiss her—en he dead en gone.

After a time pretty Miss Fannie became too weak to go to the trysting places. All day long she'd sit by her window, staring toward the road on which Peter journeyed daily. At last one evening she said, "I'm going to him—he's sad—alone." And so the sweetheart of Peter Dromgoole died.

Whether the story is true or not remains the mystery of the ages, but it is known and believed by practically every university alumnus and student. Dr. Kemp Battle, in his *History of the University of North Carolina*, believes he went south and was killed in a gunfight somewhere in Texas.

Bruce Cotton, an authority on Dromgoole genealogy and a direct descendant of young Peter's grandfather, says Peter was seen in Wilmington during the summer of 1833 and probably enlisted in the army under the name of Williams, the name of his roommate while at the university.

Dr. Battle also writes he found what was probably the spring at which the anguished sweetheart waited, and that he intended "to keep it in good order, with a drinking cup on the margin, as a trysting place for the young men and women of the present and future for whom I wish a course of true love run smoother far than hers."

—*Greensboro Daily News* (March 25, 1945)

IT'S A LONG TIME BETWEEN DRINKS

David C. Mearns

You know what the Governor of one of the Carolinas is said to have said to the Governor of the other Carolina. But do you know the origin of the phrase?

Bartlett, revised, 1948, p. 786, traces it to Kipling's *The Light That Failed*, 1890, chapter 8:

"What did the Governor of North Carolina say to the Governor of South Carolina?"
"Excellent notion. It is a long time between drinks."

According to the same source, a variant had appeared in Robert Louis Stevenson's *The Wrong Box*, 1889, chapter 8:

Do you know what the Governor of South Carolina said to the Governor of North Carolina? It's a long time between drinks, observed that powerful thinker.

The note in Bartlett reads:

Of the several traditions relating to the origin of this remark, the most reasonable one traces it to John Motley Morehead [1796-1866], who was Governor of North Carolina 1841-1845. He was visited by James H. Hammond [1807-1864], who was Governor of South Carolina 1842-1844. They engaged in discussion and argument, and when the latter waxed hot, Governor Morehead was reported by a servant to have exclaimed: "It's a long time between drinks."—Personal letter from John Motley Morehead, November 21, 1934.

Burton E. Stevenson, in *The Home Book of Quotations*, 1935, p. 404, declares on another's authority:

The expression, "It is too long between drinks," is undoubtedly an invention. There is no record of its having occurred in any conferences between Governors of the Carolinas. My guess is that when a convivial party was having a good time one night and matters became a little slow, some booster of the party asked the question, "What did the

Governor of North Carolina say to the Governor of South Carolina?"
And when they all gave it up, he furnished the answer, "It is too long
between drinks."—A. S. Salley, Secretary, Historical Commission of
South Carolina, in a letter to the compiler, 28 May 1932. The expression antedates the Civil War, and many stories have been invented to
explain it. John Motley Morehead states that there is a legend in his
family that his grandfather was the governor of North Carolina who
made the historic remark. Another legend credits it to Zebulon B.
Vance, governor of North Carolina at the time Wade Hampton was
governor of South Carolina. There are several other explanations, none
of which has any historical foundation.

This is shockingly cynical, but in a later work, *The Home Book
of Proverbs, Maxims and Familiar Phrases*, 1948, p. 632, Mr.
Stevenson wrote:

"It's a damn long time between drinks."—Edward B. Dudley, Governor of North Carolina (?), to Pierce Mason Butler, Governor of South
Carolina, at the home of Mrs. Nancy Anne Jones, midway between
Raleigh and Durham, N. C. (1838). The attribution is purely legendary, but in *The Saturday Review of Literature*, 18 March 1939, Lucy
M. Cobb, of Raleigh, N. C., had a letter purporting to give the cir-
cumstances.

To my amazement, this morning, I came upon the following
passage in Daniel E. Sickles' "Leaves from My Diary," *Journal of
the Military Service Institution of the United States*, vol. VI, no.
23, September, 1885, p. 268, at a point where Sickles is reporting
his command of the Carolinas during Reconstruction:

Two of the conservative cabinet were Governor Orr, of South Carolina, and Governor Worth, of North Carolina.

One day, after a long discussion over a paragraph in an order pre-
scribing regulations for the registration of voters, which provided for
the appointment of one colored man in each board of registers and
inspectors for the several precincts in the two States, the Governors,
reluctant to yield their consent to so novel a measure, asked for a post-
ponement of our deliberations until the following day. This I was
obliged to refuse.

Governor Orr then expressed a wish to confer apart with his col-
league, Governor Worth, which being assented to, Governor Orr dryly
remarked:

"The Governor of South Carolina feels constrained to say to the Governor of North Carolina, that in these military cabinet counsels, there is a mighty long time between drinks."

There! I'm sorry to rob a Tar Heel of the honor of the coinage, but at least it brings your [Jonathan Worth Daniels'] distinguished ancestor into the dialogue.

—*News and Observer*, Raleigh (March 20, 1960)

JOHN KOONER

"Scotch Hall," Bertie County, 1849

George Higby Throop

"Is this 'ere house haunted?" asked the professor, as he met me on Christmas morning.

"I hope not."

"Wal, I hope so tew. I was pretty well tuckered aout last night after so long a ride, an' so I s'posed I sh'u'l git a good night's rest, but, Lord bless ye! sech noises I never heerd!"

"Perhaps it was the 'John Kooner'!"

"The John what?"

"I will explain. The Negroes have a custom here of dressing one of their number at Christmas in as many rags as he can well carry. He wears a mask, too, and sometimes a stuffed coon-skin above it, so arranged as to give him the appearance of being some seven or eight feet high. He goes through a variety of pranks, which you will have an opportunity to see by and by, and he is accompanied by a crowd of Negroes, who make all the noise and music for His Worship the John Kooner."

"Wal, what's all this 'ere firin' and shutin' we heerd 'beout daylight?"

"A part of the celebration of Christmas, as essential to the ceremonies as the hanging up of stockings by the little folk."

The family were soon astir. "Christmas gift! Christmas gift! Wish you merry Christmas!" shouted Molly, as she came to the door.

The morning was beautiful. The air was "frosty, but kindly." A huge fire was blazing in the parlor, and an enormous bowl of egg-nogg was already in preparation. The Negroes were lounging about in holiday attire, awaiting the customary Christmas dram. This was duly given them by little Molly, who distributed the whisky with the air of a queen. The colonel came into the piazza rubbing his hands, and caught her in his arms in a genuine doting hug.

Breakfast was announced, and we had barely left the table when a loud shout betokened the arrival of the hero of the Christmas frolic. We hastened to the door. As the Negroes approached, one of the number was singing a quaint song, the only words of which that I could distinguish were those belonging to the chorus,

Blow dat horn ag'in!

One of them carried a rude deal box, over which a dried sheepskin had been drawn and nailed, and on this, as if his salvation depended on it, the man was thumping with ear-splitting din. Beside him was another, who kept up a fierce rattle of castanets; another beat a jaw-bone of some horse departed this life; and still another had a clevis, which he beat with an iron bolt, thereby making a very tolerable substitute for a triangle. The chief mummer, or John Kooner, kept up, in the meantime, all conceivable distortions of body and limbs, while his followers pretended to provoke his ire by thrusting sticks between his legs. One of the party seemed to officiate as bear-leader, to direct the motions of the unknown chief mummer. They approached the piazza, knelt on the ground, and continued to sing, one of them improvising the words while the rest sang in chorus,

O! dear maussa!
O! dear missus!
Wish ye merry Christmas!

The expected dram was given them. A few pieces of silver were thrown from the piazza, and they left us, singing a roisterly song, the chorus of which was

> By on de row!

> —*Bertie: a Humorous Novel* (1851)

THE COACHWHIP SNAKE
AND THE HORN-SNAKE

Harden E. Taliaferro

"I had a hog claim over beyant Moor's Fork, and I concluded I'd take old Bucksmasher [his rifle], and go inter the big huckleberry patch, on Round Hill, in sarch for 'um. Off I trolloped, and toddled about for some time, but couldn't find head nur tail uv 'um. But while I was moseyin' about, I cum right chug upon one uv the biggest, longest, outdaciousest coachwhip snakes I uver laid my peepers on. He rared right straight up, like a May-pole, licked out his tarnacious tongue, and good as said, 'Here's at you, sir. What bizness have you on my grit?' Now I'd hearn folks say ef you'd look a vinimus animil right plump in the eyes he wouldn't hurt you. Now I tried it good, just like I were trying to look through a mill-stone. But, bless you, honey! he had no more respect fur a man's face and eyes than he had fur a huckleberry, sure's gun's iron. So I seed clearly that I'd have to try my trotters.

"I dashed down old Bucksmasher, and jumped 'bout ten steps the furst leap, and on I went wusser nur an old buck fur 'bout a quarter, and turned my noggin round to look fur the critter. Jehu Nimshi! thar he were right dab at my heels, head up, tongue out, and red as a nail-rod, and his eyes like two balls uv fire, red as

chain lightnin'. I 'creased my verlocity, jumped logs twenty foot
high, clarin' thick bushes, and bush-heaps, deep gullies, and
branches. Again I looked back, thinkin' I had sartinly left it a long
gap behind. And what do you think? By jingo! he'd hardly begun
to run—jist gittin' his hand in. So I jist put flatly down again
faster than uver. 'Twasn't long afore I run out'n my shot-bag, I
went so fast, then out'n my shirt, then out'n my britches—luther
britches at that—then away went my drawers. Thus I run clean
out'n all my linnen a half a mile afore I got home; and, thinks I,
surely the tarnul sarpunt are distanced now.

"But what do you think now? Nebuchadnezzar! thar he were,
fresh as a mounting buck jist scared up. I soon seen that wouldn't
do, so I jumped about thirty-five foot, screamed like a wildcat,
and 'creased my verlocity at a monstrous rate. Jist then I begun
to feel my skin split, and, thinks I, it's no use to run out'n my
skin, like I have out'n my linnen, as huming skin are scarce, so
I tuck in a leetle.

"But by this time I'd run clean beyant my house, right smack
through my yard, scaring Molly and the childering, dogs, cats,
chickens—uvry thing—half to death. But, you see, I got shet uv
my inimy, the sarpunt, fur it had respect fur my house, ef it
hadn't fur my face and eyes in the woods. I puffed, and blowed,
and sweated 'bout half an hour afore I had wind to tell Molly
and the childering what were the matter.

"Poor old Bucksmasher staid several days in the woods afore
I could have the pluck to go arter him."

When Uncle Davy told one snake story, he must needs exhaust
his stock, big and little. After breathing a little from telling his
coachwhip story, which always excited him, he would introduce
and tell the story of his adventure with the horn-snake.

"Fur some time arter I were chased by that sassy coachwhip,
I were desput 'fraid uv snakes. My har would stand on eend, stiff
as hog's bristles, at the noise uv uvry lizzard that ran through the
leaves, and my flesh would jerk like a dead beef's.

"But at last I ventured to go into the face uv the Round Peak
one day a-huntin'. I were skinnin' my eyes fur old bucks, with
my head up, not thinkin' about sarpunts, when, by Zucks! I cum

right plum upon one uv the curiousest snakes I uver seen in all my borned days.

"Fur a spell I were spellbound in three foot uv it. There it lay on the side uv a steep presserpis, at full length, ten foot long, its tail strait out, right up the presserpis, head big as a sasser, right toards me, eyes red as forked lightnin', lickin' out his forked tongue, and I could no more move than the Ball Rock on Fisher's Peak. But when I seen the stinger in his tail, six inches long and sharp as a needle, stickin' out like a cock's spur, I thought I'd a drapped in my tracks. I'd ruther a had uvry coachwhip on Round Hill arter me en full chase than to a bin in that drefful siteation.

"Thar I stood, petterfied with relarm—couldn't budge a peg—couldn't even take old Bucksmasher off uv my shoulder to shoot the infarnul thing. Nyther uv us moved nor bolted 'ur eyes fur fifteen minits.

"At last, as good luck would have it, a rabbit run close by, and the snake turned its eyes to look what it were, and that broke the charm, and I jumped forty foot down the mounting, and dashed behind a big white oak five foot in diamatur. The snake he cotched the eend uv his tail in his mouth, he did, and come rollin' down the mounting arter me jist like a hoop, and jist as I landed behind the tree he struck t'other side with his stinger, and stuv it up, clean to his tail, smack in the tree. He were fast.

"Of all the hissin' and blowin' that uver you hearn sense you seen daylight, it tuck the lead. Ef there'd a bin forty-nine forges all a-blowin' at once, it couldn't a beat it. He rared and charged, lapped round the tree, spread his mouf and grinned at me orful, puked and spit quarts an' quarts of green pisen at me, an' made the ar stink with his nasty breath.

"I seen thar were no time to lose; I cotched up old Bucksmasher from whar I'd dashed him down, and tried to shoot the tarnil thing; but he kep' sich a movin' about and sich a splutteration that I couldn't git a bead at his head, for I know'd it warn't wuth while to shoot him any whar else. So I kep' my distunce tell he wore hisself out, then I put a ball right between his eyes, and he gin up the ghost.

"Soon as he were dead I happened to look up inter the tree, and what do you think? Why, sir, it were dead as a herrin'; all the leaves was wilted like a fire had gone through its branches.

"I left the old feller with his stinger in the tree, thinkin' it were the best place fur him, and moseyed home, 'tarmined not to go out agin soon.

"Now folks may talk as they please 'bout there bein' no sich things as horn-snakes, but what I've seen I've seen, and what I've jist norated is true as the third uv Mathy.

"I mout add that I passed that tree three weeks arterwards, and the leaves and the whole tree was dead as a door-nail."

—*Fisher's River (North Carolina) Scenes and Characters* (1859)

THE DRAM TREE
AT THE MOUTH OF THE CAPE FEAR

James Sprunt

Looking ahead to the farthest point in view, we distinguish an object, the passing of which was signalized in "ye olden time" by the popping of corks or by other demonstration of a convivial nature. It is an old cypress tree, moss-covered and battered by the storms of centuries. Like a grim sentinel, it stands to warn the out-going mariner that his voyage has begun, and to welcome the in-coming storm-tossed sailor to the quiet harbor beyond. Its name is significant. It is called the Dram Tree, and it has borne this name for more than a hundred years.

—*Tales and Traditions of the Lower Cape Fear* (1896)

TOM DULA

[This folk ballad is based on the murder of Laura Foster by Tom Dula, with the assistance of Ann Melton, in Wilkes County, May, 1866.]

> Hang down your head, Tom Dula,
> Hang down your head and cry;
> You killed poor Laura Foster
> And now you're bound to die.
>
> You met her on the hill-top,
> And God Almighty knows,
> You met her on the hill-top
> And there you hid her clothes.
>
> You met her on the hill-top,
> You said she'd be your wife,
> You met her on the hill-top
> And there you took her life.

—*Frank C. Brown Collection of North Carolina Folklore,*
vol. II (1952)

THE DEVIL WAS REAL

William S. Powell

North Carolinians since the very earliest days, and the Indians before them, have been on strangely familiar terms with the Devil. His name appears in folk-tales and superstitions, in the names of places, and in plain honest-to-goodness "true stories." Hardly a community in the state is without a Devil's Racetrack, a Devil's Resting Place, a Devil's Courthouse, or at least a Devil's horse's hoofprint somewhere not too far off.

Tales of the great horned one have frightened children for centuries and his appearance is so familiar to them that they often drew his picture when idly scribbling in their school books. And in North Carolina the Devil, himself, has appeared in the fields to people who had reason to be known to him. True, most of these personal appearances occurred a long time ago and the places named for him have stood for ages, but most folks wouldn't be at all surprised if he suddenly resumed his visits or left evidence of having camped in our midst or raced along our highways—surely in a speedy red convertible.

In the mountains the Cherokees discovered the location of the Devil's Courthouse and pointed it out to the white settlers who came into their midst. It is yet to be seen on the borders of Jackson and Macon counties where an immense precipice nearly a mile long and almost two thousand feet high curves in something like a half-circle shape. Part way up the side of the cliff is an opening where the throne of the Author of Evil will sit and where he will judge all bad spirits and pronounce their doom.

Not so far away from his courthouse the Devil had a favorite resting place, according to the Cherokees. The numerous scattered treeless tracts atop the mountains were his footprints, they reasoned, but in one especially large spot which they called the Devil's Old Field was found his choice napping spot. Once, on a hot summer day, a party of irreverent Indians, rambling through the dense forests of balsam and rhododendrons, suddenly came into the edge of this open ground and with their noisy chatter awoke His Majesty from a deep sleep. He was irritated, of course, and must have revenge. He immediately assumed the form of a giant serpent and swallowed fifty of the Indians before they could scramble back into the thickets. Forever afterwards the Cherokees refused to go near the Devil's nap site.

At least two natural formations in North Carolina have been named because of a resemblance, real or fancied, to the Devil.

On a ledge on the side of a mountain near Chimney Rock a large granite boulder is perched. It has long been known as the Devil's Head because it looks so much like traditional illustrations of Satan. In Burke County near Linville River is a perpendicular mass of rock some sixty feet high and about twenty feet in diameter topped by a large flat stone so placed on its pedestal that it looks as if it surely will fall on the next person who passes by. This has been called the Devil's Cap for a great many years.

In Chatham County about ten miles from Siler City it is possible to see the Devil's Tramping Ground. This is a circular path about forty feet in diameter where the Devil is said to go at night to pace round and round as he thinks up evil and mischief for mankind. Nothing grows in the path, which is about a foot wide; and sticks and stones placed in it mysteriously disappear over night. Various explanations have been offered for this strange sight, but none of them ever completely satisfies the people who have known about it all their lives and heard the story of the Devil's nocturnal walks there from their parents and grandparents.

On the highway from Smithfield to Clinton just across the Sampson County line is a stretch of road once widely known as the Devil's Racetrack. It seems that the local folks used to race their horses there on Sunday afternoons and by gradually eliminating the slower horses and less skillful riders were about to select the champion. Everything was in readiness for the final test and just as horses and riders began the race a mysterious stranger in a black flowing cape on a dark horse galloped from behind the crowd and onto the track. Although the racing horses were already well ahead he easily overtook them and sped on down the road past the end of the prescribed course and out of sight. All the witnesses were so amazed and astonished at this performance, to say nothing of their fright at the sudden and strange appearance of this rider who was almost instantly recognized as the Devil, that they never again raced there on Sunday or any other day.

The Devil seems to have made numerous appearances in North Carolina. There are some, of course, who maintain that he is constantly present and tempting poor weak mortals in various ways.

But sometimes he assumes a bolder form and has been recognized instantly as the Evil Being that he is.

Not so many years ago a not-so-good husband died in the Smoky Mountains. He may have been a good provider, but his wife wasn't exactly sad to see him go. She knew where he went, too, since she actually saw the Devil drive up to the house in a jet-black cart pulled by equally black oxen. The cart was empty when he drove up but when he left he was carrying a big black ball which the unfortunate wife instantly recognized as her departed husband's soul.

Another woman in the same region who was having difficulties of another sort with her husband was also paid a visit by the Devil who, this time, brought along Mrs. Devil and some of the Little Ones. They simply took over her home and made themselves perfectly comfortable. The wife who witnessed all this declared afterwards that she was wide awake the whole time and even lighted one torch after another to see everything the Devil and his family did while they were in her home. It was not long after this episode that her husband left her for the charms of a near-by widow. It was the Devil, she declared, who had come between her and her husband.

All of these accounts of the appearance of the Devil have something of the nature of a tall-tale about them, but there is one report of his appearance which has every mark of being true.

In June, 1785, the Rev. William Glendinning of Brunswick County, Virginia, was visiting and preaching in central North Carolina. At one time in November he was staying in the home of Leonard Smith but later went to the home of John Hargrove, about five miles away. This was in Granville and Halifax counties.

One night several of Hargrove's neighbors came to see the Rev. Mr. Glendinning and he told them that "Lucifer" would be there that night. He had no sooner uttered the words than there was a loud rap at the door. All of this Glendinning reported in his autobiography which was published in Philadelphia in 1795. A copy of this rare little book may be seen in the University of North Carolina Library.

When the door was opened Preacher Glendinning saw the

Devil's face! "It was black as any coal—his eyes and mouth as red as blood," he said, "and long white teeth gnashing together. I shut the door, and in a little time he went off: and some present then observed that they never heard it blow and rain harder.

"For some weeks Lucifer would appear two or three times a week, in the course of that winter; either in the evening, or before the family went to bed. One night before the family went to bed, I was in the house with them lying on a bed, and he then made his appearance, by the window, where I was lying. And he spoke and said in derision, 'O, that there was but mercy for the wretch that blasphemes the Holy One of Israel.' Some that were present said that it was a man's voice: But I told them it was Lucifer's, and that he was mocking of me in it. He repeated the same words a second time, and then went away, and for some months did not appear again.

"One day, as I was in the fields, near the house, in the greatest rack of misery—loudly belching out most horrid blasphemies, the children of the family came to drive me farther from the house, on account of my language. They drove me but a little way, when Lucifer appeared to view, at a distance from us. He made towards us, then turned toward the spring branch, and disappeared. It was about noon when he appeared, and the first time I ever saw him in daylight. He appeared upward of five feet high, round the top of his head there seemed a ridge; some distance under the top of his head there seemed a bulk, like a body, but bigger than any person; about 15 or 18 inches from the ground there appeared something like legs, and under them, feet; but no arms or thighs. The whole as black as any coal; only his mouth and eyes as red as blood. When he moved, it was as an armful of chains rattling together. Several of the family were present—they declared they saw it, and said they never beheld the like in their life.

"Frequently, during the summer, in the year 1786, and for near two years after, he would appear. For the most part, he made his appearance in the fore-part of the day. He would often stand in the orchard, near my cabin, and shoot out of his head something like a horn, about six or eight inches high, above the top of his head. Sometimes he would come up to my cabin, and frequently he would be on one side of the roof, or the other, and seem as if he would tear it to pieces. I would at such times, run from my cabin and fly into the house, where the white family was. He would follow me into the house, where they were, and from one room to another. I would beg of some of the family then to stand by me, and would loudly mention the name of the LORD to him, crying out, 'The Christians' God, rebuke thee, The God of Abraham, rebuke thee, God of the Prophets, banish thee, in the name of the Father, Son, and Holy Spirit, thou fallen angel disappear.' At this, he would stand trembling, while the balls of fire would be flaming out of his eyes. But he could never stand long; when I mentioned that sacred name he would draw back to some distance, and then disappear, as quick as lightning. Frequently, some of the family would then say, they saw him go off like a gust.

"One day, coming from out of the fields to my cabin, it being in the afternoon, I had a small stream of water to cross, at a little distance from the house. When I had got some distance from the brook, I saw a large black appearance, about a hundred yards from me. At first, I thought it was one Argil Hanks, son-in-law to the family and supposed he had wrapped himself up in a dark-colored great coat, in order to frighten me. I went near him, and said, 'Argil, it can answer you no end, for you to attempt to scare me.' He then began to move, and I then saw it was Lucifer; the balls of fire came flaming out of his eyes, his chains rattling, and then he appeared like a four-footed beast, as large as a calf of a year old, and seemed to have large wings. He followed me some distance towards the house, then stopped in the field, for some time. While there he made the smoke to rise, like that of a chimney. Some of the family asked me if it was smoke he was raising. I told them it was dust he was eating, and the scriptures were fulfilling, that 'upon his belly he should go, and dust should he eat, all the days of his life.' After some time he went to the creek's side and disappeared.

"One day, I was in my cabin and, as usual then, in the greatest rack of misery, crying out of my miserable condition, and belching out my most horrid blasphemies, when two of the Mrs. Sims, in that neighborhood, and Mrs. Hargrove came to see me. I told them I was eternally damned, and added that Lucifer came after me, and that he might take me bodily down into the pit. Mrs. Leonard Sims said I only thought so, it could not be so. I appealed to Mrs. Hargrove, whether she had ever seen him come after me, or not. She said before them she could not deny but she had. Since my recovery, Mrs. Leonard Sims and I have conversed on this and she said that she perfectly remembered what then passed; and that Mrs. Hargrove did then say that which is above mentioned. Mrs. Sims is a woman that, I hope, lives in the fear of the Lord, and her character is much reputed in that neighborhood."

The poor Rev. Mr. Glendinning eventually recovered from the shock of these many visits from the Devil and later preached in North Carolina and Virginia as well as in Maryland and New York. He became a close friend of Bishop Asbury and was quite active in the early years of the Methodist Church.

—*News and Observer*, Raleigh (April 27, 1952)

FAMOUS NORTH CAROLINA TREES
A SURVEY OF THE LEGENDS

Christopher Crittenden

Writing history in terms of trees is a somewhat novel approach to the interpretation of the past, and yet such a method can be aptly applied in the case of every one of the older American states. There are trees under which famous men stopped to rest, trees under which public meetings were held, trees where duels were fought, trees under which treaties were signed, trees from the limbs of which men were hanged, and trees under which treasures were buried. The stories connected with most of these trees rest upon mere legend rather than upon reliable historical evidence; but this fact need not detract in the slightest from their romantic appeal—indeed, if anything, the lack of certain knowledge serves to enhance their romance and charm.

North Carolina has its full share of famous trees. Best known of all is probably the Davie Poplar on the campus of the University of North Carolina, but there are many others, stretching from the coast to the mountains and representing every period of the state's history. Most of them are oaks, but there are also several cypresses and at least one pine, one poplar, and one persimmon.

Let us begin with the Eagle Nest Pine, which represents the first English Colony in the New World. The settlers sent out during the reign of Queen Elizabeth by Sir Walter Raleigh, favorite of the Queen, came to Roanoke Island, within the present borders of Dare County. There Eleanor Dare, wife of Ananias Dare, gave birth to a daughter, Virginia, first child born of English parents in the New World. The settlement mysteriously disappeared, and today we know it as the "Lost Colony." When John White, governor of the colony and grandfather of Virginia Dare, returned after several years' absence, he found the settlers gone and the word "CROATOAN" carved on a post and the letter "C" cut on a tree, indicating supposedly that they had gone to live with the Croatan Indians, who made their home nearby. What their fate was, we will probably never certainly know, but today there stands at the edge of Fort Raleigh an old tree, known as the Eagle Nest Pine, which is said to be the very tree on which the letter "C" was cut.

One would naturally expect that the historic town of New Bern would have a noted tree—and so indeed it has. Just off Chance Street, on the banks of the Neuse River, is a very old cypress under which the first vessel built in North Carolina is said to have been constructed and launched; under which the early colonists were reputed to have signed treaties with the Indians; under which General Nathanael Greene and other notables are reported to have made speeches; and under which George Washington and others are said to have rested.

In the town of Hertford, on the west side of United States Highway 17, are two cypress trees under which William Edmundson and George Fox, both members of the Society of Friends, are declared to have held the first religious services in North Carolina.

Teach's Oak, in the town of Oriental, takes us back to the days of our notorious pirate, Blackbeard, or Teach. Treasure is rumored to have been buried beneath its roots, and the ground all around reputedly has been dug up by treasure hunters.

Far to the westward, on the Robinson plantation in Catawba County, is an oak which stood at the home place of Henry Weidner, thought to have been the first settler in the area which later became Catawba County. The story is told that, once Weidner and his family were driven away by the Indians, an understanding was made with a friendly redskin to keep one side of the tree painted red as long as it was dangerous for them to return, and that in this way the family escaped harm.

At Guilford College, standing in the graveyard of the old Friends' meeting house, is the Liberty or Revolutionary Oak, under which are said to be buried twenty-six soldiers of the Revolution. The spot is marked by a tablet.

Standing in the town of Wilkesboro is the famous Tory Oak, on which Colonel Benjamin Cleveland is said to have had five Tories hanged. The tree is very old and is in bad condition, but is protected by a fence.

Guilford Battleground, near Greensboro, boasts two famous trees. There is the Battleground Oak, to which General Greene is thought to have tied his horse during his important battle with Lord Cornwallis. The twisted top of the tree today is said to prove that the horse ate out the top of what was then a young sapling. There stands also a fine old persimmon tree, two and one-half feet in diameter, on the very spot where Lord Cornwallis had a gray horse shot from under him.

There is, of course, a Washington Oak. It is on North Carolina Highway 30, fifteen miles east of the city of Wilmington. Here the Father of his Country is said to have rested his horse on his Southern tour of 1791. Its branches arch over the highway, and nearby is a tablet placed by the Daughters of the American Revolution.

And there is the Davie Poplar, referred to above. Here in 1792

William Richardson Davie, "father of the University," is reported to have sat while he wrote his description of the site chosen for the University. Though obviously of an advanced age, the tree is still standing. Nearby is a small poplar, rooted from a shoot of the original, which will become known as the Davie Poplar when the parent tree is no more.

And in the northern part of the city of Raleigh is the well-known Henry Clay Oak. Under its branches in 1844 reputedly sat the dashing Clay when he wrote his far-reaching "Raleigh Letter," opposing the annexation of Texas, and perhaps costing him the presidency, for which he was then a candidate.

Near North Carolina Highway 200, seven miles southwest of Monroe, is the Richardson Oak. It is said that Edward Richardson, Revolutionary hero, was about to be hanged from this tree by a group of sixteen Tories when he was rescued by a band of Whigs summoned by his young wife, Sally. Tradition adds that the Tories were then lined up and shot, one by one, by their former prisoner. It is said, too, that they were buried in one grave. Today, sad to relate, the oak is dying.

These and many other famous old trees stand within the borders of North Carolina. Each has its own past, each its own story to tell. We can but wish that the voice of the wind, as it sighs through their moss-grown boughs, could speak our language and tell us what happened underneath in years gone by.

—Booklet Accompanying Garden Club Map of North Carolina
(1937)

MAGIC IN THE MOUNTAINS

Manly Wade Wellman

Early in America's history, the most venturesome colonists headed into mountain country. Their remembered old ballads, their quaint and forceful idiom, their special morals and manners, suggest to scholars a survival of Elizabethan days and ways. Among the importations from the old, old country came a steadfast credulity about black art, as defined by churchmen and condemned by courts. That old-country belief mingled with the myths and faiths of the Cherokee Indians, and once it ruled the minds of the people. To doubt it was to be exceptional. That modern realism and sophistication would destroy this lore of the shadows is to be expected; that some of it still remains in the coves and hollows and along the side trails is testimony to its vigor.

New England wavered from witchcraft within a generation after the deplorable Salem hysteria in 1692, but the twentieth century dawned with "wise women" and "witch doctors" still enjoying respect and profit in Burke, Buncombe and Yancey counties. A few of them still exist and ply their trade, not openly as a generation ago, but they are there.

There is more than a century's echo of names and events. When Charlie Silver was murdered in the 1830's, his father sought out a sorcerer to help trace the guilty one; and Wilkes County folks still tell that Satan came in person for Ann Melton, the sorceress who helped Tom Dula kill Laura Foster. As early as 1799, North Carolina's doctors began to agitate for laws to punish those who claimed occult healing powers, and the witches laughed at them.

More recently, the laughter has faded away. Tom Peete Cross, gathering material for his *Witchcraft in North Carolina*, published in 1919, found mountain people slow to talk. Yet Sam Guy, of Zionville, pointed out his neighbor Eph Tucker as one who wanted to sell his soul to the devil and who was badly frightened by what happened when he began to say the words of the requisite spell. And in the 1930's, when Alberta Pierson Hannum came to teach school at Crossnore in Avery County, she heard about witchcraft from her pupils and their parents.

"My Aunt May died," volunteered a girl of her class. "She got spelled and fitified. . . . The old witch on yon side of the mountain done hit."

Nor were such tales confined to the dwellers in remote hollows. A housewife in a mountain town, "thoroughly intelligent, with a quick sense of humor," told Mrs. Hannum how to kill a witch by firing a silver bullet through her picture. Such persons are apt to disavow personal belief; but they tell the tales.

Just one thing about those tales. If you're listening, don't smile. Because the tale-teller shuts up, quickly.

Even those who would scorn or shiver to be called witches are ready with "home remedies" of wild herbs and plants. Indian medicine men taught the first settlers to observe the shapes of plants. "Look for an herb the same shape as the organ you want to cure," a mountain woman told Muriel Sheppard, author of *Cabins in the Laurel*. Thus, a broth of moss to rub on for baldness. Heart-shaped mint leaves for heart ailments. Pine kernels for toothache. It has been noted that a full third of the Indian medicine plants are regarded as beneficial by *United States Pharmacopeia*. "They went to the woods for them," sums up Mrs. Hannum. "We buy them over the counter."

North Carolina has not been without its tales of werewolves, enchanters who turn into animals to kill enemies or destroy their cows and pigs. The last wolf has been hunted out of the Smokies, which may explain why today's witches are said to turn into owls, cats and dogs. Silver bullets are good against them in their beastshapes, say the wise men and women; but an ordinary bullet will bounce right back at you.

Within the past two years, a Rutherford County witch doctor was said to be practising magic with the aid of a book called *Long Lost Friend*, which is now and then brought south from among the hex-conscious Pennsylvania Dutch. A copy of this curious work, lent by Pinebluff's venerable scholar, Levi Packard, claims to be a talisman in itself. If you carry it in your pocket, you cannot "drowned in any water, nor burn up in any fire." It is full of recipes for cures—for hysterics, worms, bleeding wounds, whooping cough, various ailments of horses and cattle, and so on. It also teaches you to lure fish to your hook (bathe your hands in hemlock water), to win a lawsuit (write the names of the twelve apostles on sage leaves and put them in your shoes), and to make a thief return stolen goods (bend down a juniper tree and weight it with a stone, with the skull of a "malefactor" beneath). It is hard to think that anyone would want to get rid of a book so crammed with useful knowledge; but, should the need arise, you can dispose of it only by burying it in a grave and saying a prayer, as at a funeral.

Even world-wide superstitions have their special mountain interpretations. In 1952, a Virginia doctor, wandering lonely, high trails near Hendersonville, came upon a man nailing a horseshoe over his door.

"That's for good luck, isn't it?" asked the doctor.

"Not exactly," replied the other. "But if you've got a horseshoe over the door, and you do something that brings a witch after you—well, they see the horseshoe, and some way they reckon you're not at home."

With kindly feelings toward all such superstitions, Muriel Sheppard wrote: "Where does today begin in the hills, when yesterday has not yet left off?" But that was before World War II, which changed the world, even the world of the North Carolina mountains.

A great many young mountain men went to that war, and a great many others of their kin sought the cities and defense industries. These have come back with a good freight of skepticism. The oldest folks still like to tell stories, and children still like to listen. However, listening isn't believing.

"Shucks, no," said a young farmer in Buncombe County early this year. "I don't put any weight in those ideas any more. Thirteen at a table, black cats across your path, the like of that—I don't study them at all. I'm not superstitious."

"Have you stopped planting by the moon?" he was asked.

"Now hold on—that planting by the moon ain't superstition. That's scientific fact."

—*The State* (April 10, 1954)

THE WHANG DOODLE

Alex White

Until I was a growed-up man I'd kite out like a rabbit in the tall grass if anybody so much as mentioned a Whang Doodle in my hearin'. Even now, when a body says anythin' 'bout one of them critters, my skin begins to crinkle up, and seems like I cain't keep my eyeballs from rollin'.

I ain't sayin' I ever met a Whang Doodle face to face, and I don't know as I can tell 'zactly what one looks like, but I come up on one of the varmints oncet and that's enough for me. All I seed was a big flash of gray fur, and a pair of green eyes with lightnin' in 'em, making the awfulest yowl I ever heered—but that's gettin' ahead some, I reckon.

I was jes a shirt-tail boy, this winter I'm tellin' 'bout, and I had toted in a pile of lightwood, and the chimbley jamb was heaped with logs what me and pappy'd cut in the atternoon, and it seem nice and cozy 'round the blazin' hearth, and I's thinkin' to myself, a boy's lucky what's got a good pappy and a good mammy, and a little kid brother, and good rations to eat, and a place to sleep, and a nice fire on a cold night.

Sure seem nice! Pappy was a-settin' afore the fire borin' out corncobs and fixin' hisself some new pipes. Mammy was a-burnin' a hole through the pith of some fig stems with a red-hot darnin' needle for the pipe stems. Smelt powerful good, them burnin' fig stems! Ever oncet in a while mammy'd stoop over and heat the needle in the embers. First the needle'd be black; then when mammy fotches it outen the fire it's red-hot and glowin'.

Pappy look over at mammy, and he grin, and say, "That-air needle look jes like the Whang Doodle's tongue; dog ef it don't."

Mammy, she look up quick and say, "What you tryin' to do— skeer these chillun into fits with you brash talk 'bout that varmint? Better be puttin' you thoughts 'longside with the Good Book and talkin' that kinda talk 'stead such foolishment as you talkin' now." She jerked the needle outen the fire, and when it was cool she lay it on the fireboard. She still a-scowlin' at pappy, but he not worried much 'bout mammy's scoldin'. He jes rare back in his cheer, and he shet his eyes tight, and he sing:

> Whang Doodle holler, and Whang Doodle squall,
> Look out, chillun, do he git you all.

Mammy she stop what she a-doin', and she say, "I bet iffen you don't shet you mouth like I done tole you, I'se gwine to up and bash you a good'un with this yere long-handle spider."

Pappy sort of settle down atter that. He know not to rile mammy too fur, do she bash him one sure 'nuff, like she say she will. Mammy she say, "Time you chillun git off to bed, anyhow. Moe, you git me them cardin' boards and lemme give yo'all's hair a good combin'. You sure a passel of nappy haids." When mammy gits through with Jim Baby and come my time, seem like she goin' right down to my brains. Then she say, "Yo'll wash you foots, and mind you washes 'em good, and git on off to bed."

Me and Jim Baby sleeps in the shed room where mammy keeps her strings of leather britches and hot peppers. They was hung from the rafters, and the light shinin' in from the hearth makes big shadders on the wall, a-jigglin' and a-jumpin' like spooks and hants. Jim Baby wake up and see them shadders a-traipsin' on the wall, and he grob me and say, "Moe, you reckon that's the ole Whang Doodle a-dancin'?" And I say, "Jim boy, no, them's not the Whang Doodle, them's jes shadders on the wall."

Long atter us chilluns is in bed, I's layin' awake. Seem like I jes cain't git to sleep, thinkin' 'bout that ole Whang Doodle, what pappy done tole 'bout. I 'members what Pete Bunker say,

> The Whang Doodle moaneth
> And the Doodle Bug whineth,

and I feels the goose bumps jes risin'. I slides over clost to Jim Baby, 'cause I's skeered. He holler, in his sleep, "Look out, Moe, how you scrougin' me. I's sleepy and wants you to leave me be."

I lay there, as I say, a long time, thinkin' 'bout that critter whut nobody cain't see. Pappy and mammy is a-snorin' in they bed, and it was so quiet you can hear the mice a-squeakin' and ole Dan a-scratchin' fleas under the house. It was jes one of them black-dark nights, and I keep a-wishin' I can go to sleep so's I can forgit how skeered I is.

All to oncet, out of the quiet, and seem like way off, I hears a long scream: "Ye-e-e-ow-ow-ow."

I jumps right outen the bed, and helt my breaf, and say, "Dear Lawd, look atter me and mine."

Nothin' don't happen for a spell. Ever'thing is still and quiet. Ole Dan quits a-scratchin' his fleas and the mice quit a-runnin' 'round. Then, seem like right down by the hawg lot, come that scream agin.

You never heered sech a scatterment in all you born days. I shakes and trembles. I thinks I shorely die. Pappy, he wake up, and go lookin' for his goose gun. Mammy, she wake up and gits the lantern lit.

The hawgs is a-screamin' fitten to kill, and pappy tell to me, "Moe, you git up and hustle. Somethin' is a-gittin' the hawgs."

Iffen I'd-a-had my way, I'd snuggle down in the bed and pull the civers over my haid. I know iffen I don't come out, pappy come in there and jerk me out, so I pulls on my pants, and foller him, so trembly I cain't hardly stand on my laigs.

Pappy he goes ahead with the gun, and mammy she follers with the lantern, holdin' it up high. I come behind mammy, holdin' to the battlin' board, but I reckon I couldn't hit a flea with it, I's shakin' so bad. Time we gits down the path a piece here comes Jim Baby, cryin' and hollerin', "Wait for me, wait for me—I's skeered." He brung up the rear.

We cropt, single file, 'round the wash house, 'round the spring house, past the branch, and to'rds the hawg pen. The hawgs is a-carryin' on something terrible, screamin' like's if all they throats is being cut.

Jes then the light from mammy's lantern ketched the varmint's eyeballs, and I see them big balls of green fire inside the hawg pen. Pappy raises up the ole gun, and fires, and it sounds like the roar of the heavenly cannon. The old gun kick pappy, and he tumbled back on mammy. Mammy, she drap the lantern and falls down, and seem like my laigs jes fold up and I's a-layin' on the ground, too. Jim Baby, he takes to his heels and lights out fer the house, yellerin' and bawlin' hard as he can.

That ole critter skins over the fence of the hawg pen, and I catches a glimpse of him. He looks like he as long as a cow, as high as a goat, and got big ears like a mule. He look like a pinter, but he ain't no pinter. He all gray, and woolly. He take one big jump to'rds the woods, and he lets out his yell: "Ye-e-e-ow-ow-ow."

Pappy gits to his foots and grobs me by the scruff of the neck and he say, "Godamighty, boy, run fer the house. Yonder goes the Whang Doodle."

Mammy ran, and pappy ran, and I ran, and we gits in the house, all out of breaf, and Jim Baby he already in there, hidin' in the bed with all the civers pulled up over him. Pappy pulls the door shet and bolts it tight.

Man, I don't never want to see no more Whang Doodle, no suh, ne-ver.

—*Bundle of Troubles and Other Tarheel Tales* (1943),
ed. W. C. Hendricks

NEW YEAR SHOOTERS

The crash of muskets and an ancient chant will usher in the New Year once more in the Gaston County community of Cherryville.

The ceremony that is revived annually began here about 150 years ago. Some say it originated in Germany hundreds of years ago.

Two groups of shooters will shoulder their muskets and make the rounds on homes beginning at midnight and continuing until late in the afternoon of New Year's Day.

At each stop, the muskets will boom. And it probably will be

Uncle A. Sidney Beam, or Peter Saine, who will start the chant with these words:

> Good morning to you, sir.
> We wish you a happy New Year.
> Good health, long life,
> Which God may bestow as long as you stay here. . . .

Both Beam and Saine are in their mid-80's. They joined the ranks of shooters before the turn of the century.

Neither Beam nor Saine is able to make the full round, but both are always on hand at midnight for the start of the festivities.

After the shooting and chanting, the shooters have a bite to eat before moving on to the next stop.

Cherryville is one of the few communities, if not the only one, in which the ancient custom is continued.

—*News and Observer*, Raleigh (December 30, 1958)

PEAS ON NEW YEAR'S DAY

Wellborn Cook

Concerning the origin of the custom of eating peas and hog jowl on New Year's Day, I had always heard from my father that this custom originated in the South after the Civil War. The peas and pork symbolized a hope for peace and prosperity in the coming year. This explanation had been given to my father by my grandfather, who fought in the Battle of Atlanta. The people in the South certainly had cause to hope for peace and prosperity after the ravages of the war and Sherman's march to the sea. I can remember hearing the story told in our family of how the people had to boil the dirt from the smoke house floor to obtain salt.

There are probably a number of explanations regarding the origin of this custom, and I have no way of knowing if the above explanation is the correct one.

—*The State* (April 1, 1961)

HAUNTED HOUSES

E. P. Holmes

THE HAW HOUSE

Since Revolutionary War days the old Haw Place at Hillsboro has had nightly visits from a ghost. At exactly midnight the ghost moves up and down the steep staircase with a rumbling noise.

Though many traps have been set to catch this ghost, it still operates nightly. Some ten years ago the house was entirely renovated and brick-veneered, and many thought that would be the end of the ghost. But it wasn't. The haunt still operates on schedule—thus proving that it takes more than brick veneer to keep a ghost out.

ENGLESIDE

This mansion was built in Lincoln County by order of Peter Forney (a hero of the Battle of Guilford Courthouse), whose beautiful young wife wanted a show place for a home.

Tradition says that it was built mostly by slave labor, and that an unruly slave was murdered by the overseer and buried in the third pillar from the left.

It is impossible to make white cement stick to this pillar for any length of time. And they say if you place your ear against the pillar and listen closely, you can hear the ghost of the unfortunate man threshing around in his walled-up tomb.

The Carnes Mansion

The famous "Carnes Ghost" operates in the old Carnes Mansion on the road to South Carolina between Kings Mountain and Grover.

Great efforts were made to stop the clanging and the clattering of this midnight visitor, but to no avail. Mrs. Elizabeth Carnes and her twin daughters, Clarissa and Priscilla, even went so far as to hire an Englishman by the name of Edgar Ellege, who claimed to be a professional ghost-catcher. Though Ellege lived in the home for some six weeks, a few months after Mr. Carnes' death, he was unable to get a glimpse of this haunt. But he heard it everywhere in the house, especially around midnight hours.

Finally the house was abandoned, and today it's just a shell. Souvenir hunters have carried away practically all of the woodwork and movable parts around the house.

This is one ghost that really ran everything off the place and took full charge.

The Burris House

The town of Rockford, once the Surry County seat, dates back to pre-Revolutionary days. In its old courthouse (now a home), English judges once presided, and it was here that Andrew Jackson came as a young man to practice law.

Jackson boarded at the old Burris House that was for many years a tavern. For months he went daily across the river to Judge Tate's Law School.

Many oldtimers—and present-day folks, too—tell that, on dark, windy, rainy nights, they have seen "Old Hickory" charging up and down the front veranda of the house with his long white hair flying in the wind and his clanking sword swaying from side to side.

The Roberson Home

White Oak is a little settlement in Bladen County on the banks of the Cape Fear River. About a mile from where the Tar Heel ferry crosses the river is a tumbling-down antebellum Southern mansion. Here and there one can discern a roof or a chimney that shows a trace of its fast-departing grandeur. It is known as the Old Roberson Place.

In the early 1780's Cornwallis and his retinue of officers drove up in the home's front yard and demanded lodging for the night.

As Colonel Roberson was then stationed in South Carolina near Cowpens with General Greene, Mrs. Roberson had no choice but to offer her hospitality, such as it was.

The general and his officers, after a hearty dinner prepared by Negroes on the place, immediately closeted themselves in an upstairs bedroom to map out future campaigns. While they were in conference, Mrs. Roberson spied on them. Then she sent a faithful servant named Old Jobe with the valuable information to her husband and General Greene.

Today the house is only a shell; the huge chimney bears enormous cracks. Everything is gone—but Old Jobe.

Tradition has kept him there all these years. He is seen—so they say—all around the place, resting under the huge water oaks or roaming the river banks near the house. On dark and stormy nights he has been seen standing by one of the upstairs windows peering out at the storm.

The Cabin's Silver Tree

Many folks in Randolph County always thought the cabin near Parks Crossroads was haunted. Weird tales have been told about this log cabin which is overshadowed by a big dead oak.

However, around the turn of the century, this tree was chopped down and 2,500 silver dollars rolled out of its hollow interior. The "ghost" disappeared entirely. The haunted-house tales were circulated to keep inquisitive folks away from this horde of silver money.

—*Journal and Sentinel*, Winston-Salem (October 31, 1954)

DETECTING A MURDERER

John Harden

There is an old superstition that the wounds of a murdered man will bleed again after death if his body is touched by the murderer. It was by this means that the victim in a well-known Eastern North Carolina murder case pointed an accusing finger several years ago.

A prominent farmer had been brutally slain early one morning. There was no trace of the murderer and no clue as to why the crime had been committed. And then came this interesting turn of events: In preparation for the customary country wake that was to follow, neighbors gathered and administered to the body. Things were following the customary pattern for such occasions until a certain man touched the corpse. When he did so, the wounds bled eloquently and spoke a ghostly conviction to those who were watching. But it was not a conviction that would stand up in court, and the murder—save in the minds of a few who bank their judgment on superstition—remains unsolved to this day.

—*Tar Heel Ghosts* (1954)

LOCAL SUPERSTITIONS

compiled by Joseph D. Clark

The seventh daughter of the seventh daughter is psychic.

Step on a crack and it will break your mother's back. Step on seven straight and it will mend her back.

A whistling girl and a crowing hen are sure to come to no good end.

If a baby moves first on the left side, it is a boy; if on the right, it is a girl.

Kiss a red-headed person and it will cure fever blisters.

If you bite your tongue as a bee or wasp approaches, the insect can't penetrate you.

Eat collard greens at New Year's to have paper money all year.

Eat blackeyed peas at New Year's to have pennies all year.

To dream of death is a sign of a birth.

If someone makes a mark across your path, it is bad luck to step across the mark.

Shaking hands with a crosseyed person is bad luck.

If a man comes to your house first on New Year's Day, you will have good luck. If a woman comes first, you will have bad luck.

Put money in the pocketbook when offering it as a gift.

If you turn a stray cat away from your door, you turn your good luck away.

If you get your belly wet while washing dishes, you will marry a drunkard.

If you walk over a new grave without walking back over it, you'll be next to die.

When it is raining and the sun is shining, the devil is beating his wife.

Roosters crow at midnight at Old Christmas.

Rain before seven, clear at eleven.

The number of foggy days in August is the number of snows during the winter.

Never cut firewood from trees which have been struck by lightning.

If you kill a frog, your cow's milk will turn to blood.

If a horse has one white leg, look at him; if he has two, try him; if he has three, buy him; and if he has four, leave him alone.

Bite a mule's ear to tame him.

A spotted pig has sour meat.

Plant cucumbers the first day of May before the sun rises.

A liver-shaped leaf is good for your liver.

If you stamp a white horse, you'll have good luck.

To get rid of a wart, rub a penny on it and throw the penny away. The person finding the penny will get the wart.

If the hem of your dress turns up, kiss it and you will get a new dress.

Moles on the neck mean money by the peck.

Corn thick with silks means cold weather.

It is bad luck to cross baseball bats.

If you go out of the house and forget something and have to return for it, sit down and cross your legs before leaving again.

A horse hair in water will turn to a snake.

Headless Hattie rides on the full of the moon.

—Excerpts from a much longer manuscript (1961)

WATER WITCHING

Brandt Ayers

An infant state agency must combat witchcraft and superstition as it plumbs the core of North Carolina in its quest for the miracle of water.

A mass of scientific data is being assembled by the Ground Water Division of the youthful Department of Water Resources to locate the underground preserves of this precious resource.

But intelligent North Carolinians, school superintendents, city officials, and industry presidents still seek advice from the practitioners of the occult craft of "water witching."

Through some unexplained power they still claim to be able to find water with birch, hickory, or peach twigs, coat hangers and mysterious black boxes.

These are the "diviners," "dousers," or "water-witches." They claim some magical bond with the earth which sets their forked twigs quivering and draws them irresistibly down, pointing to an unseen reservoir.

What is the State government's opinion of their gift? "Not much," says Harry M. Peek. Peek is probably the State's number-one ground-water geologist and chief of the Ground Water Division since it was established in November, 1959.

Probably the most widely known practicing water-witch is a man who came from another state. He uses a black box device, but has never revealed its contents.

One of their pseudo-scientific probes was described by a State official:

"They make everybody stand back about 100 feet and they put their box on the ground. It's about the size of an old automobile battery. After about 45 minutes of walking around the box consulting one another and moving the box around a little, they drive a stake in the ground. 'There's your water. Drill there,' he says."

Sometimes there is water. Sometimes it is much less than promised.

A few years ago the N. C. Well Drillers Association passed a resolution declaring that no member could drill the "witch" sites. The resolution still stands.

Two of the less successful ventures of a "water-witch" are well remembered by well-drillers.

An eastern North Carolina town hired a "witcher" to locate a water supply, ignoring recommendations of an engineering firm. For a $1,200 fee, he promised to get 600 gallons a minute. He got 16 gallons, enough for about three houses.

The second incident involved a manufacturing firm. The State geologist and a well-driller told the president he could find little water on his property. A "witcher" was hired, promising 200 gallons a minute. He found 40, according to the report.

Peek recalled one county superintendent of education who had consulted a "witcher" and called to say, "We already know where the water is, but we just wanted to hear what the scientific people have to say."

Dousers are unable to explain the power of their divining rods, but Peek and State Geologist Jasper Stuckey can. They explain it as a blend of psychology and muscular tension. A douser with a tight grip on his divining rod can only hold it steady so long, and if he believes he has a supernatural power he subconsciously helps it quiver and dip. Actually, they say, water is difficult to find, especially in the Piedmont sections, even with the most scientifically proved methods.

But they have found it in draws and valleys and have statistics to prove that it most likely appears there. Rocks under the Piedmont section are hard, crystalline formations where water is found mostly in underground cracks or faults. These are most likely to appear in draws and valleys.

They admit their methods are not infallible, but they say they can be trusted more surely than the clairvoyant geologists with their forked twigs.

Could a "water witch" be prosecuted? The Attorney General's office says it is unlikely. One assistant attorney general, Lucius Pullen, says no appellate court has ever made a decision in North Carolina against a "witcher" for obtaining money under false pretenses. A further check revealed that there have likely been no convictions on that charge in the entire country.

But Pullen pointed out an interesting statute in effect in Wake County and about 40 other counties. A diviner might be brought to trial under this provision which would make it unlawful to "Practice the arts of phrenology, palmistry, clairvoyance or fortune telling and other crafts of similar kind."

—*Raleigh Times* (March 23, 1961)

MOUNTAIN MEDICINE

Horton Cooper

The early *doctors* of the Carolina Appalachian Mountains were, as a rule, highly esteemed, for they had ideas. They *cooked up* things.

They had attended no medical or pharmacy schools, nor had any recognized authority issued them licenses or diplomas. But in the absence or scarcity of real physicians and druggists, they tried faithfully to make well again those who suffered from disease or hurt. Many of them succeeded remarkably well. Numerous patients recovered, while some were *tuck*, but everyone knew that, in the last analysis, death always won the final round.

The *doctors* flourished in the rural areas and small towns from the coming of the first settlers until after the turn of the century, but even now in scattered communities a few still attend the sick. Despite their serious lack of medical knowledge, they were the answer to the problem of illness and injury, childbirth and aching teeth in an isolated region where trained practitioners were not available.

Their kind did not originate in the mountains, for there were those from early colonial days in lowlands and among the hills who were relied upon in time of illness to relieve suffering. Society, wherever human beings lived, expected and demanded special knowledge of a few which could cope with the inevitable human ills as they came.

Trained physicians, surgeons and nurses came first to the Carolina lowlands, where population encouraged their practice with greater remuneration. Slowly home remedies and the formulas of the specially skilled were forgotten, while in the Appalachian Mountains, where existed the richest flora of the temperate zone outside of Japan, the many medicinal plants and the scarcity of real physicians created a situation which encouraged those who were medically inclined to experiment and learn how to be of service to their fellow citizens.

Long after trained physicians had established themselves miles apart, these old *doctors* did a thriving business, for they could be reached more quickly, their fees fitted the poor man's pocketbooks, many families were skeptical of *new-fangled* medicines and the old practitioners had earned reputations which continued to merit reliance when troubles came.

For many generations, every mountaineer was more or less his own physician in many illnesses, especially the minor ones. But relatively few had the time in which to accumulate an extensive knowledge of the curative properties of the many crude drugs that grew in abundance all about them; to mix and blend the ingredients of salves, tinctures and infusions; to learn the art of extracting aching teeth; and to learn the formulas, if available, for magic treatment.

There had to be specialists who devoted a great deal of their time to gathering and experimenting with the many crude drugs and who had the patience to produce pure medicines in their laboratories, consisting mainly of pots, pans, troughs and earthen jars. There had to be available storage space for the many crude drugs which would be turned into medicines. Anyone could treat a common cold, but few could recognize and treat pneumonia and the most dreaded diseases.

The virtue of decoctions, infusions, tinctures, distillations, salves and poultices was highly respected, and rightly so, for many *doctors* of the mountains produced some medicines which almost equalled in remedial principles those used by real physicians of the time in the largest cities of the Tar Heel lowlands. Despite this fact, the best available medicines then, as today, were unable to produce the results wished for and it was then that magic and witchcraft played their colorful parts in many cases.

There were those who called themselves *Old Indian Herb Doctors,* claiming that they had learned the virtues and preparation of crude drugs from the Indians. Most of them had never seen an Indian. Too, there were a few *Spanish Herb Doctors, Vegetable Doctors* and lots of *Neighborhood Herb Doctors.* All possessed a knowledge of simple remedies that were not without their value. Even the limited medical knowledge of these self-styled *doctors* plus the native crude drug preparations plus the willingness shown in a devotion to the alleviation of pain were unquestionably of great good when illness came and no other source of medical help was available.

The *doctors* had obtained their meager medical knowledge from various sources. A part of it had been handed down from father to son for many generations. Some of it consisted of Indian lore, a portion of it was the result of the trial and error method and much of it was a carry-over from a European setting.

Knowing some of the properties of medicine and that the action of a remedy upon the human system depends upon attributes peculiar to it, they used hot infusions of catnip, dog-fennel, ginger, boneset, sage, butterfly weed and snakeroot as sudorifics for producing sweating in the treatment of measles, colds, grippe and pneumonia. Yellow dock, mandrake, poke root, blood root and black cohosh were used as alternatives to tone up the system and establish a healthy condition. They made these into both decoctions and tinctures.

Some of them, at least, understood that alternatives may possess tonic, stimulant, laxative or diuretic properties all combined in one remedy and they combined them in various ways.

The last *Old Spanish Herb Doctor* to live in Avery County left the state around forty years ago, but while here he made anodynes to relieve pain by blunting the sensibility of the nerves from poppies grown in his lower garden, Deadly Nightshade from the fields, and the herb henbane. He used hops as a remedy for wakefulness; worm medicine was made from the seeds of the vermifuge plant, which had been introduced into the mountains by the early settlers; tonics were made from wild cherry bark and stone root; and queen's root and stillinga were for common colds.

As they became available, calomel, quinine and camphor were used extensively by most of the self-styled doctors in the treatment of various diseases.

The *Honey and Brandy Doctors* claimed to know the exact amounts of honey and brandy to be mixed, the size and timing of the doses, and the length of treatment required to cure a case of *milk sick* or *milk poison*.

This malady was caused by the use of milk, butter or flesh of an animal which had eaten a variety of white snakeroot herb when the pastures were low because of drought. The ailment caused nausea, vomiting, dizziness and extreme prostration as the disease progressed. Often death resulted.

None knew then what caused the illness and until Purdue University of Indiana discovered the origin it was thought that a poisonous dew or gas had settled upon the vegetation during late summer. So prevalent was this strange malady that a book was written calling it "the Great Scourge of the Appalachians." In most cases the patient recovered, because the honey and brandy treatment apparently had *killed* the poison, but physicians today declare that the remedy was not only valueless, but extremely dangerous.

Rheumatiz Doctors had many remedies, many of which could be administered by the patient or members of his family. Sometimes stones were heated, wrapped in cloths or pelts and applied in the aching joints. Often patients were advised to carry buckeyes in the pocket.

Occasionally the sufferer was made to carry a potato for months in the pocket, the cure coming after the potato had become *petrified*. Bee stings, snake poison and snake oil were administered by the *doctor*, but they had no real curative value beyond their psychological effect. The patient's joints were bathed for hours daily with vinegar and hot water or a mixture of lard and kerosene. Later, bracelets of copper wire were worn on the wrist.

The midwife, known as the *granny womern*, was one of the most indispensable persons of the community. She generally relied upon the practical knowledge gained over the years as a *helper*, but she was not averse to using odd remedies and magic formulas when she believed their use was justified.

To induce a quicker delivery, she held powdered tobacco leaves or snuff under the patient's nose to produce sneezing. This was known as *snuffing the patient*. She fumed and fretted when the birth was not occurring within a week before or after full-moon. Sometimes she placed an axe under the patient's bed *to cut the pains and time of delivery.*

She held herself in readiness to answer a call anywhere in her area, regardless of the hour, day or night, the distance or weather conditions. When possible, she rode horseback, but often she tramped rough paths over the mountains, waded creeks and rivers and sometimes used her own body as a bulldozer when encountering snowdrifts.

Occasionally she received money for her services, but more

often her fees were paid in such things as ginseng roots, cured pork, chickens, leather and the fruit of the loom. She expected nothing from the poorer families. In her fervor to serve her neighbors she was content in knowing that all she had *cotch* belonged to the rare breed of men who lived in the Appalachians of North Carolina and who would grow up to be tall in the sight of God.

Besides the business of catching babies, she was often consulted regarding simple remedies which other medics apparently had overlooked. She advised putting sulphur on a chronic sore, tying a yarn thread around a cracked toe, smearing a badly chapped thumb or finger with white pine *rosin* and using fresh cow dung to cure a boil. She treated *cramp colic*—probably gall bladder colic—with a decoction of dried tobacco stems. And she always kept a supply of *stalls*—cloth or leather protective shields or sheaths for sore fingers and thumbs.

The tooth-puller and the tooth-jumper were known as *Tooth Doctors*. Decayed and aching teeth were usually tolerated for a long time before most persons overcame their timidity sufficiently to have them extracted.

The pain was treated in the home by holding a bag of hot ashes on the jaw, holding cold water on the aching tooth for several minutes, plastering the cavity with snuff, smoking a corncob pipe filled with homemade tobacco until vomiting occurred, drinking a few snorts of *peartenin'* juice or picking the tooth with a splinter from a tree which had been struck by lightning. When neuralgia struck, *peartenin'* juice was sipped until one couldn't walk a crack in the floor.

When worse came to worst, either the tooth-puller or the tooth-jumper was visited for the tooth to be extracted. In either case the patient would be given two or three good drinks of brandy or whiskey and allowed to wait until the distilled spirits overcame the timidity of his own spirit.

If a tooth-puller was performing the rough work, the patient was made to lie upon the floor or ground, and the crude doctor of dental surgery knelt astride him, forceps in hand. Often the aching tooth was yanked out during what appeared to be a wrestling match as the determined tooth-puller performed the task allotted him.

The tooth-jumper was usually an expert who completed his job quickly. A hammer and a chisel about the size of a fairly large nail were used. The chisel was placed against the tooth, just under the edge of the gum, and it was given a sharp, quick tap, which caused the tooth to jump from its socket.

Sometimes accidents happened. The jawbone was fractured or the patient was hit on the nose or chin with the hammer, usually because he moved at the wrong time. Bleeding was stopped by packing salt in the vacancy left by the tooth or the gum was rinsed with a solution of tannic acid obtained by making a decoction of oak bark.

Those who were known as *Neighborhood Doctors* possessed some knowledge of the medicinal properties of a few crude drugs, held to beliefs in magic remedies and prescribed odd and strange *cures* for common diseases, especially of children. They measured a child suffering from phthisis with a whiteoak rod and placed the rod under the eaves of a house, prescribed sheep dung tea for measles and onion poultices for sore throat.

Usually there was only one person—commonly a woman—in each community who had *sufficient* faith to be a *Blood Doctor* and able to stop profuse bleeding from nose or cut by reading or reciting in a loud, clear and confident voice to the patient the sixth verse of the Sixteenth Chapter of Ezekiel. Strange to say, the bleeding usually stopped after this verse was recited three times. Sometimes it didn't; then crushed puffballs, spider webs and soot were applied. Cold compresses, applications of salt or ooze of oak bark and crushed green persimmons were used.

For warts, there were *Wart Doctors* who attempted to conjure away warts by reciting secret formulas in an inaudible voice while gently rubbing each wart. Neither they nor their patients knew that these tumorous growths usually disappear of their own accord within a short while. *Fire Doctors* were called into the homes to blow the fire from burns and scalds by blowing their breaths repeatedly upon the injured spot while thinking of a magic verse learned under oath from another fire-blower who was on his deathbed. *Thrush Doctors* were men who had never seen their fathers, and they blew their breaths three times into a baby's mouth to cure the thrush.

If no real *Thrush Doctors* were available, it was thought that the baby's drinking a few drops of water from the shoe of a blackeyed young man would work a cure. Seventh sons of seventh sons were *Cancer Doctors*, who attempted to cure cancers on the exterior of the body by rubbing them with their little fingers. *Madstone Doctors* attempted to cure hydrophobia and remove the venom from snakebites with a small porous stone called a madstone, said to have been taken from the gall bladder of a deer. *Corn and Bunion Doctors* trimmed corns and bunions with sharp knives very expertly and bathed them with liquids of strange names.

As knowledge spread and learning increased, the *Witch Doctor* slowly passed from the picture with the going of the witches. As far as the writer has been able to ascertain, the last one died in 1907.

In his day, the *Witch Doctor* was an exalted and very important personality, for it was he who was always ready to combat the wickedness of the witches of his area, either by removing their witchery on beast or human being, or by punishing them severely. He was very useful otherwise, for he taught the people how to avoid a witch's displeasure and vengeance; how they themselves might remove some of the minor witcheries; and he advised them that they could recognize the home of a witch by observing whether the sweep of the broom in that house was placed uppermost when it stood upright against the wall. He told others never to accuse a witch by name.

He himself never mentioned the name of a suspected witch when persons or livestock were reported as being *spelled*, but when the imagined offense was a major one he drew her picture on a chip with a piece of charcoal, placed it in the fork of a stooping white oak tree and shot it with a silver bullet.

The *Love Doctors* were never numerous, but they were scattered throughout the Appalachians. Like that of most of the other *Doctors*, their lore had originated outside the mountains and in many regions. They helped the forlorn in love by furnishing them Adam and Eve roots, John the Conqueror root, various love powders, and secret formulas to be recited at bedtime. They managed to obtain needles which had been used to sew burial clothes and sold them to unrequited male lovers to be stuck secretly into the shoes of their hearts' desires. They manufactured and sold *bewitching powder* to be sprinkled secretly upon the opposite sex.

The *Hex Doctors* were never numerous, but they used witchcraft a-plenty, mostly among the Negroes, for hexing almost anything. Their potions, it was believed, helped the buyers to lay burdens upon the hearts of their enemies, to win courtships, to help them understand the opposite sex, to escape the visitations of ghosts, and to be successful in various undertakings.

The *Horse Doctors,* some of them fair veterinarians, treated not only domestic livestock, but frequently human beings as well. They had *picked up* a limited knowledge of the simpler remedies, learned how to use splints and reset dislocations and they often performed operations on farm animals. They knew some of the properties of crude drugs. A seventeen-year-old youth once suffered a severe colic from eating several half-ripe apples and lay groaning in pain. Suddenly his father shouted to another son, "Sam is bad-off. Go and fetch the hoss doctor."

Although they lacked the *know-how* of the trained physician, the mountain *doctors* served their communities well. Even those who used magic formulas in an effort to cure were psychologically beneficial. All together these men and women who were so great a part of the social life of that day contributed much to the rich folklore of the Carolina Appalachians.

—*News and Observer,* Raleigh (March 27, 1960)

NOTES ON CONTRIBUTORS

NOTES ON CONTRIBUTORS

AVERY, ISAAC ERWIN, was city editor of the *Charlotte Observer* until his death in 1904.

AYERS, BRANDT, native of Anniston, Alabama, is the Washington correspondent of the Raleigh *News and Observer*.

BARLOWE, ARTHUR, was one of Sir Walter Raleigh's captains of the 1584 expedition to Roanoke Island.

BARRINGER, MARIA MASSEY, of Concord, wanted her book to correct Northern misconceptions about Southern cooking.

BELL, HOLLEY MACK, worked as a newspaperman in Charlotte, Windsor, and Greensboro before joining the U. S. Information Agency.

BELL, THELMA HARRINGTON, Detroit native now living at Sapphire with her artist-writer husband Corydon Bell, specializes in juvenile books.

BLYTHE, LEGETTE, lives in his native Huntersville and is author of more than a dozen books.

BOYD, JAMES, Southern Pines novelist who died in 1944, wrote *Drums* (1925).

BRAWLEY, JAMES S., of Salisbury, is particularly interested in the history of Rowan County.

BROCKMAN, ZOE KINCAID, poet and essayist, is on the staff of the *Gastonia Gazette*.

BURTON, W. C. ("Mutt"), Reidsville feature writer, has a column in the Sunday *Greensboro Daily News*.

BUTLER, BION H., newspaperman of Southern Pines, died in 1935.

BYRD, WILLIAM, diarist and aristocrat, rarely had a good word to say for the state south of his beloved Virginia.

BYRON, GEORGE GORDON, LORD, the English romantic poet, never visited America.

CARPENTER, UNCLE JAKE, kept a record of the deaths at Three-Mile Creek, Avery County.

CHAMBERLAIN, HOPE SUMMERELL, who lived in Raleigh from 1891 to 1926, died in 1960.

CLARK, JOSEPH D., professor of English at North Carolina State College, gathers much of his folklore material from students.

COKE, THOMAS, English missionary of Methodism, preached in North Carolina on several journeys to the state.

COOK, WELLBORN, Georgia native and graduate of Clemson College, is Charlotte district manager for a business firm.

COOPER, HORTON, folklorist and historian, is principal of the Minneapolis School in Avery County.

CRAYON, PORTE, is the pen name of David Hunter Strother, travel writer and artist from Virginia.

CREECY, RICHARD BENBURY, of Elizabeth City, published his *Grandfather's Tales* at the age of eighty-eight.

CRITTENDEN, CHRISTOPHER, director of the State Department of Archives and History in Raleigh, is normally a historian, very rarely a folklorist as in this book.

DANIELS, JONATHAN, editor of the Raleigh *News and Observer*, is a versatile writer of books.

DAVIS, BURKE, of Greensboro, has written several volumes on Civil War subjects.

DAVIS, CHESTER, newspaperman from Winston-Salem, has been much interested in Moravian lore and history.

DEDMOND, F. B., is head of the English Department at Gardner-Webb College in Cleveland County.

DOS PASSOS, JOHN, American novelist, inserted bits of biography into his *U. S. A.* as commentary on the lives of his fictional characters.

DUGGER, SHEPHERD M., whose *Balsam Groves* is a literary curiosity and delight, died at Banner Elk in 1938.

FLETCHER, INGLIS, author of the multivolume Carolina Series of historical novels, resides at Bandon Plantation in Chowan County.

FOWLER, MALCOLM, long-time resident of Harnett County, is an authority on the history of the Cape Fear River country.

FREEL, MARGARET WALKER, formerly of Andrews, is a county historian now living in Canton.

FRIES, ADELAIDE L., of Winston-Salem, wrote extensively in the field of Moravian history till her death in 1949.

GILL, EDWIN, native of Scotland County, has been State Treasurer since 1953.

GOERCH, CARL, Raleigh writer and speaker, still contributes regularly to *State* magazine, which he founded.

GOLDEN, HARRY, New Yorker who settled in Charlotte in 1942, is a journalist and biographer.

GREEN, PAUL, Pulitzer Prize dramatist from Harnett County, was for many years a teacher of philosophy at Chapel Hill.

GRIFFIN, EVELYN L., of Shawboro in Currituck County, is a genealogist.

HARDEN, JOHN, Greensboro businessman, has written books on North Carolina mysteries and ghosts.

HARIOT, THOMAS, whose *Brief and True Report* is the first book in English written in the New World, was with Sir Walter Raleigh's settlers on Roanoke Island in 1585.

HARRIS, BERNICE KELLY, novelist of Seaboard, grew up in Wake County and often writes about her childhood there.

HODGES, ED, is a Durham newspaperman and husband of columnist Betty Hodges.

HOLEMAN, FRANK, native of Raleigh, is Washington correspondent of the *New York Daily News*.

HOLMES, E. P., Charlotte feature writer and author of several books, died in 1961.

JOHNSON, CAPTAIN CHARLES, is very likely a pseudonym.

JOHNSON, GUION GRIFFIS, is a sociologist and clubwoman from Chapel Hill.

JOHNSON, L., was professor of mathematics at Trinity College in Randolph County.

JOHNSON, MILLIE, wife of Congressman W. J. Bryan Dorn of South Carolina, was from Coats and attended U.N.C.

JONES, WEIMAR, after a successful career in journalism, returned to his home town in 1945 to edit the *Franklin* (N. C.) *Press*.

KOHRS, KARL, native of Iowa and editor of a book on opera, is on the staff of *Parade* in New York.

KOTERBA, ED, of Czech parentage, was a columnist for United Feature Syndicate until his death in 1961.

LAWSON, JOHN, early settler of Bath, did not live to see his famous book re-titled *History of Carolina* (1714).

LEDERER, JOHN (Johann), German explorer, was only twenty-six when he traveled into the undiscovered Carolina hinterland.

LEFLER, HUGH TALMAGE, professor at Chapel Hill, had written extensively on North Carolina history.

LOUGEE, GEORGE, newspaperman and Durham native, has a grandfather who made bullets for the Confederacy.

MCKNIGHT, JOHN, Mayflower Award winner from Shelby, has in recent years been with the U. S. Information Agency.

MCNEILL, JOHN CHARLES, Scotland County poet, published prose essays in the *Charlotte Observer*.

MALLISON, DALLAS, former Pamlico County educator, is a free-lance writer now living at Carolina Beach.

MASON, MARY ANN, native of New Bern, was wife of an Episcopal rector in Raleigh.

MEARNS, DAVID C., is Chief of the Manuscript Division at the Library of Congress in Washington, D. C.

MEDLEY, MARY LOUISE, is a poet and newspaperwoman living in Wadesboro.

MICHAUX, ANDRÉ, French botanist, hoped that various indigenous American trees could be transplanted to France.

MOORE, LOUIS T., of Wilmington, was a frequent writer on the history of the lower Cape Fear region till his death in 1961.

MURPHY, ISABEL G., of Kill Devil Hills, issues the weekly *Surfside News* during summer vacation months.

NYE, BILL (Edgar W.), popular American humorist who died in 1896, spent his last years at Buck Shoals, Buncombe County.

OATES, JOHN A., lawyer of Fayetteville, collected vast materials on the history of his city and region.

PARRIS, JOHN, native of Sylva, has written copiously on the western North Carolina mountain area.

PIERCE, OVID WILLIAMS, Weldon novelist, teaches at East Carolina College in Greenville.

POE, CLARENCE, publisher of the *Progressive Farmer* in Raleigh, has written on numerous subjects.

POLK, WILLIAM, Warrenton lawyer and Greensboro newspaperman, died in 1955.

POWELL, WILLIAM S., is custodian of the North Carolina Collection at the Library in Chapel Hill.

POWERS, LARRY, formerly an actor from Indiana, has been a free-lance writer in Clinton since 1929.

RAGAN, SAM, native of Granville County, is executive editor of the two Raleigh daily newspapers.

REED, WINGATE, retired Army colonel of Washington, N. C., is historian of Beaufort County.

REID, CHRISTIAN, is a pen name used by the prolific Salisbury novelist, Mrs. Frances Christine Fisher Tiernan (1846-1920).

RUSSELL, PHILLIPS, biographer, was professor of journalism at the University of North Carolina till his retirement in 1956.

SCHEER, JULIAN, Charlotte newspaper reporter, has written books on "Tweetsie" and "Choo-Choo" Justice.

SHARPE, BILL, of Raleigh, often makes books from his articles in *State* magazine, which he edits.

SPENCER, CORNELIA PHILLIPS, newspaper correspondent and magazine contributor, lived most of her life in Chapel Hill.

SPRUNT, JAMES, of Wilmington, wrote several books on the lore of the Cape Fear River country.

STEM, THAD, JR., is a politician, poet, and essayist of Oxford.

STICK, DAVID, Outer Banks real estate businessman, specializes in the history of the coastal country.

TALIAFERRO, HARDEN E., Baptist preacher born in North Carolina, won a reputation as humorist of the backcountry.

THORNTON, MARY L., was until 1958 the Librarian of the North Carolina Collection at the Library in Chapel Hill.

THROOP, GEORGE HIGBY, itinerant schoolmaster from the North, wrote two novels about North Carolina in the early 1850's.

VERRAZZANO, GIOVANNI DA, Italian navigator and discoverer, was the first European to write of the Carolina coastline.

WALSER, RICHARD, native of Lexington, is professor of English at North Carolina State College.

WASHINGTON, GEORGE, kept a diary of his Southern tour in 1791.

WELLMAN, MANLY WADE, now living in Chapel Hill, is a folklorist, historian, biographer, and novelist.

WHITE, ALEX, Negro of Polk County, insisted that the story he told Mrs. Aydleen G. Merrick was true.

WHITE, JOHN, grandfather of Virginia Dare, was governor at Roanoke Island in 1587.

WHITMAN, WALT, American poet with a vivid geographical imagination, never traveled in North Carolina.

WILLIAMS, JONATHAN, who has a distinctive literary style, is a poet and publisher living in Highlands.

WOLFE, THOMAS, wrote "Return" on the first visit to his native Asheville after the explosive reception there in 1929 of his novel *Look Homeward, Angel*.